P9-AOD-582

BEFORE HIS EYES

Essays in Honor of Stanley Kauffmann

Edited by

Bert Cardullo

UNIVERSITY
PRESS OF
AMERICA

LANHAM • NEW YORK • LONDON

All University Press of America books are produced on acid-free
paper which exceeds the minimum standards set by the National
Historical Publications and Records Commission.

TABLE OF CONTENTS

INTRODUCTION

I played baseball for twelve years, from ages ten to twenty-two, and I think that Stanley Kauffmann the baseball fan will forgive me if I compare him as a teacher to my best coaches on the advanced level. The job of such coaches is not to teach you how to play, but to make you a *better* player; if you've made the team, it's known that you can play. I believe that Professor Kauffmann saw his function in the same way during his years at the Yale School of Drama, where he was my teacher—a better word would be mentor—as well as that of the rest of the contributors to this volume. He simply was not a teacher in the conventional sense: an imparter of information, ideas, and theories, a conveyor of knowledge. He wasn't on hand to make you smart; he knew that you were and tried to guide you into becoming the best critic possible. He did this primarily through the model of his own writing, through the editing of yours, and through wide and illuminating reference to primary and secondary literature. Class was less a time for dissecting a particular text or film than for feeling our way around inside it and within the period out of which it arose. Professor Kauffmann eschewed "definitive" interpretations, preferring instead to prepare us to make our own attempts at definitiveness in our future roles as critics.

Often we would do something so old-fashioned in this era of deconstructionist criticism as to read parts of a text aloud. Professor Kauffmann wanted to be sure that we had *heard* and savored and embraced a play before we began to reconstitute it critically; that we had understood it *theatrically*. He contributed to our understanding by reading parts himself—especially from Shaw's plays—and spontaneously directing our readings, revealing in the process the theatrical training that has made him so acute a critic of acting, of *performance*. During films he would play the role of guide, directing our attention quickly, unobtrusively, to this camera angle, that cut; this use of color, that use of space. He gave us a feeling for the form. It was in our papers for him that we were expected to think about what it all meant, to discover what *we* thought. In his teaching he was more the artist than the critic, could indeed be described by the title of an anthology to which he once contributed: the critic as artist. Formerly a novelist and playwright himself, he gave us the artist's perspective, making us feel present at the creation and thus enabling us to write more authoritatively about that creation.

Perhaps more than anything else, though, Stanley Kauffmann cared about his students, about their social well-being in addition to their intellectual development. He knew that book-learning alone did not a good critic make, and he therefore generously offered us his friendship, his worldly ebullience, outside the classroom as well as his wisdom within it. He often would extend to us the pleasure of his company (and the pleasure of a favorite restaurant) in New York when we sought to escape the pressures of the Drama School there. I myself cannot express how much his caring meant to me in this era of cool relations between faculty and students, of education as business, of a grade as something to be negotiated rather than earned and an instructor as someone to be manipulated instead of appreciated.

Stanley Kauffmann's many professional achievements outside the class-room speak for themselves and have been widely recognized; they are docu-mented in both the chronology that comes immediately after the preface and the bibliography that follows the essays. (The bibliography is complete to date—as I write, Professor Kauffmann still writes!) I am sure that he will be remembered as the greatest film and theatre critic of his generation, if not in this country's history. I know that I speak for the contributors to this volume as well as for his former students who were unable to contribute because of space limita-tions or their own prior commitments—Roger Copeland, Robert Marx, Russell Vandenbroucke, and Susan Yankowitz among them—when I say that it was a pleasure to have known him, to have been touched by his magnanimity and influenced by his genius. We offer him this collection of writings as a small token of our gratitude and in honor of his retirement from Yale University at the age of 70.

> Bert Cardullo
> Baton Rouge, Louisiana
> April 1986

PREFACE

This volume is divided into three parts, which constitute Stanley Kauff-mann's three areas of major interest as a writer: dramatic, theatrical, and film criticism. Several of the theater and film figures discussed are par-ticular favorites of his—Shaw, Keaton, Bergman. Bonnie Marranca's "Acts of Criticism," which directly follows the chronology, is perhaps a more fitting preface to the book than this one. Like Professor Kauffmann, Marranca has received the George Jean Nathan Award for her writing, and with him and the rest of the contributors, she shares a passion for the act of criticism.

Some of the essays in this volume overlap areas. For instance, Alisa Solomon's article on the American Ibsen Theater, placed in the section entitled "Performance Criticisms," contains dramatic criticism as well; and Art Borreca's piece on Pinter, placed under "Plays, Playwrights, and Playwright-Critic," includes criticism of a recent New York production of *Old Times*. Some of the contributions have endnotes, others don't. I have not added notes to the latter articles in the belief that these pieces can stand without them, were in fact not conceived with notes in mind.

It remains for me only to convey my warmest thanks to Professor Kauff-mann's wife, Laura, and his agent, Carl Brandt, for their support of and assistance on this project; to my family for their love and understanding during the editing process; to the contributors for their hard work and patience with their editor; and to Stanley Kauffmann himself, whom I can still hear urging us, *imploring* us, to go out and become the very best writers and thinkers possible.

B.C.

STANLEY KAUFFMANN

Born 24 April 1916, the son of Joseph H. Kauffmann and Jeanette (Steiner) Kauffmann

B.F.A., New York University, 1935

Married 5 February 1943, to Laura Cohen

Positions

Member (Actor-Stage Manager), Washington Square Players	1931-1941
Associate Editor, Bantam Books	1949-1952
Editor-in-Chief, Ballantine Books	1952-1956
Editor, Alfred A. Knopf	1959-1960
Film Critic, *The New Republic*	1958-1965
	1967-present
Drama Critic, WNET-TV, New York	1963-1965
Host of Series "The Art of Film," WNET-TV, New York	1963-1967
Drama Critic, *The New York Times*	1966
Associate Literary Editor, *The New Republic*	1966-1967
Theatre Critic, *The New Republic*	1969-1979
Professor of Drama, Yale University	1968-1973
	1977-1986
Distinguished Professor of English, York College of the City University of New York	1973-1976
Visiting Professor of Drama, City University of New York Graduate Center	1977-present
Theatre Critic, *Saturday Review*	1979-1985

Awards

Emmy for "The Art of Film," WNET-TV, New York	1963-1964
Honorary Fellow, Morse College of Yale University	elected 1964
Ford Foundation Fellow for Study Abroad	1964, 1971
George Jean Nathan Award for Dramatic Criticism	1972-1973
Rockefeller Fellow	1978
Guggenheim Fellow	1979-1980
George Polk Award for Film Criticism	1982

Travel Grant from the Japan Foundation
    for Interest in and Support of Japanese Films   1986

Distinctions

Member, Theatre Advisory Panel
    of the National Endowment for the Arts   1972-1976
Two-Time Juror, National Book Awards   1969, 1975

Acts of Criticism

Bonnie Marranca

Performing Arts Journal

The following speech was delivered by Bonnie Marranca on April 15, 1985, on the occasion of her receiving the 1983-1984 George Jean Nathan Award for Dramatic Criticism.

I thought that, since today is April 15, I might speak of the taxonomy of criticism, and, in particular, of what it is I think I'm doing and why I'm doing it. One of the reasons I do what I do, that is, write, is that it is all I have ever done or wanted to do as a way of being in the theatre. I think of it less and less as criticism and more and more as, simply, writing.

In the Anglo-Saxon tradition there is too much distinction between what is called criticism and what is called writing. I look forward to seeing those borders abolished in a new cosmopolitanism of the pen. With the same stroke, I look forward to seeing advances in the social sciences incorporated into the humanities for a richer, more pluralistic account of the contemporary world and all its artifacts. Anthropology and literary criticism are beginning to have the same texture of desire.

What is wonderful about writing is its power to re-imagine worlds in endless possibilities, and what is more remarkable, even dangerous, about theatre is its ability to demonstrate the potentiality of future worlds in the very possibility of their being acted by human beings living now.

Increasingly, what intrigues me is to read the future in works of the past and to read the past in works of the present—simply, to find a way to make writing live in historical and aesthetic time. In Edward Said's graceful phrasing, the world, the text, and the critic form an ineluctable trilogy that shapes being in the state of writing. This state also has a politics that is, finally, a matter of taste.

The question before us now is not so much how to make a living in the theatre as how to make a life in the theatre. Where does theatre, with its obvious identity crisis, fit in the culture at this time of crisis in contemporary life? Even more to the point, what will theatre do now that life itself is experienced more and more according to a theatrical paradigm? What is it that will make being in the theatre important to us today?

I just returned last month from ten weeks of teaching at the University of

California in San Diego. During that time I lived near the Pacific Ocean and spent many hours walking along the beach, thinking about these questions. The ocean in front of me was like an endless blank page that my thoughts could never fill up. Consequently, all the writing I did in this period was in invisible ink. I was writing only in the landscape. Italo Calvino once wrote, "There is no better place to keep a secret than in an unfinished novel." I believe the same can be said of the essay.

I began to think of the promise of culture as horticulture and of myself as a naturalist, so to speak. Theatre appeared as an endangered species. This way of thinking seemed to me to point to an all encompassing humanism that would embrace biological, social, ecological, and political issues in the study of an art form in relation to its environment, its culture—in other words, its livingness. In this context, critical writing is not merely an activity but a way of life, an attitude toward living. It is the same verb, to cultivate, that gives definition to cultivation of the land, of the mind, and of the human body. And sometimes in history knowledge grows on trees.

It is the promise of worldliness that makes writing so powerful a way of being. I love the idea of "worldliness." That is what attracts me to beloved writers such as Anton Chekhov, Marguerite Yourcenar, and Hannah Arendt. In fact, it was Arendt who wrote, "Art works clearly are superior to all other things; since they stay longer in the world than anything else, they are the worldliness of things."

Each of these wonderful writers honors the world in all its objecthood, in all that space and time between its past and its futureness. In their deep and abiding humanism they love the thingness of the world, in all its incomprehensible splendor. At times I feel that they exist to help me understand how to live in the world and how to live the life of the world, and perhaps how to write it, or know it cannot be written.

To live life fully is to live it as an act of criticism. Writing is thinking and thought is language, and to choose words is to imagine worlds. One reason to live is to have the luxury to know writing. If all this is beginning to sound a bit mystical, perhaps there is something to that. It was Nietzsche who said, "We have not gotten rid of God because we still believe in grammar."

The language of the stage is only one of the many kinds of writing. There is so much work to be done in the field of theatre writing, especially in these glorious days when scholarship, at its best, is so open to what Bakhtin brilliantly articulated as "the dialogic imagination." Very early on he discovered that there were languages within languages, worlds within words. Later it was Roland Barthes who seduced us with the pleasure of the text.

These are good days for criticism and theatre as intellectual pursuits. If once all the arts were said to aspire to music, now it seems that art—in addition to psychoanalysis, politics, sociology, and literary theory, not to mention painting and dance—has been drawn to the notion of the theatrical as a way of understanding human activity.

Of all new languages it is the theatrical vocabulary that has most revitalized American scholarship in the last two decades. But too few theatre people have contributed to the grammar of this startling event.

Those of us who write, should write more often, and more fervently. Not only for ourselves but also to leave new species of writing for those who come after us. Writers are a little like gardeners. They are drawn to the activity of hybridization as a way of generating new forms. They are cultivators of their own and other people's backyards.

Just as we here tonight have fed on the good books of our time, perhaps future generations will be as fortunate to discover the pleasures of worldliness in simple acts of writing.

I. PLAYS, PLAYWRIGHTS, AND PLAYWRIGHT-CRITIC

"I must get out of this into the air": Transfiguration and Ascent in Three Plays by Bernard Shaw

Jane Ann Crum

University of North Carolina

Deeply imbedded in Christian theology is a tension between life in the world and life beyond it. Christ, as the manifestation of God, enters the world in the humblest form imaginable to live among men as a teacher and healer. But underlying the story of his Passion—by far the most dramatic portion of his life—is the impulse to escape this world for another, more satisfying one. The flogging and crucifixion underscore the "man-ness," some would say "meanness," of Christ's existence on earth, but the resurrection and ascension point toward escape from worldly constraints. The belief that ascent toward God (the "other world") is man's natural destination, is reflected in the medieval chain of being, which is organized hierarchically from the natural to the supernatural. Man, as an imitation of Christ, must operate in the world but at the same time seeks to leave it. His departure is always seen as an ascent—an escape from the earth's gravity. The metaphoric ascent of man is most easily seen in the Gothic cathedral, whose flying buttresses make possible the immense, vaulted spaces that hint of freedom from the mundane. Kenneth Clark remarks that, before the Gothic style, architecture had always been limited by problems of stability and weight, and "in the end it kept [man] down to earth"; the new style "made stone seem weightless: the weightless expression of [man's] spirit."[1]

Bernard Shaw's plays reflect the tension between gravity and ascent that makes up so much of the legacy of Christian thought. The use of these motifs isn't surprising in a playwright who has been described as "not only a profoundly religious man but a profoundly religious playwright"[2]; their presence in his work, however, also suggests something of the inner conflict of the artist who would transcend his art—become, as it were, his own audience—at the same time he creates it. Comedy requires more detachment from life than most forms of art, as many critics have observed; Shaw's own detachment results in a comic style that is more contemplative than experiential. Even at the height of emotional involvement, his characters are able to pull up short in order to speculate or to question the nature of their next action. Not every rhetorical or "set" speech in Shaw is an instance of a character's transcendence to a higher realm, but these speeches are often evidence of a schism between a character and the world of his or her play, a schism that begins to deepen as Shaw's

5

theory of Creative Evolution takes shape.

My purpose is not to trace Shaw's relationship with Christianity, but I must emphasize J. Percy Smith's observation that the theatre for Shaw was more than a means toward social progress.[3] It was "a temple of the Ascent of man"; "a place 'where two or three are gathered together.' "[4] In the lay sermon "The New Theology," which he delivered in London on May 16, 1907, Shaw outlined his own hierarchy of being:

> If there are three orders of existence—man as we know him, the angels higher than man, and God higher than the angels—why did God first create something lower than himself, the angels, and then actually create something lower than the angels, man? I cannot believe in a God who would do that. If I were God, I should try to create something higher than myself, and then something higher than that, so that, beginning with a God the higher thing in creation, I should end with a God the lowest thing in creation.[5]

This is a radical inversion of other systems of belief, but Shaw's model still retains a vertical quality. Unfortunately, the "continual struggle to create something higher and higher," to make social as well as spiritual progress, has been marred by "innumerable experiments and innumerable mistakes,"[6] so that the tension between gravity and ascent has continued to inhere in human existence.

My interest is in some of the moments in Shaw's dramaturgy, specifically, in *Major Barbara*, *Misalliance*, and *Saint Joan*, when the balance between these forces cannot be held, and the impulse toward escape catapults his characters upward into a realm of "otherness." Northrop Frye has discussed the movement in Shakespeare's comedies away from the normal world toward a "green world," in order that a metamorphosis can occur, and then back to the normal world, where order will be restored.[7] Shaw's plays are not so tightly patterned as this, nor are escapes in them always followed by a return to the status quo. There is also considerable variation in the tone surrounding these ruptures that ranges from the sublime to the ridiculous. The characters who undergo transfiguration in Shaw have a remarkable tendency to be women. Without pausing to discuss Shaw's principle of the Divine and its connection with women, I note Barbara Watson's thesis that female characters offer themselves as mouthpieces for his ideas because they are outside the idealist world of male society; and Norbert Greiner's counter argument that woman, "because of the educational processes that she [is] subject to, adopts and realizes men's ideals."[8] In fact, what these female characters have in common is the spirit of rebellion, the original spirit of the Protest-ant (as Shaw insisted it be pronounced) that Warwick describes in *Saint Joan* as "the protest of the individual soul against the interference of priest or peer between the private man and his God."[9] The operative word here is "private," and it is a moot point whether these women seek privacy via escape from the tentacles of a problematic world because their traditional roles have not allowed them privacy, or whether they seek such privacy because their immersion in male ideology has given them the conviction, and the power, to demand their rights. What remains are women who, with heroic effort, lift themselves out of the morass for sometimes brief, sometimes eternal moments of transcendence.

Since I have used the word "transfiguration," it is necessary to return to Christian theology in order to define the term more completely. The story of Christ's transfiguration is told in three of the Gospels (Matthew 16:24-28, Mark 9:2-8, and Luke 9:23-27) and varies little from version to version. The chief points about the event are that it begins as prayer at a high place and that it grows into an intense religious experience only dimly perceived by Peter, John, and James. The aura of unnatural brilliance that surrounds Christ at the moment of transfiguration ("having an un-earthly appearance") foreshadows his appearance as the Messiah after the resurrection. But just as important as the transfiguration itself is its context within Christ's tenure on earth. The transfiguration follows directly after the feeding of the multitudes and the healing of the blind man. It is one of the few moments of meditation and escape from the constant activity surrounding Christ before his entrance into Jerusalem. As soon as he descends from the mountain, he is again caught up in the sickness of the world: he casts out the "demon" from an epileptic boy.

Two contrasting views of the transfiguration can be found in Fra Angelico's and Raphael's paintings, the one a static presentation of it, the other a dramatic representation. Fra Angelico's Christ stands on sculptured rock, surrounded by an aura of pure white, his hands outspread in prefiguration of the crucifixion to come. His separation from the kneeling apostles is complete, except for a downward glance that suggests his attachment to the beings who cower in terror below him. This *Transfiguration* (1438-45), painted as a fresco for an individual cell in the Monastery of San Marco, presents a single, meditative subject from which the rest of the world retreats. Raphael's *The Transfiguration of Christ* (1517), by contrast, shows both the glory of Christ and the gloom that pervades his life on earth. Christ is in mid-air, his arms and head raised to the heavens as if to greet the divinity above him. Down below the windswept apostles, in the foreground, impatiently await his return, the confusion of their gesturing enveloping the demonic boy and his father. The world beneath Christ is dark—it is only half-lit by the radiance of his transfiguration.

Raphael's version of the transfiguration dramatically captures the eruption of the spirit toward privacy, away from the strictures of a demanding society. A similar moment is captured in the last scene of *Major Barbara* as the now enlightened Barbara, stripped of her uniform and her idealism by her realist father, begins her new mission of saving souls without the "bribe of bread."[10] Shaw describes a scene of visual contrast here: the emplacement of concrete overlooks the town of Perivale St. Andrews, which is spotlessly clean and "only needs a cathedral to be a heavenly city instead of a hellish one." Included in this picture are the instruments of war—a huge cannon, sheds for explosives, and dummy soldiers who, "more or less multilated, with straw protruding from their gashes," and strewn about "like grotesque corpses," are constant reminders of the destructive forces controlled by the gigantic will of which Andrew Undershaft is a part. Barbara stands on the firestep, "looking over the parapet towards the town." Often during the scene she is above the action, and at one point she steps onto the mounted cannon so that her father must reach up to grasp her hand. Other scholars have established Barbara's link with the saint of the same name, the patron saint of the hour of death and liberation from the earthly prison. It is no coincidence that St. Barbara's imprisonment in a tower by her father is suggested by Shaw's placement of Barbara on the parapet and on the cannon, where she is above the earthly powers at her feet, but still connected to them.

Barbara is silent until Cusins declares the circumstances of his birth, but her presence is noted by Shaw as Undershaft announces the death of 300 soldiers and follows this announcement by "kicking the prostrate dummy brutally out of the way." At this moment Barbara and Cusins exchange glances, and when Cusins sits on the step and buries his face in his hands, "Barbara gravely lays her hand on his shoulder." As Cusins explains his status as a foundling, Barbara climbs onto the cannon and remains there during most of what has been called "Undershaft's apologia." Only when her father touches her hand and demands a definition of power does Barbara confess her anxiety—she waits in "dread and horror" for the second shock of the earthquake that has caused her world to "reel and crumble" around her. Barbara erupts with "sudden vehemence" in response to her father's scoffing remark about her "tinpot tragedy" and demands that he show her "light through the darkness of this dreadful place." Shaw has been careful to present Perivale St. Andrews as beautiful, spotless, and enlightened, both in his stage descriptions and through Sarah's, Stephen's, Lomax', and Lady Britomart's surprised and even possessive approval of the place. Barbara, the divine spark in the play (Cusins. "I adored what was divine in her, and was therefore a true worshipper"), reveals the correct perception of this gleaming factory. Though it may glow in respectability and middle-class morality, it remains a factory of death and destruction, a "dreadful" place; by the end of the play, it will have become the object of Barbara's energy, the demonic child from which she will cast out the devil.

Barbara's relative silence during this scene, in contrast with Undershaft's and Cusins' loquacity, suggests that her focus is turning inward. Her responses become increasingly reflective; they seem to arise out of a sedate and even somber mood—and these from a character who, for the two previous acts, has been outspoken, persuasive, and humorous. When Lady Britomart demands that they leave since their father is obviously "wickeder than ever," Barbara's rejoinder is simply, "It's no use running away from wicked people, mama." The word "wicked" is repeated, though subtly changed, as Shaw contrasts Lady Britomart's superficial objection to Undershaft's social behavior with Barbara's heartfelt insight into the major dilemma of the play—that "there is no wicked side: life is all one."

In the final scene the trio of Undershaft, Barbara, and Cusins is reduced to a duet, and Barbara's responses and questions continue to give no hint of what her final action will be. Cusins' rationalized defense of his decision grows more and more aggressive, until his final cry is characterized by the repeated use of the first person: "Dare I make war on war? I dare. I must. I will." When he turns and asks Barbara if their relationship is over, in "evident dread of her answer" (stage direction), she replies, "Silly baby Dolly! How could it be!" Barbara has responded to Cusins' weakness in the only way her nurturing nature will allow, but his garish response to her answer, his "levity," as Shaw describes it (which understandably would follow his previous dread), is too raw for the intensity of the moment, and Barbara reacts by transcending in word and thought the "mereness" of the world: "Oh, if only I could get away from you and from father and from it all! If I could have the wings of a dove and fly away to heaven."

Barbara is gradually transfigured as the pull of her mission raises her above the paltry concerns of her family and lover to reveal the agony of the soul that finally faces evil without illusions, that must endure evil "whether it be sin or suffering." The second act has removed the bribe of bread, and in her transfiguration Barbara dismisses the "bribe of heaven." God's work is to be done "for its own sake," and, in indirect reference to the quotation above from Shaw's unique theology, Barbara vows that she will forgive God, an inversion that places her higher than the Creator, since He will be in her debt. Like the apostles in the Raphael painting, Cusins has become a disciple at her feet, and his question, "Then the way of life lies through the factory of death?" elicits from Barbara the mystical outpouring that has puzzled so many, and that can itself be explained as a gloss on Shaw's new hierarchy of being:

Yes, through the raising of hell to heaven and of man to God, through the unveiling of an eternal light in the Valley of The Shadow.

Her religious ecstasy here oddly parallels Luke's own at the transfiguration of Christ:

. . . a cloud came and overshadowed them; and they were afraid as they entered the cloud. And a voice came out of the cloud, saying, "This is my Son, my Chosen; listen to him!" And when the voice had spoken, Jesus was found alone.[11]

Eric Bentley has said of Vivie at the end of *Mrs. Warren's Profession*: "A soul is born."[12] A description of Barbara at the end of *Major Barbara* might be: a soul is illuminated. Fighting the limitations of the world, seeking escape through private meditation, Barbara reaches out toward the eternal, only to find it in herself. Her return from the metaphorical mountain (the parapets of the gun factory) results in marriage to Cusins and both the start of a new dynasty and the continuation of the Undershaft inheritance—proof of Shaw's optimism in 1905.

Death is for many of us the gate of hell; but we are inside on the way

out, not outside on the way in. Therefore let us give up telling one
another idle stories, and rejoice in death as we rejoice in birth; for
without death we cannot be born again . . .

Preface to Misalliance[13]

When Lina Szczepanowska drops out of the sky into the Tarleton
household, her perceptions become the lens through which the antics of these
summer folk are judged. Without Lina, Misalliance would be a somewhat
pointless romp through the fertility rites of an eccentric family. Shaw sets up
a tension between the family's inconsequential activities and the foreign Lina's
consequential actions—ones taken at the edge of existence. While they tell
one another "idle stories," Lina rejoices over life lived in flirtation with death.
Hypatia complains about the continual "talk, talk, talk, talk" of the Tarleton
clan and wants to become an "active verb," but her aspirations become mere
lip service to a high-sounding ideal when contrasted with Lina's decisiveness,
vitality, and bravery.

Lina is more than a means for perspective, however. Like Barbara, who
precedes her, and Joan, who is to follow, Lina contains the divine spark.
Her development takes a different tone from that of the other two heroines,
primarily because the disquisitory nature of Misalliance does not permit the
social drama of Major Barbara or the tragic agon of Saint Joan. Yet certain
elements in Lina's character find their counterparts in both Barbara's and Joan's:
her contemplative side (Summerhays. "What is the Bible for?" Lina. "To
quiet my soul"), her compassion for others, and her ego, which enables her
to divorce herself from the crowd. Her transfiguration is essentially comic
because it arises not out of a crisis of soul, but from outrage and frustration.
But it is a transfiguration nonetheless and through its energy propels the play to
the bursting point, where the significance of a world that, by its nature, must
remain earthbound is placed in question. Her vocation is to defy gravity, as
Summerhays describes: "The last time I saw that lady, she did something I
should not have thought possible . . . she walked backwards along a taut wire
without a balancing pole and turned a somersault in the middle."

Lina's outburst, "I must get out of this into the air: right up into the
blue," springs from the same impulse as Barbara's more tormented cry. In only
an hour, every male in the house except Percival (who has had his hands full
with Hypatia) has made love to Lina. As she says, she has forgiven Tarleton
because of his affection for his wife, Lord Summerhays because his position
as ambassador demanded such behavior, and Bentley because of his youth and
obvious weakness. All this she has borne "in silence," even though she has come
to regard the atmosphere of the house as "disgusting" and "not healthy." But it
is Johnny Tarleton's proposal—priggish, complacent, and condescending—that
elicits the fury and scorn of a woman who is accustomed to living in the world
as an active agent, whose privacy and honor have been violated:

This to me, Lina Szczepanowska! I am an honest woman: I earn my
living. I am a free woman: I live in my own house. I am a woman of

the world: I have thousands of friends: every night crowds of people applaud me, delight in me, buy my picture, pay hard-earned money to see me. I am strong: I am skillful: I am brave: I am independent: I am unbought: I am all that a woman ought to be . . .

Coming as it does immediately after Hypatia's "Papa, buy the brute for me," Lina's exclamation that no one can buy her becomes a comment on the previous action. Through her eyes the children are seen as spoiled and caddish, and the older generation is regarded as garrulous and pathetic. There is no possibility of redemption for anyone here except the cowering Bentley, who vows to accompany Lina after she exhorts, "You must learn to dare." Lina's transfiguration results, not in comic restoration, but in her actual ascent. "There may be a storm tomorrow. And I'll go: storm or no storm. I must risk my life tomorrow." The storm that lies on the horizon of *Misalliance* suggests Shaw's growing pessimism about reform of the indolent, vapid upper classes—a pessimism that will culminate in *Heartbreak House*. Lina cannot single-handedly cast the demon out of this society; she can save only the weakest member, then return to her circus of unbought souls.

In *Major Barbara* and *Misalliance*, the heroines break out of the confines of society but return to their respective missions: Barbara will save souls at the Undershaft factory and Lina will return to performing in the "otherworldly" circus, where people exhibit bravery and skill every day. At the end of *Saint Joan* the *status quo* returns, as the epilogue emphasizes, but it is a status quo without the heroine. Joan bursts the boundaries of the world and, in doing so, proves herself unwilling and unable to return to the society that has rejected her. The spark that illuminates Shaw's heroines is magnified in Joan to the point where she prefers divine to human company:

I see now that the loneliness of God is His strength: what would He be if He listened to your jealous little counsels? Well, my loneliness shall be my strength too: it is better to be alone with God; His friendship will not fail me, nor His counsel, nor His love. In His strength I will dare, and dare, and dare, until I die.

As Maurice Valency has noted, Shaw shares with Strindberg and Ibsen an interest in the tragic dilemma "of the extraordinary individual in the world of ordinary people."[14] The cry with which Joan ends the play, "How long, O Lord, how long?" is at the core of modern tragic thought. Joan's *agon* results from the disparity she perceives between herself and the world.

The first three scenes of *Saint Joan* mark the ascent of Joan's ideals— nationalism, Protestantism, and individual genius. God's blessing is evident throughout this ascent as the natural world responds in harmony with her actions: hens lay eggs, the wind shifts, and an arrow in her throat cannot prevent Joan

from winning the battle at Orléans. The next three scenes mark the decline
of her ideals at the hands of the government, the Church, and other pedestrian
souls. The natural world becomes crass and threatening, and by the beginning
of Scene 6, physical pain is depicted onstage—something Shaw had not done
in his previous plays. Joan is weak from imprisonment, ill from bad food; her
feet are chained to a block of wood, and the instruments of torture have been
shown to her. She suggests that she is a caged bird, an image that fits Barbara
and Lina as well as Joan, but that is crueler and more hopeless in Joan's case:

> D'ESTIVET. You tried to escape?
>
> JOAN. Of course I did; and not for the first time either. If you leave
> the door of the cage open the bird will fly out.

It is the pain of death by fire that confronts Joan. Her flesh shrinks from
flame: "I have dared and dared; but only a fool will walk into a fire." At
the moment she signs the recantation, Shaw describes her as "tormented by the
rebellion of her soul against her mind and body." The glorious simplicity of Joan
as a child of God, pursuing nearly impossible goals with unbroken confidence
and through direct communication with her own divinity, is destroyed by the
scratch of a pen. At the sentence of life imprisonment, however, her body and
mind rejoin her soul. In her moment of transfiguration she rejects the cage and,
with it, the world:

> His ways are not your ways. He wills that I go through the fire to His
> bosom; for I am His child, and you are not fit that I should live among
> you. That is my last word to you.

Like Barbara, Joan goes "right up into the heavens," but her soul's impulse to
escape confinement cannot be tempered by love, marriage, and good works.
As Lavendu takes the cross from her sight on the lighted pyre, she looks up
to heaven and utters her final word, to God. Ascent follows, with only her
unsinged heart left behind.

Charles Krauthammer has written that "among the purposes of
remembrance are pedagogy (for those who were not there) and solace (for
those too much there). But the highest aim of remembrance (for us, here) is
redemption."[15] Christ asked that the Last Supper be held "in remembrance of
Me"; and the Eucharist celebrates the redemption of mankind as well as Christ's
memory. Shaw's play about the young woman from Lorraine is neither ped-
agogical, consolatory, nor redemptive. *Saint Joan* is not so much remembrance
as *testament* that, after 400 years of so-called civilization, the world is still
trapped in the Dark Ages of misery and persecution. Joan asks, "Must I burn
again?" and Shaw's answer between the world wars was a profound, despairing
"yes."

The sinking of Joan's heart to the bottom of the river with the rest of
Rouen's garbage is a metaphor for Shaw's dark belief that the world is governed

by waste. Despite the tendency of the spirit in *Major Barbara, Misalliance, Saint Joan*, and other plays of Shaw's to fight gravity through transfiguration and ascent, to achieve moments of weightlessness, it must finally return, like Raphael's Christ, to a world that crucifies and burns those who would lead it to salvation.

NOTES

[1] Kenneth Clark, "The Great Thaw," Ch. 1 in his *Civilisation* (New York: Harper & Row, 1969), pp. 59-60.

[2] J. Percy Smith, "The New Woman and the Old Goddess: The Shaping of Shaw's Mythology," in *Woman in Irish Legend, Life, and Literature*, ed. S. F. Gallagher (Totowa, New Jersey: Barnes & Noble, 1983), p. 74.

[3] J. Percy Smith, p. 74.

[4] G. B. Shaw, *Our Theatres in the Nineties* (Standard Edition, 1932), p. vi. Shaw cited by J. Percy Smith, p. 75.

[5] G. B. Shaw, "The New Theology," in *The Portable Bernard Shaw*, ed. Stanley Weintraub (New York: Penguin, 1977), p. 312.

[6] G. B. Shaw, "The New Theology," p. 313.

[7] Northrop Frye, *Anatomy of Criticism* (Princeton, New Jersey: Princeton University Press, 1957), p. 182.

[8] See Barbara Bellow Watson, *A Shavian Guide to The Intelligent Woman* (New York: Norton, 1964). Norbert Greiner, "Mill, Marx and Bebel: Early Influences on Shaw's Characterizations of Women," in *Fabian Feminist: Bernard Shaw and Woman*, ed. Rodelle Weintraub (University Park, Pa.: Pennsylvania State University Press, 1977), p. 96.

[9] G. B. Shaw, *Saint Joan* (Baltimore, Maryland: Penguin, 1951). All subsequent references to the play will be to this edition.

[10] G. B. Shaw, *Major Barbara* (New York: Penguin, 1960). All subsequent references to the play will be to this edition.

[11] Luke 9:34-36, in *The New Oxford Annotated Bible* (New York: Oxford University Press, 1977), p. 1258.

[12] Eric Bentley, *Bernard Shaw, A Reconsideration* (New York: New Directions, 1947), p. 107.

[13] G. B. Shaw, *Misalliance* (New York: Brentano's, 1914). All subsequent references to the play will be to this edition.

[14] Maurice Valency, *The Cart and The Trumpet: The Plays of George Bernard Shaw* (New York: Schocken Books, 1983), p. 381.

[15] Charles Krauthammer, "The Bitburg Fiasco," *Time*, 29 April 1985, p. 90.

Mayakovsky's Tragic Comedy*

Jonathan Kalb
Yale School of Drama

All roads led into the mire in my time.
My tongue betrayed me to the butchers.
There was little I could do. But those in power
Sat safer without me: that was my hope.
So passed my time
Which had been given to me on earth.
— Bertolt Brecht, "To Those Born Later"[1]

Certain revolutionary societies have produced artists who felt cosmically liberated—freed from the very way that civilization had moved through history before them. These artists extolled their new social orders with a moral fervor that shocked even their leaders, and, inevitably, the revolutions that produced them killed them. With some, such as F.T. Marinetti, the inability to leave a political movement gone sour changed their fervor into self-righteous, amoral ecstasy. Others, such as Vladimir Mayakovsky, retained their moral standards at the cost of professional success and official sanction; they could then only channel their energy into negative forms, creating a literature of attack.

Manifestations of such attacks have a tendency to become time-bound, relevant only to the time of their authorship. According to general opinion, Mayakovsky's last play, *The Bathhouse: A Drama in Six Acts, with a Circus and Fireworks*, is a fitting example. A satire on Soviet bureaucracy, it focuses on familiar Russian situations and character types, and contains a great deal of *na litso*, or barbs against named people of the era. If one is to believe the few critics who have offered a judgment (very little serious criticism on *The Bathhouse* exists in any Western language), this topicality relegates the play to historical obscurity.[2]

> In spite of the occasional flashes of Mayakovsky's genius that are in it, *The Bathhouse* is now quite dead, and probably could not be revived. (Edward Brown)

---

*This essay was originally written as part of the author's work as dramaturg on a production of *The Bathhouse* at the Yale School of Drama, April, 1985.

Plot is secondary in both *The Bedbug* and *The Bathhouse*; the poet's
meanings depend on caricature and on parody understandable only to
contemporaries. (Vera Alexandrova)[3]

Analysis of the text, however, shows that *The Bathhouse* has been unduly
neglected, for much of its significance lies in dramatic elements that supersede
topical references. The play is not naive, as the simple label "topical satire"
implies, but is a work of tragic proportion whose ending contains profound
ambiguities concerning reward, punishment, and inanition.[4]

The setting is Russia, 1929-1930. The "compromising" capitalism and
relative freedom of NEP (a palliative measure that Mayakovsky hated) had
been over for two years, and the industrial surge of the first Five-Year Plan
was in full swing. Stalin, having consolidated his power, was in a position to
clamp down firmly on peasant opposition to mass collectivization, and in the
next several years about 10 million people would be killed or displaced. In
literature, official encouragement was given to RAPP (Russian Association of
Proletarian Writers), which favored psychological approaches to character. For
years Mayakovsky had been violently opposed to RAPP, but on February 6,
1930—when the script of *The Bathhouse* had been delayed by the censor for
over two months—he was finally forced to join. Permission to produce the play
was granted on February 9.

By that time the Soviet bureaucracy had become such a huge, sprawling
monstrosity that strict measures had to be legislated to curb its waste. Strangely,
as James Symons points out, in this one sense *The Bathhouse* was consistent
with Party policy.[5] On a banner in the Meyerhold State Theater in Moscow
(where the play opened on March 16, 1930) Mayakovsky wrote:

> You can't wash away at once the whole swarm of bureaucrats. There
> just aren't enough bathhouses or soap. And besides, bureaucrats get
> help from the pen of critics like Ermilov.[6]

V.V. Ermilov was a shallow and doctrinaire critic who had viciously attacked
The Bathhouse in a *Pravda* article (March 9, 1930) after having read only part of
it. He was a member of RAPP, which subsequently pressured the Meyerhold
company into removing the banner.[7] 1930 audiences would have associated
Ermilov's name with the popular debate on "psychologism vs. theatricalism."
To Mayakovsky, "psychologism" had become a bugbear for all the superficiality
to be found in ideological art; and the allegorical action and spectacle in *The
Bathhouse* were a rebellion against that naiveté.

The play's characters are divided into two camps, parodying the simplistic
classification of people into types in official speech. An "honest worker,"
Chudakov (the name means "eccentric"), invents a Wellsian time machine
and needs government funding to complete his project. He is opposed by
the "bourgeois opportunist" Pobedonosikov ("nose for victory"—connotation:
overbearing), head of the Federal Bureau of Coordination, who only inhibits
with red tape "those struggling to build Communism." The zeal of Chudakov

and his worker friends (which both exemplifies *and parodies* the ideal of the new Soviet citizen, whose motto is "The Five-Year Plan in Four Years") is suppressed by the utterly corrupt bureaucrats. Thus, the plot comes to an almost clichéd stalemate mid-way through the play—"petty-bourgeois ignorance and vulgarity" at loggerheads with "true Soviet ambition."[8]

Chudakov's machine, however, becomes functional prematurely, and a Phosphorescent Woman from "the Age of Communism" appears, announcing that she will take back with her to the year 2030 "anyone who possesses even one trait making him kin to the collective of the commune."[9] Though Pobedonosikov then tries to take credit for the invention, the Phosphorescent Woman installs herself in his office and listens to petitions, which reveal to her the inequities of the 1930 system and Pobedonosikov's hypocrisy. When the time comes for the select group to leave, all the characters (including the bureaucrats, who push their way in) gather in Chudakov's workshop and sing a rallying chant, "The March of Time." Then the machine explodes and the bureaucrats are left alone onstage. Pobedonosikov delivers the last line:

> She, and you, and the author—all of you! What have you been trying to say here? That people like me aren't of any use to communism?

The comedy of the play centers on the satire of bureaucrats, who are presented as manifestations of insensitive, machine-like behavior. Their satire might be seen as an illustration of Henri Bergson's concept of "mechanical inelasticity."[10] Pobedonosikov and his secretary, Optimistenko, run an organization through which every official proposal must pass but which has no real purpose except to perpetuate itself. The Bureau is like a robot with Pobedonosikov at its head. He is a clownish caricature, the main butt of the satire, who performs meaningless official tasks with mindless reflexivity. He dictates importantly about arbitrary subjects:

> *TYPIST.* We stopped on: "And so, comrades . . ."
>
> *POBEDONOSIKOV.* Oh, yes. "And so, comrades, remember that Leo Tolstoy was a very great and never-to-be-forgotten wielder of the pen . . .
>
> *TYPIST.* Pardon me, comrade. Before, you were talking about a streetcar, and now for some reason you've put Leo Tolstoy in it while it's moving along . . .
>
> *POBEDONOSIKOV.* What? What streetcar? Oh, yes! All these continual greetings and speeches! . . . Where did we stop?
>
> *TYPIST.* On "And so, comrades . . ."
>
> *POBEDONOSIKOV.* "And so, comrades, Alexander Semyonich

Pushkin, the peerless author of . . .

At times, Pobedonosikov's relentless mechanical behavior becomes more than ridiculous, even evil, like a disease people catch when they come too near him: e.g., the petitioners in the line outside his office "imitate one another's movements like so many cards being shuffled."

The play also has another, non-satirical aspect that centers on the general sense of hopelessness, the feeling that the social situation may never improve. Chudakov speaks of his invention in Act I in a tone that is not wholly optimistic:

> I shall compel time to stop . . . People will be able to climb out of days like passengers out of a streetcar or bus. With my machine you can bring one second of happiness to a halt and enjoy it for a whole month—or until it bores you. With my machine you can make long-drawn-out years of sorrow flash by like a whirlwind . . . thus bringing your days of gloom to an end.

His compulsory ambition to serve the state is mixed with a rejection of the present, an impulse simply to escape. In subsequent scenes he and his worker-allies occasionally appear to be normative characters, because their bureaucratic opponents are so ridiculous, but none of them ever really displays a clear, exemplary moral standard against which we may measure the other characters' iniquity.

Thus, simply labeling *The Bathhouse* a satire is too simple. It also contains something of the tragic—the old agon of vision and possibility, the real and the ideal. Mayakovsky balances an ecstatic hope for the future (questions of immortality) against an almost totally iniquitous environment (questions of immorality). Ionesco's idea of tragicomedy would seem to apply:

> . . . it seems to me that the comic is tragic, and that the tragedy of man is pure derision. . . . I tried . . . to confront comedy and tragedy in order to link them in a new dramatic synthesis. But it is not a true synthesis, for these two elements do not coalesce, they coexist: one constantly repels the other, they show each other up, criticize and deny one another and, thanks to their opposition, thus succeed dynamically in maintaining a balance and creating tension.[11]

Unlike his earlier plays, *Mystery-Bouffe* and *The Bedbug*, *The Bathhouse* places the comic and tragic in a tension that is never resolved; the comic and tragic refuse to coalesce, and the play ends with an ambiguous view of the future.

Some of the humor in the first two acts is based on exaggeration and enlargement, but more of it is based on frustration. Chudakov's opening conversation with his friend from the Young Communist League, Velosipedkin ("bicycle man"), is an example of the former type:

VELOSIPEDKIN. (rushing in.) What's new? Does the vile Volga still empty into the Caspian Sea?

CHUDAKOV. (*waving a blueprint.*) Yes, but it won't for long. Better pawn your watch or sell it.

VELOSIPEDKIN. I'm in luck—I haven't even bought one yet.

CHUDAKOV. Well, don't! Don't buy a watch under any circumstances! Before long those flat, tick-tocking things will be more . . . useless than an ox team on a highway.

The language is inflated to exaggerate enthusiasm and to create a framework for the sci-fi terminology that goes with the time machine. But as Optimistenko remarks in Act II, "nobody needs your enthusiasm." Much of the action shows the workers' inflated rhetoric, indeed all individual enterprise, being damped by the bureaucrats' bullying. This kind of humor of frustration dominates both Mezalyansova and company's visit to Chudakov in Act I and the workers' visit to the Bureau in Act II:

CHUDAKOV. . . . If we can't shift our experiment to the space above the city, there may even be an explosion.

OPTIMISTENKO. An *explosion*? That's enough of that! Don't you dare threaten a government agency! It's not proper to get us all worked up and nervous! And if there *is* an explosion, we'll report you to Certain Competent Authorities.

One might expect the character of Chudakov, who is introduced as the protagonist, to be developed further through contact with his chief adversary, but in Act II he is reduced simply to the "persistent knocker," as cardboard a figure as Pobedonosikov. The drama becomes wholly preoccupied with depicting the bureaucrats as entirely without social value; they commit one after another of the most flagrant abuses, and Mayakovsky spares them no malice.[12]

Though all satire is born of moral rage, the rage in the first two acts of The Bathhouse is unusually close to the surface. Mayakovsky's anger is so fierce that it threatens to burst the formal confines of the play, which it actually does in Act III. Its urgency might be illustrated by comparison with The Inspector General, a more realistic play than The Bathhouse but nevertheless based on some of the same satiric principles.[13] In Northrop Frye's words, "Satire demands at least a token fantasy, a content which the reader recognizes as grotesque, and at least an implicit moral standard."[14] In Gogol's play, the grotesquerie or fantasy (far from token) lies in the magnification of the townspeople's corruption and philistinism. Within that framework the plot is fueled by an internal logic (based on a mistaken assumption) that causes a sequence of events to continue unmasking new aspects of vice until the guilt and shame of the society, represented by the townspeople, stand "naked" in the final tableau.

In Mayakovsky's play, the represented society is "naked" almost from the beginning. Since the piece is theatricalist, fantasy elements such as the endless line of petitioners and the declamatory language are expected, and grotesquerie exists in the exaggerated caricatures of the bureaucrats. The plot, however, is only sporadically logical. Until the entrance of the Phosphorescent Woman, the characters are powerless to affect their situation even in slight ways. The same (or nearly the same) hypocrisy regarding the socialist ideal is seen in character after character, and the same problem of Pobedonosikov's obtuseness is demonstrated in situation after situation, as if Mayakovsky needed to flay the society he had already stripped bare. Sometimes the dialogue degenerates into insults:

> NOCHKIN. All you care about is following precedents and paragraphs, you old stuffed briefcase! You paper clip!

In fact, the play becomes almost unbearable by the end of Act II—not because of boredom (there is too much laughter based on recognizable foibles for that) but because of the futility one feels in watching any helpless situation. If Act III were a continuation of the same dramatic approach, *The Bathhouse* would indeed be a forgettable topical satire.

Act III surprises us, however, by taking a different line of attack on the bureaucrats and diffusing the audience's sense of frustration. Pobedonosikov and his entourage are seen attending a performance of *The Bathhouse*, and during an ostensible break in the action the Chief admonishes the play's director, who appears as a character:

> We don't have officials like that. It's unnatural. Not lifelike. Not the way things are.

The Director listens for a time with strained patience, but then answers with an outburst by staging, on the spot, a sarcastic symbolic ballet in mockery of the type of theater officially seen as "appropriate" in 1930—which, of course, Pobedonosikov likes. We have a significant change of tactics. Mayakovsky turns the guns of the theater on the critics before they get a chance to criticize his play. He shows the real bureaucrats in the audience their own reaction to *The Bathhouse* while they are having it, which in 1930 must have been a powerful device (if not a particularly lauded one). The symbolic ballet is a satire of Reinhold Glière's *The Red Poppy*, recently performed at the Bolshoy and considered by Mayakovsky and Meyerhold to be typical of the simple-mindedness of Soviet drama.

An understanding of Act III's structural relationship to the play as a whole, however, does not depend on recognition of this topical reference. The beginning of the act reads as follows:

> (*The stage represents an extension of the orchestra seats. There are several empty seats in the first row. A signal: "We are beginning."*

*The audience looks at the stage through opera glasses, and [actors on]
stage look back at the audience through opera glasses. People begin
to whistle and stamp their feet as they shout, "Time to start!")*

> DIRECTOR. Comrades, don't get all worked up! Owing to cir-
> cumstances beyond our control, we've had to delay the third act a
> few minutes.

A Pirandellian mirror is turned on the spectators, and *their* viewing of the play
now becomes part of the play's subject. Mayakovsky, perhaps finding himself
incapable of sustaining the black humor of Acts I and II, exchanges oblique
cynicism for direct address. Topical satire alone is insufficient to contain his
bitterness, and he must go beyond it. It's as if the issues are so urgent to him
that they burst out of the plot into a metatheatrical grimace. Up to this point
the audience has had a wry response due to the lack of potential for change,
but now the possibility of change arises. The sudden shift in technique invites
spectators to perceive a sense of option, if not hope, for the first time.[15]
Accompanying that sense, however, is a parallel one of dark foreboding.
Like Mayakovsky, the Director loses composure in the face of arrant hypocrisy.
He says, apparently placating Pobedonosikov,

> I see what you mean, of course. So we'll make the necessary changes
> in the play, introducing cheerful and graceful supplementary scenes.

But later he adds to Velosipedkin, who corners Pobedonosikov at the theater in
order to ask him for money,

> Comrade Velosipedkin, please don't make a scene! . . . Please! I
> don't want them to catch on. You'll receive full satisfaction before the
> play is over.

His words might be seen as a threat: a note of defiance against the bureaucrats
and a kind of curse on the rest of the play. He invests Acts IV through VI with
an undertone of vengeance, saying in effect, "I'll make this play mean what I
want it to mean, even at the most extreme risk."
R.C. Elliot has written that the origins of satire in Greek literature before
Old Comedy were magical rites in which invective, ridicule, and other violent
language were used ritually to kill off evil spirits that plagued the society; in
other words, the phrase "stinging satire" was once used literally.[16] Metaphorically, modern satire's purpose is also to kill; the act of writing it is an aggressive
attack on the target, using the weapons of wit and humor. In structuring Act III
of *The Bathhouse* as a metatheatrical reversal, Mayakovsky turns this aspect of
his satire inward, against itself. Formerly clear distinctions between subject and
object are distorted, and the satire's target now must include the satire (more
specifically, its present performance). Under this pressure the satire dissolves,
no longer sustaining a pretense of storytelling, and criticizes storytelling itself.

A metaphoric satire becomes a direct attack, made with all the "homicidal" viciousness of the original assault, and a self-criticism that is not so vicious but does ask a very apt question: can the Soviet theater, under present conditions, still serve significant social ends? The answer may well be "no," and for the remainder of the play, a suspicion of futility accompanies the apparent prevalence of hope.

In a sense, Acts IV through VI shrug off the objections made in Act III by returning to the metaphoric satire. Now the element of hope has been firmly introduced, however, through the presence of the Phosphorescent Woman. She creates a stir in Pobedonosikov's former office (now called the "Bureau for Selection and Transfer to the Age of Communism") that resembles "all the excitement and disorder of combat conditions, as during the first days of the Revolution." The workers treat her as their socialist Messiah, almost pleading for each one's individual redemption and admission to the Communist Heaven of 2030:

> *POLYA.* Please forgive me for intruding but I have no hopes at all. What hopes could I have? It's ridiculous. But I just wanted an answer to one question: What is socialism?
>
> . . . .
>
> *TYPIST.* Can it be that where you come from, people will notice a girl even if she doesn't use lipstick? If that's true, then give me a look at that life there . . . please send me right now.

The bureaucrats, when they can gain access to her, treat her as a very senior official, fawning on her as if she determined their next job promotion:

> *POBEDONOSIKOV.* Greetings comrade! Forgive me for coming late—awfully busy, you know. But I still wanted to drop in on you for a minute. You see, at first I declined to make the trip. But nobody would hear of it. "Go," they said, "and represent us!" Well, since the collective had asked me, I had to agree. But you must bear in mind, comrade, that I'm a top-level executive.

The Woman, for her part, seems to see through the Chief's arrogance fairly quickly:

> *THE PHOSPHORESCENT WOMAN.* No matter what you talk about, it's always "I don't," "I don't," "I don't." Isn't there anything you "do, do, do"?

One of the funniest ironies in the play is that all the characters, bureaucrats and workers, hope to leave with her and be free from their era. In Act VI they gather in a provisional brotherhood and sing "The March of Time" together like old friends:

                    O
                        Time,
                                march on!
                    Quicken your pace,
                                        dear land of mine,
                    Old ways
                                are dead
                                        and gone!
                    March
                            on-
                                ward,
                                        Time!

When that song ends, Pobedonosikov bullies his way aboard the machine like
a misguided Ubu blurting out demands for his personal comfort even after he is
deposed, and starts articulating his own foibles as if a malfunction had occurred
in his mechanical mind:

> This apparatus of liberated time was invented in my apparatus, and
> nowhere else, because in my apparatus there was as much free time as
> you could want. The present, current moment is characterized by the
> fact that it is a stationary moment . . .

Sponging has become such second nature to him that he leeches onto every
new opportunity without even thinking about what it is. Thus, he comes almost
inadvertently to *want* the Communist utopia (which would presumably deny him
his present bourgeois excesses), and the audience gets to feel that justice is done
when he is denied something he wants. The society marches off ecstatically
to an age of perfection, leaving the evil ones to suffer the most horrible of
punishments: staying in their world.
      Neither that justice nor its benevolent quality, however, is guaranteed.
They are never more than desired possibilities, and this is the firmest basis for
finding the play partly tragic. The final gesture is ambiguous, rapture colored
with negativity, and the elements of that ambiguity are present earlier in the
play. Consider, for example, the speech of justification that the Phosphorescent
Woman delivers when she is installed at the head of the Bureau:

> Comrades, our meeting today is rather rushed. But I'll be spending
> years with many of you, and I'll tell you many other details of our
> joyful experience. Almost immediately, when we learned of your
> experiment, our scientists went on continuous watch. They helped
> you a lot, anticipating your inevitable miscalculations and correcting
> them. You and we came toward each other like two crews of workmen
> digging a tunnel, until we met—today . . .

Her speech has the oddity of containing no information about what solutions the future holds. In fact, one cannot tell from anything she says whether she really knows any more about the future than the people in 1930. She speaks in generalities, and the righteous, immaculate air that surrounds her seems to forbid close questioning. Furthermore, except for the promise of the time machine, the political situation in Act V is almost exactly the same as in Acts I and II; only the top authority has changed, and Pobedonosikov is now among the disadvantaged. We are back in a chaotic urgency similar to that of the opening acts, modified only by the hope the characters place in the time machine and the Woman.

Both the time machine and the Woman mean much more to the characters, and the author, than is explicitly stated. To read their functions in the story only literally (i.e., as the instruments of an actual journey through time), as does Victor Terras, for instance, is at best to discern only half the play's meaning.[17] A science-fiction fantasy is predominantly important for what it reveals about the people who must cope with it. The Woman herself says, "I came here only to convince you people of our existence," and she might be seen as coming from their imaginations. As a wish fulfillment she can satisfy several pressing desires: miraculous assurance that the toil of building socialism will ultimately end in success; the consolation of a confessor, to whom the workers unburden their present frustrations; and immediate gratification of the general desire to escape. The time machine, too, is a kind of wish fulfillment and should not be read *only* literally. It is invented by Chudakov as a solution to the world's ills and might even be seen as the play's protagonist. What or who else could be the "bathhouse"? In this interpretation, the Phosphorescent Woman is the volitional force behind the time machine, and whether that force is benevolent or evil depends on how one views Mayakovsky's idea of Time.

The theme of Time always figured prominently in this author's work. In *Mystery-Bouffe* Time is seen as the Heroic Destroyer, Revolution's greatest ally, which will eventually kill off all its enemies. In *Vladimir Mayakovsky: A Tragedy* and *The Bedbug*, it is also a destroyer but its ally, Revolution, does not improve Man's condition; Time is the Indifferent and Somber Gravedigger, independent of any socio-political design. In all three earlier plays, however, Mayakovsky shows us the future, if not as proof of socialism's triumph then at least as proof of its survival. In *The Bathhouse* we never see the time machine's destination. After showing us the Communist Paradise in *Mystery-Bouffe*, after showing us the year 1979 in *The Bedbug*, Mayakovsky, significantly, declines to use his penchant for futurism at the end of *The Bathhouse* to show us the year 2030. *The Bathhouse* contains no vision of the past, only a hypothetical vision of the future, and a present action that is aborted at the moment when Time is about to leave it behind. The resulting feeling of incompleteness may be seen as a critique of the whole idea of progress. Perhaps Time is a metaphor for the act of writing, and Mayakovsky is doubting whether either can any longer achieve progressive goals.

The characters' leaving, their dismissing the present world, is a brutal denunciation of the Soviet system and the propagandist notion of "struggling to build it." "There just aren't enough bathhouses" to wash away the bureaucrats, says the banner: the slogan has a double edge. People in this "bathhouse" wash their hands, so to speak, of the whole iniquitous environment, and then the future world is excluded from the play with a vengeance. It's as if the Director of Act III manipulated events up to the last in order to show how sinister an apparently carefree spectacle can be. The theatricalist subtitle, *A Drama in Six Acts, with a Circus and Fireworks*, might itself be satirical, for the action surely amounts to the most distressing "circus" ever imagined.

Perhaps here we can appeal to biography, for it seems likely that the true impetus of *The Bathhouse* was the loss of a world in which Mayakovsky could continue being an artist. The brand of Romanticism that flourished in pre-revolutionary Russia was not fundamentally different from that which informed modernism elsewhere at the time. Robert Brustein writes,

> Ibsen and Strindberg, both nourished on a revolutionary Romanticism, were occupied with the friction between their *personal* rebelliousness and the opposing forces of the social, religious, and metaphysical reality.[18]

Few people would challenge the assertion that Mayakovsky's Romanticism was originally similar to Ibsen's and Strindberg's. The lonely Futurist, touring provincial towns where no one understood him, was a veritable model of quixotic Byronism: full of abstract ideals, the artist-hero lives entirely on hopes and possibilities—the hope that the masses of Man will rise to his level, the possibility of achieving communion through his works. There is a widespread misconception, however, that this aspect of Mayakovsky disappeared after the revolution. It did not.

> Why am I alone in the cage? Dear ones, my people! Come in with me! Why am I suffering? Citizens! (*The Bedbug*)

Mayakovsky may have worked diligently for the state, he may have believed in Communism, but he remained a staunch Romantic to the end of his life. His great mistake was the same as Eisenstein's and Gorky's—assuming that the Russian revolution would expedite its artists' regeneration of and integration into society. As the 1920s drew to a close, Mayakovsky saw taking place what must have been the most terrifying of changes—the disappearance of all possibility. The Romantic is accustomed to living without approval or public understanding (especially the modernist, who uses abstract formal innovations in order more purely to express subjective impulses, and consequently distances himself even further from audiences), but he cannot live without hope.

A basic contradiction always existed in Mayakovsky's use of partly abstract theatricalist forms to communicate the Messianic ideals of Communism. Thus, *Mystery-Bouffe* tries to be both utopian and iconoclastic and enjoys the odd reputation of being both the greatest Bolshevik and the greatest Futurist drama. It is important to remember that Mayakovsky never denied the Party's position that the theater *should* be an arena for political propaganda; his difficulties with authority were the result of his insistence that plays must also be entertaining spectacles, a criterion that the Moscow Art Theater's "psychological" theater did not meet. Twenty years after his Futurist "Slap in the Face of Public Taste," Mayakovsky delivered *The Bedbug* and *The Bathhouse* as theatricalist "slaps," despite the fact that they still contained propaganda. The usual penalty of didacticism, however, is accessibility—anathema to the type of modernist who distrusts success as probable shallowness. Mayakovsky wanted simultaneously to be popular and avant-garde (i.e., understood by certain select souls). As propagandist, he harbored perennial hope and wanted clearly to articulate proper goals for his society (and his role as satirist is the mirror image of that impulse), but some time before *The Bedbug* he began to experience horror and desperation as well. By the time of *The Bathhouse* he could not breathe, could not talk freely about his inability to breathe, and the result was a tragic play about suffocation written with the lighthearted trappings of regenerative farce.

In a way, *The Bathhouse* offers a resolution to these contractictions in Mayakovsky because of its unique fusion, or balance in Ionesco's terms, of the tragic and comic. The fusion is achieved mostly through the brilliant device of Act III, which serves an author who is both propagandist and avant-gardist. Bluntness of direct address (which returns in the last line) allows him to give his audience a clear political choice, and the temporary stripping away of metaphor provides a self-consciousness of suffering that distances spectators somewhat from the anguish. The result is that *The Bathhouse* can take an ambiguous stand on the future without becoming unclear. The ending may be read as an ecstatic victory or as a gesture of futility; it is equally likely that 2030 will bring perfection or nothingness.

Meyerhold once compared *The Bathhouse* to Molière—a comparison that illuminates Mayakovksy's ending.[19] Since Molière never violated the neoclassical rule of consistency of character, his dramaturgy is based on an assumption that characters cannot change: all reversals in Molière are of plot, not character. One result of such a reliance on plot reversal is that endings can be very strange: e.g., in *Tartuffe*, where the characters speak as if they have changed (after all, there's been a catastrophe!) even though they are exactly the same; or in *Le bourgeois gentilhomme*, where Molière does not manage a plot reversal and resorts to pure theatricality, providing closure but no ending. Mayakovsky uses these principles in *The Bathhouse*. Since the characters are all types and cannot change, the plot must effect change, which it does in the form of the Phosphorescent Woman. This deus ex machina, however, carries too much irony to be used unambiguously to resolve the play, so Mayakovsky resorts to theatricality as a final gesture that proclaims the ambiguities of meaning while providing closure.[20]

By way of conclusion, I would like to offer a slightly a-textual interpretation of the play's ending, suggested by the proximity of *The Bathhouse* to Mayakovsky's suicide and by recent events in, of all places, the Americas. This interpretation depends on viewing the possibility of futility in the ending as more likely than the possibility of victory.

Consider the Phosphorescent Woman as a malevolent force leading her society to a figurative mass suicide. Seeing her as something of a Jim Jones figure, the characters in the final acts could degenerate from revolutionary zeal to a glassy-eyed, mindless obedience. The rapture of "The March of Time" would then seem sarcastic, paralleling the ballet satire in Act III, and would sharpen the fury of the final action. The March could even approach the macabre if staged metatheatrically, inviting the audience to join in the "escape." Instead of disappearing in the time machine, all the characters could, for instance, jump systematically into a vat of boiling oil while the Phosphorescent Woman stands beside it guffawing. After this gesture, a second (ironic) ending might be added depicting an ecstatic Communist victory. The last act of *Mystery Bouffe* could be adapted to show the characters in *The Bathhouse* arriving in triumph at 2030. Such a double ending would have a theatricalism consistent with the play's aesthetic and would literalize a dualism similar to that of the text's ending. The new choices would be punishment and inanition, instead of reward and inanition, creating a clear allegory of an entire society being massively duped into following a charismatic leader (who believes in the evangelical concept of "rapture"!) who cannot even properly explain how his policies will accommodate the people in the country's future. The future that is envisioned is an idealistic fairy tale.

NOTES

[1]Bertolt Brecht, *Poems: 1913-1956*, ed. John Willett and Ralph Manheim (New York: Methuen, 1976), p. 319.

[2]A noteworthy exception is Angelo Maria Ripellino, *Maiakovski et le théâtre russe d'avant-garde* (Paris: L'Arche, 1965).

[3]Edward Brown, *Mayakovsky: A Poet in the Revolution* (Princeton, New Jersey: Princeton University Press, 1973), p. 335; Vera Alexandrova, *A History of Soviet Literature* (Garden City: Doubleday, 1963), p. 65.

[4]Obviously, many of the specific references mentioned in the script (e.g., P.S. Kogan, L. Friedland, the Dnieper Power Plant, the Izvestia skyscraper) had for 1930 audiences a direct effect that probably cannot be regained. In a contemporary production, especially one outside the Soviet Union, some of those references would have to be cut or changed. A surprising number of them, however, can remain unaltered. For example, Chudakov's interpretation of the coded letter announcing the Phosphorescent Woman's arrival:

> VELOSIPEDKIN. . . ."R-V-1-3-2-24-20." What's that, the telephone number of somebody named Comrade Arvey?

> CHUDAKOV. It's not just the letters r and v, it's "arrive." They write in consonants only, which means a saving of twenty-five

percent on the alphabet. The numbers 1, 3, and 2 show the sequence of the vowels: A, E, I, O, U: "arrive." See? The figure 24 means the 24th day of the month—tommorrow. And 20 indicates the hour. He, she, or it will arrive at eight o'clock tomorrow night.

His speech satirizes the orthographical reforms that had tried to do away with unnecessary letters in the Russian alphabet, but it is also funny in context because of the improbable speed with which he grasps the code. It is worth pointing out that both *The Bedbug* and *The Bathhouse* were popular successes when they were revived in the Soviet Union in the 1950s. Comments on Valentin Pluchek's 1953 production of *The Bathhouse* may be found in Ripellino, pp. 247-249, and in Marjorie Hoover, *Meyerhold: The Art of Conscious Theater* (Amherst: University of Massachusetts Press, 1974).

[5]The 15th Congress of the Soviet Communist Party had in 1927 declared a campaign against bureaucratic waste. James Symons, *Meyerhold's Theatre of the Grotesque* (Coral Gables: University of Miami Press, 1971), p. 186.

[6]Victor Terras, *Vladimir Mayakovsky* (Boston: Twayne, 1983), p. 35.

[7]In his suicide note written in April, Mayakovsky said: "Tell Ermilov that it is too bad I took down that slogan, ought to have fought it out." Terras, p. 35.

[8]Meyerhold's production emphasized these divisions in many ways; for example, the workers all wore coveralls and moved with acrobatic agility while the bureaucrats wore business suits and sat about in armchairs. Descriptions of the production may be found in Konstantin Rudnitsky, *Meyerhold the Director* (Ann Arbor: Ardis, 1981) and Edward Braun, *The Theatre of Meyerhold* (New York: Drama Book Specialists, 1979).

[9]All quotations from *The Bathhouse* are from *The Complete Plays of Vladimir Mayakovsky*, trans. Guy Daniels (New York: Washington Square Press, 1968).

[10]Henri Bergson, *Laughter: An Essay on the Meaning of the Comic*, trans. Cloudesley Brereton and Fred Rothwell (New York: Macmillan, 1917), p. 10.

[11]Eugène Ionesco, *Notes and Counter Notes*, trans. Donald Watson (New York: Grove Press, 1964), p. 27.

[12]At one point, Pobedonosikov rails to his typist,

> I must ask you to refrain from making objections. Here I am, working away with great consistency and perfectionism, pursuing a single theme without in any way digressing, while you . . . For that matter, Tolstoy and Pushkin—and even Byron, if you like—may have been born at different times, but we're still going to celebrate their birthdays all together, and in common . . . You know, I'm thinking of writing just one general article as a guide. Then you could break it down into individual subjects . . .

This speech refers to a situation that, despite claims to the contrary, was a tremendous source of frustration to Mayakovsky: the creation of policies forcing all literature (all creative endeavor) to mean exactly the same thing. Edward

Brown has written,

> [Mayakovsky] made a consistent and conscious effort to lend his poetic gift to political uses. The pressures on him to do this were complex and varied, but they came largely from inside himself. The image we sometimes have of a genuine poet required by a state bureaucracy to give up his real self in favor of agitation and propaganda is totally false. (p. 8)

The fact that Mayakovsky was a willing, enthusiastic Soviet poet—the great majority of his writings after 1917 were for propaganda purposes—has all but blinded critics like Brown to the scope of disillusionment in *The Bathhouse*. In *Comedy in the Soviet Theater* (1956), Peter Yershov states that Mayakovsky did not feel that the problems were faults of the Soviet system but of people like Pobedonosikov. These are highly misleading critical views and are exactly the Soviet defenses of the play. The script itself, especially when seen in light of Mayakovsky's problems with RAPP, is perfectly clear on the issue: self-expression and loyalty to the state can no longer be reconciled even for the most steadfast of Bolsheviks; for the new Stalinist order views the artist as either a useless, non-working bourgeois, a charlatan/entrepreneur (as in the biting characterization of the "painter," Belvedonsky), or a mouthpiece for *realistic* state propaganda.

[13]Andrew MacAndrew also compares these two plays in the introduction to his translation of *The Bathhouse*, in *Twentieth-Century Russian Drama* (New York: Bantam, 1963), pp. 261-262.

[14]Northrop Frye, *Anatomy of Criticism* (Princeton, New Jersey: Princeton University Press, 1957), p. 224.

[15]Another interpretation of Act III may also help to explain its tentative sense of hope: since the fiction onstage now represents real life, the Director's actions represent manipulation of real life, the very thing that was impossible in Acts I and II.

[16]R. C. Elliot, Ch. 1 in his *The Power of Satire* (Princeton, New Jersey: Princeton University Press, 1960).

[17]Terras, p. 112.

[18]Robert Brustein, *The Theatre of Revolt* (Boston: Little, Brown, 1964), p. 138.

[19]Rudnitsky, pp. 448-449.

[20]Mayakovsky originally planned another, more spectacular ending that was changed due to budgetary considerations, to the actors' dismay. One of them wrote,

> The time machine was to have thrown out the bureaucrats, headed by the chief high leader Pobedonosikov, and that would have put a period on the finale. But this was not contained in the prop design. Everyone went upward somewhere on the construction, with suitcases and bags, and the spectator could not understand what was happening. This was a great omission. (Rudnitsky, p. 464)

It was indeed a great, and fortuitous, omission. The new ending was less straightforward in moralistic terms, and could thus take on far greater thematic significance.

Love at the Margin: F.X. Kroetz's *Through the Leaves*

Colette Brooks

Interart Theatre

It is but a small part of a man's wants which the produce of his own labor can supply . . . every man thus lives by exchanging, or becomes in some measure a merchant.

—Adam Smith, *The Wealth of Nations.*[1]

Though Freud viewed the accomplished adult as one able both to work and to love, each in full measure, the latter skill has long been employed in industrialized cultures as if it were compensatory rather than satisfying in itself, providing not for instinctual need but for relief from the isolation and disappointment commonly endured in the bourgeois workplace. Our modern images of love and work, in consequence, are not so much complementary as conflated, the two spheres intermingled, each liable to adopt the coloration of the other. Such unbidden confusion is to be found in every moment of *Through the Leaves*, Franz Xaver Kroetz's play about the relationship between a woman butcher and her boyfriend. From Martha's declaration "I just know I love my job"[2] to Otto's fear of being laid off as a lover, the two characters are engaged in a struggle for clarity that transcends the more limited male-female conflict alluded to in the play. *Through the Leaves* opens with a toast, a celebration of their newly-pronounced commitment as a couple; ensuing scenes explore the nature of desire and need as Martha and Otto carry out the transaction that each sought but only dimly comprehends.

The principle which prompts to expense is the passion for present enjoyment . . . the principle which prompts to save is the desire of bettering our condition.

—*The Wealth of Nations.*

There are indications of a possible misalliance early on; Martha and Otto spend little more than moments together before it is clear that they are temperamentally at odds, disinclined to join except in mutual reproach. Otto is a spendthrift, an hourly worker conditioned to a life of spasmodic experience— a day's pay for a day's work, sex on demand, whatever can be encompassed within an imagination bounded by the moment. He has no sense of the future,

31

nor any use for the past. Martha, however, is a businesswoman, prone to budget, to plan, to make steady and constant provision for the future; full gratification is forever deferred, the pleasures of the moment subordinated to the promise of greater reward in a kind of eternal tomorrow. (This is, as it were, what economists refer to as "abstinence," a condition crucial to the accumulation of capital.) What Otto offers are fitful sexual interludes, shorn of even the most perfunctory accoutrements of sexual partnership: he won't give warning of his arrival, he seldom spends the night. What Martha wants, however, is a relationship—a succession of shared moments and experiences that can be bound together, a store of memories to be tapped, if need be, on some presumably distant rainy day: "You got to hold on to the good things you come up against in life, then you've got something to look back on." Martha's willingness to forfeit present pleasures for the sake of such a stock is embodied in the diary that she begins upon meeting Otto. It is an exemplary means of hoarding experience, and she interrupts their evening together to make the initial entry. Nothing is to be forgotten.

Profit is so very fluctuating, that the person who carries on a particular trade cannot always tell you himself what is the average of his annual profit . . . It varies, therefore, not only from year to year, but from day to day, and almost from hour to hour.

—The Wealth of Nations.

Apart from serving as a bank of memories, the diary constitutes a chart of accounts by which Martha can track the most minute variations in her newly active personal life. The relationship is, in effect, audited; running accounts of its ups and downs are prepared with as much precision as she can muster:

> Otto is moody. Maybe he has a complex because I'm not good-looking. But he's not so good-looking either. But I don't tell him, because he thinks he's really something. Otherwise I'm doing fine and so is Otto. He really lives here now. Exclamation point. Maybe that's why we fight so much. He always has to have the last word, but I'm right most of the time. Because he always says just the opposite of what I say, no matter what. He always has to be the smart one and show he's better than me. Maybe once he's knocked me down far enough he'll pick me up again? Maybe a person ought to just close their eyes to it because he needs it as a man. Resolution colon be more diplomatic exclamation point. A lot of times I'd like to talk to someone and I realize I don't have one really good woman friend. I'll have to make some. Business is bad. Much too hot. Yesterday we went to the Löwenbräukeller and sat outside in the garden. It was nice. Otto was in a good mood. He didn't get drunk at all. I love him a lot. Does he love me too question mark.

The impulse behind writing "every little thing" down, as Otto would have it, is ultimately to try to force meaning out of a situation that is ever more bewildering, to marshal facts and feelings as though through doggedness or vigilance alone she can still a sense of spiraling uncertainty. As Otto's behavior becomes less predictable, Martha's need to understand, to "figure" him out, becomes more urgent: "February 16. Otto, where are you. Parenthesis: desire. Close parenthesis."

There is scarce perhaps a single instant in which any man is so perfectly and completely satisfied with his situation as to be without any wish of alteration or improvement of any kind.

—*The Wealth of Nations.*

Though Otto is more obviously the chronic malcontent, always surly and by her admission "never satisfied," Martha also harbors expectations that are exacting. His is the consumer's lingering suspicion that a more appealing model might be available elsewhere—Martha, as is, can't possibly be the "real woman" he wants. (At one point—looking under the hood, as it were—he lifts up her skirt for a "sex check.") She, in turn, is concerned more with rewards just out of reach than with what she has on hand. Despite the caviar available, she "can't do nothing at the shop," but the meal she could prepare in her own home, with the same ingredients, would be immeasurably superior; Otto, if cajoled, influenced, changed, might one day more closely resemble the man she sees in her forecasts. (In one scene, in which both at her behest don costumes from *My Fair Lady*, she sees her laborer transformed in a tux that makes him acutely uncomfortable.) Neither one is really willing to grant the truth of her repeated pieties: "you have to make the best of things the way they are," "when a person's got something they don't know what it's worth." Things as they "are" invariably fail to satisfy, and both Otto and Martha are haunted by unappeased desire for something other than what actually is.

That part of a thing which he is only just induced to purchase may be called his marginal purchase because he is at the margin of doubt whether it is worth his while to incur the outlay required to obtain it.

—Alfred Marshall, *Principles of Economics.*[3]

Neither Otto nor Martha, however, is likely to find peace, whether together or apart; for the play seems to offer only the starkest of choices to those aware of what their lives may lack. "If you go walking through the leaves, you'll have to put up with the rustling. . . ."[4]; one must elect either to abide in relationships riven by doubt or to opt for "freedom" that simply masks isolation without solace or end. The irony, however, is that these are not genuine alternatives; rather, they are states that shade into one another, sometimes indistinguishably. In the modern world no one is truly alone, yet we may well lack the means to achieve more than the semblance of intimacy with others. Smith foresaw such a paradox when he observed of man at the dawn of the Industrial Age, "In civilized society he stands at all times in need of the cooperation and assistance of great multitudes, while his whole life is scarce sufficient to gain the friendship of a few persons." Martha and Otto are indeed able to develop the superficial contacts required in the economic realm, but they have no inkling of how to sustain the very different, deeper forms of human association such as friendship. They can only attempt to transfer the skills and expectations of the one realm to the other; to invest their energies and hopes in that tangle of impulses that they forlornly label "love."

NOTES

[1]Adam Smith, *An Inquiry into the Nature and Causes of the Wealth of Nations*, ed. Edwin Cannan (London, 1904; rpt. Chicago: University of Chicago Press, 1976). All quotations from *The Wealth of Nations* will be taken from this edition.

[2]Franz Xaver Kroetz, *Through the Leaves*, trans. Roger Downey (New York: Theatre Communications Group, 1983). All quotations from the play will be taken from this edition.

[3]Alfred Marshall, *Principles of Economics*, annot. C.W. Guillebaud, 2 vols. (London: Macmillan, 1961).

[4]This is a Bavarian proverb that Kroetz uses as an epigraph to the play.

An "Exquisite" Memory: Henry Irving and Bernard Shaw at *Waterloo*

W. D. King

The American National Theater

> To my own mind *Waterloo* as an acting play is perfect, and Irving's
> playing in it was the high-water mark of histrionic art. Nothing was
> wanting in the whole gamut of human feeling. It was a cameo,
> with all the delicacy of touch of a master-hand working in the fine
> material of the layered shell. It seemed to touch all hearts always.
>
> —Bram Stoker.[1]

Arthur Conan Doyle had written the story "A Straggler of '15," then
turned it into a one-act play that, "greatly daring,"[2] he sent to his theatrical idol,
Henry Irving. Irving, the first actor to be knighted by his sovereign, the man
whom Stoker called the Napoleon of the mimic stage, was the "Governor" of
the Lyceum Theatre and the foremost actor and producer of the English theatre
from the 1870s to the turn of the century. The great man agreed with Stoker,
his personal secretary, that the play was "made for" him and, changing only
the first few pages of Doyle's script, he entered it into his repertory in 1895
under the title *A Story of Waterloo*, later simply *Waterloo*.

Doyle noted in his *Memories and Adventures* that his eyes "were moist
as I wrote it and that is the surest way to moisten those of others." Stoker's
reminiscence, quoted above, confirms this opinion of the play's effectiveness,
and 343 performances of it over the ten years between its opening and Irving's
death in 1905 supply the overwhelming evidence. The critics almost universally
acclaimed the work, in terms as extreme as Stoker's. Sir George Arthur, in
From Phelps to Gielgud, wrote:

> Pinero, in one of his plays, insists that in the life of every individual
> there is one supreme hour which is never repeated; it is possible to
> think that on a dark December afternoon Henry Irving as an actor had
> his hour.[3]

Each time the "hour" was repeated—as all the critics noted—the work was met
with "a surge of emotion" and "thunders of applause." Doyle and Irving had

achieved, in some combination, a certain perfection of theatrical engineering, a mechanical miracle that regularly produced the highest yield of response. *Waterloo* might be described as an apotheosis of the spirit of the nineteenth-century theatre, in the form of an heroic actor, amidst a thunderous crowd, revealing the ideal. And, in a way, the slow curtain at the end of *Waterloo* might be seen as the closing of an era, the passing away of spirit at the opening of the twentieth century.

The curtain fell slowly because the scene was the death of Corporal Gregory Brewster, last survivor of the regiment that held Hougoumont at the Battle of Waterloo. The audience had witnessed the final day of this aged hero's life, from his rising to find that this day his grandniece has arrived to care for him, to his demise in a blaze of reminiscent glory.

The curtain rises on the corporal's humble lodgings. Enter the grandniece, Norah, a bit uncertain, for she has journeyed here to keep house for the old man and does not know quite what to expect. She surveys the meager details of his existence—medicine bottles and poor food—and immediately sets about to make improvements. One thing stands out in the room: over the fireplace, there is "a rude painting of an impossible military man in a red coat with a bearskin,"[4] and on one side of it a framed newspaper clipping, on the other a framed medal—a memorial to a heroic deed.

A man of about Norah's age, Sergeant Archie McDonald, knocks and enters. As a member of the corporal's old regiment, he's come to pay his respects to the distinguished survivor: "Aye, he's been a fine man in his day. There's not many living now who can say that they fought against Napoleon Boneypart." He reads the newspaper clipping, which reports that at a critical point in the battle the corporal had been dispatched to the rear for more ammunition. Returning with two tumbrils of powder, he found that his way was blocked by a burning hedge:

> The first tumbril exploded, blowing the driver to pieces, and his comrade, daunted by the sight, turned his horses; but Corporal Brewster, springing into his seat, hurled the man down, and urging the cart through the flames, succeeded in rejoining his comrades. Long may the heroic Brewster . . . live to treasure the medal which he has so bravely won, and to look back with pride to the day when, in the presence of his comrades, he received this tribute to his valor from the hands of the first gentleman of the realm.

The story impresses the sergeant and Norah both. It is true legend from the age of giant heroes, when the uniform of service could mean glory, but a legend now strangely reduced to a bit of newspaper beside the liniment bottle in a sparsely furnished room.

The old soldier has still not appeared, but the sergeant is "due at the butts," so, promising to return later, he departs. The grandniece has barely enough time to register how impressive and kind the visitor has been and to express her pride in her heritage before the "Straggler of '15" (played by Henry

Irving) makes his heart-rending entrance:

> Enter Corporal Gregory Brewster, tottering in, gaunt, bent, and dod-
> dering, with white hair and wizened face. He taps his way across the
> room, while Norah, with her hands clasped, stares aghast first at the
> man, and then at his picture on the wall.

At 86, the man is a ghost of his former self, a pathetic remnant of the Waterloo
hero. He doesn't recognize Norah, takes her for the daughter of his brother,
"Jarge," and when she explains that George, her grandfather, "has been dead
this twenty years," he seems not to hear.

Indeed, it soon becomes apparent that he has but a dim awareness of the
past after 1815. His health has declined—his "toobes" give him trouble, and he
"cuts the phlegm" with paregoric—but his spirit is still active in the service. He
presents himself as ready at any moment to be called up to "the glory to come"
when he joins his old "ridgement" as they go on to fight the "battle of Arm—
Arm—The battle of Arm–." He struggles with the word "Armageddon," as he
struggles with the household flies that are so "owdacious," but he "'spec's the
3rd Guards will be there" at the battle, and they need only him to make up a
full muster.

He has been the good soldier these many years, dutiful even in following
the terms of his commendation: living long to treasure his medal and looking
back with pride to the occasion of his valor. But, when the sergeant returns,
it becomes clear that Corporal Brewster has not kept up with change; the ways
of the modern army are different. Always, when faced with the disturbing
changes, he defers judgment to Wellington: "It wouldn't have done for the
Dook. The Dook would have had a word there." When he breaks his clay
pipe, "he bursts into tears with the long helpless sobs of a child." Nothing but
time could defeat the man, and time now—30 minutes from curtain rise, 15
from curtain fall—is having its way.

The corporal is surprised and honored by the arrival (after the second
departure of the sergeant) of the colonel of the regiment, Colonel Midwinter.
He snaps to attention, then almost collapses from the effort. Midwinter has
come to hear of the historic battle from the heroic survivor himself. The old
man vividly re-creates the scene, using his medicine bottles to represent the
various forces. It is so clear, he "sees it afore me, every time I shuts my eyes."
The scene of receiving his commendation is also vivid in his memory, more
vivid than the life that surrounds him now:

> CORPORAL. That's what the Regent said. "The regiment is proud
> of ye," says he. "And I'm proud of the regiment," says I—
>
> COLONEL. And so you are actually he.
>
> CORPORAL. "And a damned good answer, too," says he.

The record is nearly complete; the spectator has had ample certification of the greatness of this man and his deed, amounting to victory over the Emperor Napoleon. But the heroic picture is not perfect. Because of the passage of time, it is difficult to fit the action to the broken and childish figure of the man.

Before the colonel departs, he grants the request of Corporal Brewster that he be given a proper military funeral when he's "called." At this, the veteran sinks back in his chair, apparently asleep. Already, you might say, the slow descent of the curtain had begun; but one effect remained to unify the work, to bring the moment of the past together with the moment of the present. Otherwise, the work is weirdly skewed: too quaint for the heroic, too heroic for the pathetic, too pathetic for the comic, too comic for the inspirational, too inspirational for the quaint.

So, the sergeant enters yet again and finds, as at the beginning, that the old man is "out"—asleep at center stage. He offers Norah his comforting opinion: "Yes, he don't look as if he were long for this life, do he? Maybe a sleep like this brings strength to him." The youngsters (about the same in social standing, and both unmarried) converse for some time, sketching, merely sketching, a possible romantic interest. The sergeant gets Norah to promise she will pay a visit to the barracks some day. But their scene is literally beside the point. Marriage and domestic comfort have had no place in the corporal's life, and the spectator's attention does not depart from the still figure of the sleeping man. Suddenly (how marvelous! how horrible! how pathetic!) the figure stirs:

> CORPORAL. *(in a loud voice.)* The Guards need powder. *(Louder.)* The Guards need powder! *(Struggles to rise.)*

> NORAH. Oh, I am so frightened.

> CORPORAL. *(staggering to his feet and suddenly flashing out into his old soldiery figure.)* The Guards need powder, and, by God, they shall have it! *(Falls back into his chair. Norah and the Sergeant rush toward him.)*

> NORAH. *(sobbing.)* Oh, tell me, sir, tell me, what do you think of him.

> SERGEANT. *(gravely.)* I think that the 3rd Guards have a full muster now.

CURTAIN. SLOW.

Waterloo is a play of contrasts: the old and the young, the present and the past, the quaint and the heroic, the realistic and the ideal. The final moment brings these contrasts together in a full figure, a transfiguration of the impossibly real into the really impossible, uplifted by the surge of feeling, before the curtain descends on nothingness. Out of the machine came spirit.

In writing an "acting play," as Stoker calls it, Doyle had neatly set up this opportunity for the actor, carefully constructing the ground (aged, quaint, realistic) from which the figure (youthful, heroic, ideal) would rise. Irving received praise for his detailed portrayal of old age, and in general the alternation of humorous and pathetic moments was accepted and admired as a means to realism. But the moment that shook the critics and the audience and established *Waterloo* as a work of the greatest magnitude was the apparition of Brewster/Irving/spirit rising mightily to death. Sir George Arthur describes the tremendous effect of this moment:

> When the curtain sank there was a silence, intensely significant but almost unbearable in its tension; men who had never before been "moved by theatrical stuff " were furtively wiping their eyes, women were quite unashamedly "having a good cry," a wave of emotion swept the whole house. . . . The stage manager knew his job and kept the drop down until people had a little recovered themselves and were able to give Irving an ovation which admittedly, in volume and sincerity, exceeded anything he had hitherto enjoyed.[5]

Alfred Darbyshire proclaimed, in *The Art of the Victorian Stage*, that Irving's creation of Gregory Brewster and Charles the First would not only be thought of as "works of high art," but they would also "remain as exquisite memories 'as long as memory shall hold her seat.' "[6]

And yet, the passing of the spirit of Corporal Brewster foreshadowed the passing of Henry Irving and the passing of something that is called "the age of great acting." Darbyshire calls Irving's performance an "exquisite" memory, a memory literally without question, and yet without question Irving's performance stands now as merely a strange anecdote, a memory without seat, in a number of dusty theatrical annals and *Personal Reminiscences*. That is perhaps the fate of the actor's art: it commands attention without question, and then without question it passes. It was question—one voice of question amid all the exclamations—that arrested the passage of Irving's *Waterloo* into nothingness.

If *Waterloo* is without question a forgotten play, it is outstandingly forgotten because of the extraordinary response of one critic, Bernard Shaw. Shaw made the play unforgettably forgettable, immortally dead, in the course of his review. He did so by standing alone and outside the concealed position of the other critics, and by breaking the mechanical laws of their complicity with the theatre.

A few critics were less enthusiastic about the play than the ones quoted earlier, cautiously so since by this time Irving's Lyceum was proclaimed in England and abroad as the foremost theatre of the nation. What's more, Irving was almost universally respected, admired, and loved for his service to the art and the country, for his generosity, dignity, and good nature. Still, critics must be critics, and *Waterloo* presented an interesting test of tact and discrimination. There was a widespread difference of opinion, even among the hyperbolically enthusiastic, between the majority who felt the credit was due to the *actor* and the minority who felt it was due to the *playwright*, both with the belief that the merits of the one had in some measure compensated for the demerits of the other and that the whole had exceeded its parts. This sort of disagreement, known as a healthy dispute, is practically essential to a good show of criticism. The terms remain a bit unsettled, but the basic contract of service to the theatre is subscribed.

It was Shaw who completely buried the work and marked the tomb with an unforgettable epitaph. "Mr. Irving Takes Paregoric" was the heading of his column in *The Saturday Review* of May 11, 1895.[7] Paregoric, an opium derivative, lessens pain, clears the old "toobes." The idea is that Irving used *Waterloo* (and the concurrent production of *Don Quixote*, in an adaptation by Wills) as a drug to clear himself, temporarily, of the "sustained dignity" demanded by serious drama on the stage and professional eminence in life— the pains of the art. But how much more severe the pain "at the point of the pen" when Shaw began to cut through Corporal Gregory Brewster to show that the "toobes" had been clear of vital essence all along: "There is absolutely no acting in it—none whatever." Doyle deserved all the credit for his "ingenious exploitation of the ready-made pathos of old age," while Irving's contribution amounted to "a little hobbling and piping, and a few bits of mechanical business with a pipe, a carbine, and two chairs."

And yet the machine handles the sentiments of the audience so neatly that the simplest business appears inspired, as Shaw indicates in the pattern of his inventory of the play's effects, alternating between objective description and subjective exclamation:

> He makes his way to his chair, and can only sit down, so stiff are his aged limbs, very slowly and creakily. This sitting down business is not acting: the callboy could do it; but we are so thoroughly primed . . . that we go off in enthusiastic whispers, "What superb acting! How wonderfully he does it!" The corporal cannot recognize his grandniece at first. When he does, he asks her questions about children—children who have long gone to their graves at ripe ages. She prepares his tea: he sups it noisily and ineptly, like an infant. More whispers: "How masterly a touch of second childhood!" He gets a bronchial attack and gasps for paregoric, which Miss Hughes administers with a spoon, whilst our faces glisten with tearful smiles. "Is there another living actor who could take paregoric like that?"

Shaw acknowledges the effectiveness of the machine in stimulating strong feelings. His quotations of the "enthusiastic whispers" (whispers we doubt ever got whispered) register the pure subjection—subjection without objection—of the audience to the sentiments of the scene and performance.

And Shaw does not, at least at first, detach himself from the subjected mass, but neither does he relinquish his center of objectivity and of simple objection. He represents this condition of semi-detachment rhetorically in his review, not explicitly but implicitly in his playing out of the entire sequence of events in *Waterloo*. Effectively, he dramatizes the role of the critic, showing the critic as an actor who stands apart from the crowd and yet participates in its sentimental involvement. Again and again in his reviews, Shaw addresses the problem of the critical sensibility—the admixture of engagement and disengagement, of subjectivity and objectivity, that the critic must control.

The problem of critical sensibility mirrors that of the actor's sensibility. As Diderot argues in *The Paradox of the Actor*, the actor can or perhaps must remain sentimentally disengaged from the performance. Irving debated Diderot's conclusion, allowing that detachment is possible and even essential to the extent that it is necessary for the technical execution of the part, i.e., for the efficient operation of the machine, but asserting that a great actor must go beyond the limited power that detachment permits, beyond the machine in a burst of spirit. In his rather hostile preface to a translation of Diderot's dialogue, Irving quotes the great actor Talma as his authority:

> "I call sensibility," says Talma, "that faculty of exaltation which agitates an actor, takes possession of his senses, shakes even his very soul, and enables him to enter into the most tragic situations, and the most terrible of the passions, as if they were his own. The intelligence which accompanies sensibility judges the impressions which the latter has made us feel; it selects, arranges them, and subjects them to calculation. It aids us to direct the employment of our physical and intellectual forces—to judge between the relations which are between the poet and the situation or the character of the personages, and sometimes to add the shades that are wanting, or that language cannot express: to complete, in fine, their expression by action and physiognomy." That, in a small compass, is the whole matter. It would be impossible to give a more perfect description of the art of acting in a few words.[8]

Thus, Irving answers the paradox with a promise of "exaltation," spiritual elevation beyond the capacity of judgment, beyond description, beyond criticism. But if the actor is the one who exercises this "faculty of exaltation which . . . enables him to enter into the most tragic situations . . . as if they were his own," what about the audience member or critic who is also expected to "enter," in some fashion, these situations? To what degree should the *critical* "sensibility" follow that of the performer?

An agitation, possession, soul-shaking, similar to that described by Talma, swept the audience of *Waterloo*, and the critics mostly attempted to represent this sensibility in descriptions, assigning the actor as the source of the exaltation. It could be said that they credited the actor with the emotions of the audience, such that the actor represented the feelings of the crowd "as if they were his own." This appropriation of sentiment seems to be the basic condition of "acting" plays and the "actor's" theatre—a giving over of sensibility to the actor. The actor must, as Talma writes, be disciplined by the "intelligence which accompanies sensibility." Meanwhile, the audience is allowed what might be called the free play of sensibility, since the responsibility is deferred, even to the extent that the audience member is permitted to enter into the tragic situations as if they were *not* his own. The audience can receive the stimulation—the agitation—without being obliged, as the actor is obliged, to select, arrange, and subject the impressions to calculation, according to "intelligence."

But the essence of criticism is discrimination, recognition of difference, judgment, amounting to intelligence in league with sensibility. When the critic is deprived of this responsibility, through the appropriation of sensibility, then he can do little more than register the surge or stimulation of the work, without the discipline of intelligence, without differentiating among the causes of the sentiments, without judging "the process" as a process. Shaw's revolution in criticism (indeed in the theatre generally) was the reappropriation of intelligence, and the establishing of a critical "sensibility" dramatically opposed to the actor's.

Consider the second quotation that Irving supplies from Talma:

> The inspired actor will so associate you with the emotions he feels that he will not leave you the liberty of judgment; the other, by his prudent and irreproachable acting, will leave your faculties at liberty to reason on the matter at your ease.[9]

In effect, Talma (and Irving) turn the paradox of the actor into the paradox of the critic or the critical "sensibility" in the crowd—the "you" that becomes "we" when the "liberty of judgment" is denied. Shaw, like Talma but from an opposite point of view, dramatizes the paradox of the critic in terms of the paradox of the actor. The one reflects the other.

The one critic and the one actor on the two-way stage of the theatre play out the drama of crowd control. When of acting there is "none whatever," then the critic can come forward to object against the subjection of the crowd, as in Shaw's review of *Waterloo*. When of criticism there is none whatever, then the critic remains in the crowd, wholly subject, as in most of the other reviews of *Waterloo*. More often, both critic and actor come forward, in conflict, the former objecting, the latter subjecting, until one or the other accedes. The critic accedes when the acting is as Talma describes, when it "takes possession of his senses, shakes even his very soul," denying him, the critic, the "liberty of judgment." It is open to debate in this century (since Shaw, one might argue) whether this subjection is the proper goal of theatre, but Shaw (even Shaw) seems to desire it. On the other hand, the actor must accede in the conflict when the criticism is as powerful as Shaw's. His exposure of the machine and stout objection to its effects should show the actor that he has lost a part of the crowd in judgment and that something more will be required to overcome the critic's objectivity. But the critic must fight for the crowd outside the theatre, in publications (though the judgments are born in the alienated privacy within the theatre), and so there is an unavoidable time lag in the conflict of actor and critic. The critic works on a larger time scale, changing the future of the theatre on behalf of the future crowd.

Shaw pushed for that future by satirizing the present theatre, hurting to improve, and he involved the present crowd in his satire. He worked for their improvement by catching them in the experience of reading themselves as dramatized in the figure of the critic—a painful condition. In his review of *Waterloo*, Shaw shifts his mode of addressing the audience (and his position toward them), first addressing them as individuals, then joining them in the crowd, then leaving them alone among themselves. The account begins in the second person, with the private moment before the individual is drawn into the crowd ("you read the playbill; and the process commences at once with the suggestive effect of . . ."). Soon the singular meshes with the plural since "the process" ensures that the effects are universal ("You are touched: here is the young soldier come to see the old—two figures from the Seven Ages of Man"). Then the review switches to the third person and it becomes clear that the "you" is not personalized, not flattered into a sense of individuality. In other words, the play addresses the audience as an undifferentiated crowd, a herd of low aptitude ("the pair work at the picture of the old warrior until the very dullest dog in the audience knows what he is to see, or to imagine he sees, when the great moment comes").

The "great moment" is the entrance of Irving, and it is at this point in the account that Shaw introduces the first person plural. It is as if Irving's entrance brings Shaw into the crowd to join "you" and "the very dullest dog." Irving is the drawing force that brings together the production, the crowd, the critics, and especially Shaw. Irving binds the group into a "we," but Shaw does not soon forget the undistinguished role that had been accorded him by the "the process," a role no more demanding than that given the dull dog and certainly no great opportunity for the excellent or exceptional critic. So the "we" becomes more and more ironic: one doubts that a tearful smile broke on Shaw's face while he watched the corporal take his paregoric. He pushes the limit when he parodies the absurd claims made by those who praise naturalistic acting: "We feel that we could watch him sitting down for ever."

Toward the end of the account, the "we" drops out altogether, and the quoted exclamations appear unattributed, still more enthusiastic, and *wholly* ironic ("A masterstroke! who but a great actor could have executed this heart-searching movement?"). Shaw's resistance of the machine grows as the figure of the corporal weakens and the effect on the surrounding crowd becomes overwhelming. "The curtain falls amid thunders of applause," of course, but one feels certain that Shaw, the *eiron*, did not join in the thunder.

He was already in the next paragraph, where the subject of address changes once again: "Every old actor into whose hands this article falls will understand perfectly from my description how the whole thing is done." As Irving is concealed by the curtain of seriousness, drawing the waves of emotion and thunders of applause from the crowd, Shaw is concealed by the curtain of the ludicrous, laughing scornfully but envious of the actor's opportunity. In an exceptional, bad review of *Waterloo*, Austin Brereton (who found the play "deficient in virility") was nevertheless very enthusiastic about Irving's performance, but along the way he pointed to the line that Shaw ventured to enforce:

In dealing with such a part, an actor might be forgiven if he overstepped

the bounds of common sense and lapsed into the ludicrous. It is easy
to conceive that an actor, even of average talent, could not wholly
retain the serious interest of any audience in such a part. Mr. Irving,
however, succeeds, unquestionably, in so doing.[10]

In Shaw's view, however, Irving succeeded questionably, and Shaw is more
than ready to press the question and challenge Irving's hold on the "serious
interest" of the audience. Brereton warns that the actor must stay within "the
bounds of common sense," but the same bounds apply to the audience. When
the audience oversteps these bounds, failing to question their assumption of
"serious interest," then they lapse into the ludicrous, as Shaw indicates in his
review. Shaw does not question the common sense of Irving, who, like "every
old actor," understands perfectly how the whole thing is done. It is done by
drawing the audience beyond the bounds of common sense under the guise of
"serious interest," leading them to "go off in enthusiastic whispers" over "the
commonest routine of automatic stage illusion." Shaw catches the audience out,
in ludicrous posture, then serves them their due of scornful laughter.

His satire enforces a realistic perspective on the construction, the machine,
that had held them captive to an ideal. In the Preface to his "Pleasant Plays,"
Shaw declares that his intention is not "to please the people who are convinced
that the world is held together only by the force of unanimous, strenuous,
eloquent, trumpet-tongued lying."[11] The crowd itself presents a problem, both
within and without the theatre, when its binding force, its unanimity, is not
well-founded. He continues:

> To me the tragedy and comedy of life lie in the consequences, some-
> times terrible, sometimes ludicrous, of our persistent attempts to found
> our institutions on the ideals suggested to our imaginations by our half-
> satisfied passions, instead of on a genuinely scientific natural history.[12]

Unanimity is, literally, singleness of spirit in a crowd, a contract binding the
numerous "half-satisfied passions" to an ideal. It is a construct, even a rhetorical
figure or mode of expression, having more to do with the enforcement of belief
than the recognition of truth.

In his reviews, Shaw does not go so far as to demand of himself or of his
readers a "genuinely scientific natural history." In his preface to *Our Theatres
in the Nineties*, a collection of his theatre reviews, Shaw writes:

> I beg my readers not to mistake my journalistic utterances for final es-
> timates of their worth and achievements as dramatic artists and authors.
> It is not so much that the utterances are unjust; for I have never claimed
> for myself the divine attribute of justice. But as some of them are not
> even reasonably fair: I must therefore warn the reader that my theatre
> criticism is not a series of judgments aiming at impartiality, but a siege
> laid to the theatre of the XIXth Century by an author who had to cut
> his own way into it at the point of the pen, and throw some of its

defenders into the moat.[13]

He does not aim at "impartiality" or claim "the divine attribute of justice"; instead, he adheres to "the bounds of common sense" as the proper field for partiality, allowing and even expecting the part to stand out from the unanimous whole. The line between common sense and common sensation is tenuous, even for Shaw, but when the breach of that line is as clear as the one by the *Waterloo* crowd, then the ludicrous spectacle is easily represented.

To break the crowd of its dependence on unanimity is to demand growth or maturation beyond constructed ideals, beyond the institutions that, like the family (the primal crowd), protect the immature. In a musical review some years earlier, Shaw wrote:

> When the critics were full of the "construction" of plays, I steadfastly maintained that a work of art is a growth, and not a construction. When the scribes [sic] and Sardous turned out neat and showy cradles, the critics said, "How exquisitely constructed!" I said, "Where's the baby?"[14]

The strategy of opposing question to exclamation and always asking who will *grow* in the work of art continues in his review of *Waterloo*. In refusing to acquiesce to the half-satisfaction of his passions, Shaw demands the growth of the theatre *and* of its correlative institution, the audience. The enjoyability of cradles is beyond question, is exquisite (Shaw openly acknowledges his enjoyment of sketches such as *Waterloo, when* they are in the music hall), but the "baby" of full potential should be the concern of the theatre. Shaw jars the crowd to this conclusion by showing them the ludicrous consequences of their belief in a false ideal—and this is painful.

The pain involves the loss of a fulfilled past: the loss of exclamatory feeling in the opening of questions, the loss of the subjection in the opening of an objective, the loss of the crowd in the opening of the individual. In a sense, Shaw asks the crowd to accept (or even precipitate) the death of father Irving, father actor, as a necessary stage of growing up—*or* of growing into the groove cut by Shaw, which is the groove of individuality, self-sufficiency, freedom to judge, critical independence. In other words, growing into Shaw.

Shaw sacrificed *Waterloo*, sacrificed even his own acknowledged enjoyment of the performance, for a higher cause, killing in the name of progress. *Waterloo* survived this Waterloo seemingly unharmed—for ten years and hundreds of performances, for the remaining life of Irving, and it was even revived by Irving's son, H.B. Irving, with similar success. Laurence Irving (the grandson) wrote of his father's performances:

> Many times I watched Corporal Brewster die as he relived the defense of Hougoumont, and as often I was borne along by a surge of emotion that broke over the footlights with the thunder of applause.

It is as if the work were immortal, living on from performance to performance, generation to generation. But the work stuck in theatre history primarily by its fall, soon after its opening, beneath the fatal and fateful hand of Shaw— beneath the curtain he lowered on an era that would become the theatre's Past so that a new theatre could become the Present.

Shaw was having trouble attaining this new stage for his dramatic works. Few had been performed, and their reception (not to mention their presentation) had been, in his view, all wrong. Irving, as a matter of fact, because of his eminence and the aesthetic to which it seemed to bind him, appeared to Shaw as a main obstacle to overcome. In the meantime, though, Shaw wrote a weekly column for *The Saturday Review*, and the Present theatre was *Waterloo*, so it was through his reviews that he began to "cut his own way."

Shaw took the art of theatre criticism to its limit, to the point where the critic's writing itself becomes the occasion of theatrical discovery. From the history of theatre criticism before Shaw one can cite comparable examples of excellent writing in the service of the art, but it is only with Shaw that the theatrical art comes fully into the service of critical writing. Shaw took the machine of criticism from behind the wings, where it had served the theatre in the quiet, anonymous, even perfect way of theatrical machinery, and gave it the effect of spirit, heroism, annunciation on a new stage, a stage of news.

Theatre criticism had been noisy and controversial and incisive, of course, but essentially it had played to the contentment of the crowd, not to the discontent of the committed individual. It had addressed the existence of the art, including its innovations, but not, as with Shaw, the becoming of new imperatives. Even that statement might seem unfair to the great writing of Lamb, Hazlitt, Lewes, and others.

Consider it this way. Shaw realized the full sense of "dramatic criticism" by making criticism genuinely dramatic. Instead of assisting the *closure* of the work in memory—elaborating its impressions with description and evaluation— Shaw *reopened* the work to further play, taking positions or parts according to the premises of the work and testing the resultant conclusions against a hard and responsible logic. The rhetorical fireworks for which Shaw's reviews are famous—the wild jokes, the multiplicity of voices, and especially the development of the G.B.S. character—do not serve merely as amplifications of the principal point of address but instead serve as manipulations of the reader's experience. Shaw operates on the reader's memory and understanding, using a play's performance as a pretext (literally) for the exposure of the artifices— tricks and mechanisms—that lie behind the seemingly natural processes of apprehending a performance and, by extension, any human action.

Shaw continually makes a show of upsetting the hierarchy of opinion by breaking all the "laws"—speaking the unspeakable in the name of honesty, taking advantage openly where it had always before been taken covertly. No mode of address could be more vexing to a guardian of the law and order of public opinion. But in some of his reviews he goes beyond this positional rhetoric to a fully dramatized sense of his text in which conflict stands as conflict.

"Mr. Irving Takes Paregoric" is a particularly good example of this sort of review. And *Waterloo* was a particularly ripe occasion—because its substance was compact and simple enough to represent thoroughly, and because the disparity between its apparent effects and its actual causes was especially great. Shaw reduces the audience's profound impressions to mere reflexes triggered by "the commonest routine of automatic stage illusion." He does this, as outlined above, by re-creating the whole work and anatomizing its impressive effect, piece by piece, to show that it works by "ready-made feelings and prearranged effects."

At the same time, he admits his own susceptibility to the "routine," his *enjoyment*, which cannot be denied because it comes from feeling genuinely felt, even if mechanically produced. It was the machine at the core that brought out Shaw's will to challenge, because machines don't die a natural death. In fact they improve, so that even critics, even Shaw, find themselves vulnerable to the "organized and successful attack" on the emotions:

> The whole performance does not involve one gesture, one line, one thought outside the commonest routine of automatic stage illusion. What, I wonder, must Mr. Irving, who of course knows this better than anyone else, feel when he finds this pitiful little handful of hackneyed stage tricks received exactly as if it were a crowning instance of his most difficult and finest art? No doubt he expected that the public, on being touched and pleased by machinery, should imagine that they were being touched and pleased by acting. But the critics!

Yes, the critic, too, might be haunted, beyond disbelief, by an effective spirit— the ghost in the machine—which no amount of violent stabbing or funerary rite can lay to rest—*in the theatre*. In a review, though, a different order of burial service applies—scientific methods of counterattack, killing, entombment, and commemoration. At the cost of the spiritual effect, which is left behind, untouched.

Shaw thus plays a double-agent role in his representation of *Waterloo*, a role that is (satirically) figured in his preface to this representation:

> . . . Mr. Conan Doyle has carried the art of constructing an "acting" play to such an extreme that I almost suspect him of satirically revenging himself, as a literary man, on a profession which has such a dread of "literary plays."

Shaw, the literary man, describes *Waterloo* to death in order to give it new and delightful life in his description. He makes a literary play on words, a satirical figure, out of Doyle's "good acting play," and in this action, this upstaging of Irving, he posits a different sort of play. This is the "literary play," as specifically defined by Shaw in this review: "a play that the actors have to act, in opposition to the 'acting play' which acts them." Shaw places his textual performance, his literary playing, in the "none whatever" gap that Irving opened—he metaphorically "acts" *Waterloo* by showing how *Waterloo* acted Irving.

This is the way of satire—improving by a substitution of point of view. Replace performance with description and watch how the spirit drops out of the machine. Irving sinks, and Doyle rises, but finally it is Shaw who comes forward, vengeful and marvelous, as the one who really acts, the one who makes a performance of the text. The "ready-made feelings and prearranged effects" work for him like the equipment of the actor, but the trick that Shaw accomplishes, in the way of Irving himself, is to make a moving presentation, a performance that goes beyond what can be described. This is precisely Shaw's new direction in criticism: going through description beyond what can be described—towards a new theatre. Shaw presents the new actor by outlining the void that the actor will fill once the old Napoleon is buried, and then he begins the rush toward that void in a criticism that leads rather than follows the theatre.

The skeptic will challenge Shaw's interpretation—maybe it is itself a piece of cheap magic, a sham substitute for the real thing—but it is *Shaw* who must be addressed, and only through a reexamination or *review* of memory and understanding. *Waterloo* itself recedes into the past, and a new drama begins in the present one of reading, on Shaw's stage. Thus, even in his criticism, Shaw writes a drama of the forgotten or repressed or misunderstood in the act of becoming present.

NOTES

[1]Bram Stoker, *Personal Reminiscences of Henry Irving* (New York: Macmillan, 1906), I, p. 251.

[2]Sir Arthur Conan Doyle, *Memories and Adventures* (London: Hodder and Stoughton, 1924), p. 119 (both references: this one and the one in the second paragraph).

[3]Sir George Arthur, *From Phelps to Gielgud* (London: Chapman & Hall, 1936), p. 81.

[4]Sir Arthur Conan Doyle, *Waterloo* (London: Samuel French, 1907). All quotations are from this edition of the play.

[5]Sir George Arthur, *From Phelps to Gielgud*, p. 80.

[6]Alfred Darbyshire, *The Art of the Victorian Stage: Notes and Recollections* (London, 1907; rpt. New York: Benjamin Blom, 1969), p. 107.

[7]Reprinted in *Our Theatres in the Nineties*, Part 1, Vol. 23 of the Ayot St. Lawrence Edition of *The Collected Works of Bernard Shaw* (New York: William H. Wise, 1931), pp. 119-127. All quotations of Shaw's review are taken from *Our Theatres in the Nineties*.

[8]Henry Irving, Preface to *The Paradox of Acting*, by Denis Diderot, trans. Walter Herries Pollock (London: Chatto and Windus, 1883), p. xvi.

[9]Henry Irving, Preface to *The Paradox of Acting*, by Denis Diderot, pp. xvi-xvii.

[10]Austin Brereton, Review of *Waterloo*, in *The Theatre*, 1 Oct. 1894, p. 181.

[11]Bernard Shaw, Preface, *Plays Pleasant*, Vol. 2 of *Plays Pleasant and Unpleasant* (London: Constable, 1931), p. xvi.

[12]Shaw, Preface, *Plays Pleasant*, pp. xvi-xvii.

[13]"The Author's Apology" to *Our Theatres in the Nineties*, Part 1, Vol. 23 of the Ayot St. Lawrence Edition of *The Collected Works of Bernard Shaw* (New York: William H. Wise, 1931), p. vii.

[14]Corno di Bassetto (pseudonym for Bernard Shaw), Review of 7 March 1890, in his *London Music in 1888-1889* (London: Constable, 1937), p. 323.

Michel de Ghelderode's *La Balade du Grand Macabre:* The Triumph of Life

Alain Piette

State University of Mons, Belgium

Death is omnipresent in Michel de Ghelderode's theater, a recurrent theme that often betrays his inclination toward the gloomy and the gruesome. American audiences are probably more familiar with the dark and biting irony of *Pantagleize*, set, in 1929, "on the morrow of one war and the eve of another" and intended by the dramatist as "a farce to make you sad."[1] *Mademoiselle Jaïre*, written in 1934, presents an even darker embodiment of that theme: the sexual frenzy of the protagonist Blandine after she rises from the dead at times verges on necrophilia and is the epitome of natural horror. In the same year, Ghelderode wrote *La Balade du Grand Macabre*. Although this play also centers on the theme of death, it has little in common with *Mademoiselle Jaïre* or *Pantagleize*. As its subtitle, "Farce for Rhetoricians,"[2] suggests, the author's purpose is to present us with a surprisingly merry view of death.

The "Grand Macabre," the Grim Reaper of the title, is Nekrozotar. He introduces himself as the Angel of Death and says that he has come to earth to claim his toll: he announces the destruction of the world by a gigantic comet at midnight. In his peregrinations through Breugellande, where the play is set, he meets a series of colorful characters who never take him seriously: the charming lovers Adrian and Jusemina, the jocose drunkard Porprenaz, the philosopher Videbolle and his shrewish wife Salivaine, King Goulave of Breugellande and his two ministers Aspiquet and Basiliquet. After the characters have a night of revelry and frenzy in reaction to the impending end of the world, we witness what at first seems to be the predicted cataclysm. But Nekrozotar's efforts at destruction are not successful, because no one is killed. Ironically, the Angel of Death himself dies as the inhabitants of Breugellande start reorganizing their lives.

This inability to carry out his threats turns out to be the mark of Nekrozotar. When he appears on stage, he seems to be the embodiment of death itself, a tall figure whose outward appearance matches the darkness of his soul: he is bald and skeletal; he wears black clothing and heavy black boots. We are not meant to be deluded for long by this dismal apparition, however, since we see Porprenaz kick his bottom during their first encounter. Their initial conversation sets the tone for the rest of the play. Porprenaz makes us feel that there is nothing to be afraid of, despite Nekrozotar's declared intention to destroy the world at midnight:

NEKROZOTAR. Are you happy in this life?

PORPRENAZ. Immensely.

NEKROZOTAR. You will die.

PORPRENAZ. I know.

NEKROZOTAR. Your belly will burst.

PORPRENAZ. It will release a strong smell of beer.

NEKROZOTAR. You won't be hungry anymore and you will be eaten.

PORPRENAZ. The worms will feast.

NEKROZOTAR. You won't be thirsty anymore and the earth will swallow you.

PORPRENAZ. Stop! What are you saying?! Not thirsty anymore?[3]

Thirst is the only "evil" Porprenaz cannot bear to think of. Only this is capable of arousing his anger, and he prepares to beat Nekrozotar. As early as the first scene, then, Nekrozotar is portrayed as a clownish, totally harmless creature whose character sometimes verges on the grotesque. When the curtain rises, he is hiding in a tree, one of his legs hanging from the foliage. Seeing the leg, the facetious Porprenaz starts pulling it with all his strength, with the result that the sound of bells comes from the tree. Nekrozotar falls, and we discover that he wears bells around his waist: we are urged, therefore, to perceive this character as an eccentric court jester rather than as a potential threat.

This image of Nekrozotar is reinforced when he starts gathering the instruments he needs to carry out his mission. The scythe he brandishes has too often been associated with death to remain a significant symbol. He wears a ridiculous leather hat and a leather coat that is too long, and he plays the *Dies Irae* out of tune on his copper trumpet. Clearly, this shabby image of death is not to be taken seriously. On the contrary, as we witness the confrontation between the emaciated buffoon and the fat drunkard, we cannot help feeling that we are being presented with reincarnations of Don Quixote and Sancho Panza. And indeed, Porprenaz agrees to become Nekrozotar's servant. He even consents to be his mount, his Rosinante, for the fallen knight does not own a horse. As Nekrozotar and Porprenaz leave the stage, it seems that, instead of going off to trigger the predicted cataclysm, they are on their way to their own version of Cervantes' windmills.

The quizzical characterization of Nekrozotar does not come to an end with this ridiculous exit. Throughout the play, he is given comical names: Your Highness, Your Meagerness, Your Ugliness, Your Translucence, and Your Paleness, among many others, some of them invented by Ghelderode (and therefore untranslatable). These mocking names are perfectly in keeping with the protagonist's own name, which connotes his madness and ridiculousness. As Jean Decock has pointed out, the word "Nekrozotar" is an odd combination of ancient Greek, Flemish dialect, and Latin.[4] "Nekro-" is a Greek prefix meaning "death"; "-zot-" is a Flemish adjective meaning "mad"; and "-ar" is a Latin suffix that means "having the quality of."

Ghelderode, then, presents death as a potentially deranged character from the start. By the end of the last scene, Nekrozotar himself confirms our initial suspicions about his madness. The announced apocalypse has not taken place, and Nekrozotar piteously confesses that he is only an embittered, distracted senex who wanted to revenge himself on his former wife, Salivaine, a ruthless, mannish shrew who used to beat and scold him (and who is now married to Videbolle):

> *NEKROZOTAR.* I was young and strong, loving life and my fellow man.

> *GOULAVE.* Doesn't your head ache sometimes?

> *NEKROZOTAR.* There are rocks in it. So many blows! It is cracked.

> *GOULAVE.* How did it happen?

> *NEKROZOTAR.* The whip . . . the broom. And my love died. And I ate the yeast of hatred. (p. 121)

Exhausted by his confession and by events leading up to the aborted cataclysm, the old man dies and, in a puzzling peripeteia, all the characters show compassion for him. This death is dramatically prepared in the opening scene, when Porprenaz pulls Nekrozotar from the tree while uttering these ominous words: "Okay, I pull, and like the hangman I will swing with the convict" (p. 37). The figure of death is thus given a human dimension: the Angel of Death becomes a vulnerable mortal, and consequently is more easily demystified by us as well as by the characters.

Porprenaz and his friends never seem to feel threatened by Nekrozotar's presence. In fact, the atmosphere of the play is never gloomy, in contrast with the rest of Ghelderode's work. We are often reminded in *La Balade du Grand Macabre* of the Dionysian ambience that pervades a Flemish kermis as depicted by Breughel in many of his paintings, the influence of which Ghelderode always asserted. (In recognition of this quality in the play, the French director René Dupuy entitled his 1953 Paris production of it *La grande Kermesse.*) *La Balade du Grand Macabre* is set in Breugellande, and the stage directions describing the scenery are almost the colorful strokes of a painter:

> *GREEN.* The grass, the bushes, and a round tree . . .
>
> *VIOLET.* The sky . . .
>
> *WHITE.* Left, a tomb falling into ruins. It is a whitewashed cube with a pediment and a door at the back.
>
> *FAR.* The misty city of Breugellande, battlemented with domes and belltowers.
>
> *NEAR.* A part of an abandoned yard at the end of a spring day. Proud loneliness. (p. 31)

Even though death is always present in the canvases of Breughel, we derive from them a general impression of unrestrained joy and popular celebration, as we do from Ghelderode's play in spite of its protagonist and the tomb on stage. In Scene 1, Porprenaz walks on stage playing an accordion and singing an irreverent tune. Drinking bouts abound, and we are even presented with a mock circus parade advertising the performance:

> *PORPRENAZ.* Alarm! He is arriving, he has arrived! Who? The Phantasmagoric, the Thread-Cutter, the Bogeyman, the Boneless, the Histrion of Doom, the Producer of Cataclysms, the Director of the Ultimate Shindy, the Master of the Worms, the Piercer of Paunches . . . He is coming, the one that nobody expects . . . Book your seats. At midnight, the theater will burn, explode, collapse, and nothing will be grand anymore . . . Come and see what you have never seen and never will again. We play only once. There is room for everybody. (p. 79)

"The Histrion of Doom, the Producer of Cataclysms, the Director of the Ultimate Shindy . . . At midnight, the theater will burn, explode, collapse . . ." In this almost surrealistic juxtaposition of theatrical and cataclysmic terms—a juxtaposition that applies to the clownish yet deathlike figure of Nekrozotar himself—lies an aspect of Ghelderode's artistry. He suggests here that we conceive of the whole play as a gigantic show, a grand spectacle, a treat for the eyes. The flourish of colors and forms, the movement of resplendently attired characters through a picturesque landscape, far from obliterating the thematic substance of the play, actually serves Ghelderode's purposes. The baroque beauty of the set and of the colorful costumes induces in us a feeling of bliss rather than fear, thus undercutting the potential horror of death. The dramatist is attempting in this play to "kill" death by ridiculing or demystifying it, while inviting us to share his philosophy of life, which strongly recalls Horace's "carpe diem."

In the *Ostend Interviews* Ghelderode declared, "All my life has been a dance around a coffin . . . In order to get rid of your specters, you have to write about them." But he was not simply trying to get rid of his private specters in *La Balade du Grand Macabre*. It was written in 1934, when the ghost of fascism was already beginning to threaten Europe and the world. The play is the striking visualization not only of the dark premonition of a lucid dramatist, but also of the deepest belief of a genuine humanist. For Ghelderode does not rest content to warn us against the impending catastrophe, he gives us an alternative to it, as every true artist can be said to do. The structure of the play is circular. It opens and closes with the same image: that of the young lovers Adrian and Jusemina, whose flirtation is interrupted at the start by Nekrozotar (who places them in confinement in the tomb) but resumes as if nothing had happened at the end of the last scene (when they walk out of the tomb). Their conversation at the close of the play is the exact continuation of their opening dialogue. The tomb has proved unable to imprison the two lovers for eternity; death has been deflated. The theme of love, as conveyed through the relationship of Adrian and Jusemina, the only really appealing couple in all of Ghelderode's plays, is meant to enclose *La Balade du Grand Macabre* in a parenthesis. As Jean Decock has observed, their lovemaking is the ideal antidote to the ravages of death: procreation and proliferation—underlined by the abundant vegetation that is slowly taking over the stage—annihilate the effects of destruction. Indeed, as Adrian takes Jusemina away, he speaks of birth and renewal. "Everything has been purified and washed. You walk slower because you have a treasure buried in your flesh. From now on, I shall listen to your silence to hear that minuscule heart beating under yours" (p. 127). The theme of rebirth and fertility is further emphasized by the time symbolism. The action begins on the evening of a misty spring day and ends as the sun rises on the following morning. As the parenthesis of love is being closed, we realize that we have been presented, not with the image of death contained in the title of the play, but rather with the triumph of life. Porprenaz himself is aware of this triumph, and at the sight of Adrian and Jusemina emerging from the tomb he voices the dramatist's innermost conviction: "The human race cannot perish" (p. 127).

In the *Ostend Interviews* Ghelderode said, "The only purpose of the theater is to portray man, the human being. I wanted to show man as he is now and, through him, the eternal man" (p. 79). *La Balade du Grand Macabre* does just that. In it, Ghelderode attained a unity of intent and expression that remained unequalled throughout his work. The play is, in my view, the major achievement of this important dramatist and true humanist. Like Cervantes' *Don Quixote*, *La Balade du Grand Macabre* has its roots in the anthropomorphism of the culture of the folk, but grows out of these roots to address universal and eternal concerns.

NOTES

[1]Michel de Ghelderode, *Pantagleize*, in *Ghelderode: Seven Plays*, trans. Georges Hauger (New York: Hill and Wang, 1960), I, p. 143 (2nd quotation), p. 150 (1st one).

[2]Roger Iglesis and Alain Trutat, ed., *Les Entretiens d'Ostende* (Paris: L'Arche, 1956), p. 168. Hereafter referred to in the text by page number. All translations are my own.

[3]Michel de Ghelderode, *La Balade du Grand Macabre*, in *Théâtre II* (Paris: Gallimard, 1952), p. 39. Hereafter referred to in the text by page number. My translations.

[4]Jean Decock, *Le Théâtre de Michel de Ghelderode: Une Dramaturgie de l'Anti-Théâtre et de la Cruauté* (Paris: A.G. Nizet, 1969), p. 113.

The Artist in Society: Bond, Shakespeare, and *Bingo*

Lou Lappin

Yale College

In *Bingo*, Edward Bond does not claim to uncover any new dramatic truths. Instead, he dramatizes what is known, yet must be said—that human nature cannot exist independently of the society that formulates it. The play, he explains, reveals

> what everyone knows about the way our wishes and intentions and consciences and ideas are turned awry—by money. WS's 'crime' isn't a very bad crime—he doesn't wilfully exploit anyone, or steal wilfully from them, or punish them for criticising him . . . It is all only part of his security and prosperity . . . The play is about the compromises WS makes. But what right has he to call on the poor to make these compromises . . . Even if he shows . . . restraint he still has to make compromises with his own humanity . . . The crime relates to WS. It is brought out by his life. By his pact with society.[1]

At the end of his career Shakespeare is unable to achieve the kind of peace that a life of self-reflection might provide; instead, the opposite is true—he is restive and uneasy. Through the life of art, Bond implies, the artist reproduces his own moral sanity. In *King Lear*, for instance, Shakespeare "insisted on certain moral insights, certain priorities of conduct and you did those things even if it meant your death . . . You did those things because there is no other life that's bearable. For Lear. And Shakespeare must have known that, otherwise he couldn't have written the play."[2] Yet the figure Bond creates in *Bingo* is incapable of mediating the fictive world of his plays and the actual circumstances of his life. The tension in the play is created by the dialectic between an art that is spontaneous and humanitarian and a personal experience that denies those impulses. Shakespeare, living in retirement late in his life, is not alienated from the moral propositions of his art; but he is unable to act in accordance with them. Ethical decision-making has been possible for him only through creative artifice. The disjunction between what is possible in art and what is practical in life provides the axis on which the play rests.

Art, for Bond, satisfies the need of an artist to endow reality with human significance; it provides a means for affirmation of the self as well as the world. Through art Shakespeare had created a moral imperative for action that had determined his relationship with the world; his art was a form of self-creation designed to satisfy his own moral needs. But Shakespeare no longer has the power of artistic expression, and he cannot integrate himself in the material circumstances of his world. The result is that he is unable to correct the inequities that occur around him—unable to combat the material acquisitiveness of Combe, to feel anything but pity for the displaced farmers, and unable even to treat his family with tenderness. Although he had transformed his interior world through the power of his expressiveness, Shakespeare has failed to transform the world outside through the power of action.

In the society of Stratford, having and using constitute his relations with the world. In the process, Shakespeare has altered his essence; political expediency and material concern determine his behavior. The result is exhaustion and loss. Though art should function as the most effective medium between the artist and the world, Shakespeare has lost touch with human specificity. The more he realizes the disparity between his art and his actions, the more he understands his own impoverishment. Estranged from his creative powers and guiltily recoiling from other men, he denies the spirit of his artistic achievement.

Bond's accomplishment in the play does not arise from the revelation of an individual's psychology or the sweeping portrayal of man's behavior in an irrational universe. Instead, that accomplishment rests on the following assumption: "If you are an unjust person it doesn't matter how cultured you are, how capable you are of producing wonderful sayings, wonderful characters, wonderful jokes, you will still destroy yourself."[3] Since the ethical world of Shakespeare's plays remains an implicit reflection of the artist's personality, those plays stand as indictments of his public gestures. Paradoxically, Shakespeare is separated from his own art. What he comes to realize is that he has given birth to that art at the cost of his own well-being; as symbolic extensions of his own powers, his plays are lost to him.

At the beginning of *Bingo*, Shakespeare is divided, at once the creator of the canon and the landed proprietor of New Place—a private moralist and a public materialist. The one role stands for authentic creation, the other for false needs. The result is that Shakespeare, vaguely conscious of such internal division, experiences life as fragmented. As a principal landowner, he is influenced too readily by laws governing the market. Shakespeare's alienation is an economic phenomenon that has been inculcated in him through a system of fake needs; membership in the landed gentry has forced certain pressures upon him and created false allegiances. His alienation is signified by his loss of connection with the moral truth of the plays and consequently with the formal life of art. Through his surrender to the values of Combe, the artist is separated from his product.

Shakespeare's ability to perceive reality with moral persistence remains undiminished, however. Instead of taking action, he aestheticizes reality—the artistic impulse remains intact but is cut off from its moral center, divested of commitment and practical application. It formulates itself in epiphanic, half-conscious utterances on bear-baiting, gliding swans, and clean white snow.

The power of expressiveness remains but is stripped of its moral imagination. What remains are glimmerings of creativity, recalibrated fragments of the plays, broken shards of his own mental life. They concretize the gap between the "cultural hero" and the figure who signs what amounts to new poor laws to ensure his own material well-being. The attempt to aestheticize reality in images or in stylized formal address (primarily to Judith) reflects the artists's attempt to come to terms with his own disaffection, perhaps to overcome his dilemma by assimilating it artistically. In the process artistic creation ceases to be a productive and integral activity.

The inability to act has its correlative in the way Shakespeare perceives the act of writing: "Fat white fingers excreting dirty black ink. Smudges. Shadows. Shit. Silence."[4] Through art Shakespeare had created an imaginative world of human measure, yet his practical decisions deny that creation. Only by creating a humanized reality through practical measures can he lead a moral life. The dissociation of art from the artist is complicated because it is partial and incomplete. Silence and detachment: have undermined Shakespeare's artistic credentials. He has in part renounced the idea of human significance; he has silently internalized the inequity between the function of art and the role of the artist in society. This division represents a fracture in the personality of the artist and the surrender of his most essential nature: the result is his separation from other men. Shakespeare retreats into a sphere of egoism, withdraws into a solipsistic self. He is isolated from the community, preoccupied with his private interests, and haunted by images that signify his failure to act. In other men he can see only the limitation of his own freedom, and his despair at this is a measure of his separation from human values.

Bond's argument is that the root of Shakespeare's alienation lies outside his own persona and is embedded in the artificial needs that provide the basis for his social and economic relations with society. Bond asserts that, if one is to change the order of things, one must restructure the socio-economic system:

> To show that our society is irrational and therefore dangerous—and that it maintains itself by denigrating and corrupting human beings—that is what *Bingo* is about. . . . If you want to escape violence, you don't say 'violence is wrong,' you alter the conditions that create violence. . . . Society has to bear the consequences of what it is. If you want to avoid those consequences, the only way you can do it is not by applying a remedy on top but by altering the nature of the problem below. So it seems to me that *Bingo* is a demonstration of the working-out of certain truths about society which are rational and coherent and from which the audience can learn.[5]

Bond concludes that, despite Shakespeare's authority, his stature as a symbol of culture, he "is subject to the same laws as you and I or the man who drives your bus."[6] The paradox is that Shakespeare is tied to the limitations of a class system, while his art is not. He is tied to Combe's economics, yet he is socially and culturally bound to a class that doesn't share the same material relations.

If the material world of the artist is denatured, the creativity of the artist is also undermined; the aesthetic cannot be divested of its social relation. If it is, the artist is split by the world he intends to create for. As capitalism gains ascendancy in *Bingo*, life becomes increasingly impersonalized and reified. Shakespeare ceases to identify with capitalistic values; he refuses to exalt an inhuman reality, but he no longer has an artistic form at his disposal in which to announce his refusal.

In the material reality of *Bingo*, art and society are opposed; Bond's interest lies in the disruption of the relationship between the artist and the community. In this context one might ask whether Shakespeare is a victim or a victimizer. Is he denied the power of artistic expression by an inhuman society, or do his actions simply reflect his own insensitivity? Capitalistic society may resist the artist as he tries to express truth in his art, but, since Shakespeare is no longer actively creative, his problem is not how to create but how to resist, how to affirm his presence in an inhuman world. Bond's premise is that the solution is not beyond Shakespeare's control; human relations need not be abstract and impersonal. Even a mythic figure like Shakespeare cannot find refuge in his creative individuality. By disavowing responsibility and by resigning himself to passivity, he creates a society that is antithetical to artistic activity. Ultimately, Shakespeare becomes rootless in a hostile world no longer designed to manifest human presence.

Bond's imaginative re-creation of Shakespeare's disillusion treats him as if he possessed the knowledge of a modern man. Rather than criticize Shakespeare, Bond condemns the segment of our contemporary culture which ignores the truth that art has practical consequences. He argues that

> cultural appreciation ignores this and is no more relevant than a game of Bingo and less honest. . . . [*Bingo* is] a sort of attack on that kind of culture which is seen as something outside life, a sort of gilding on life, or something removed from life . . . It [culture] should be about our lives and it should help us to be able to solve our problems. . . . It would be wrong to say that our problem is such and such now because of something that happened in the past. Our problem is created all the time, constantly re-created [in art as well as in life]. And it's because we don't interfere with the re-creations of our problems that we can't solve our problems.[7]

Bond passionately insists that, for our society to survive, acceptance must turn into action: "You can go quietly into your gas chambers at Auschwitz, you can sit at home and have an H bomb dropped on you."[8]

*   *   *

Bond's early stage directions indicate the tone of the play and implicitly suggest the path its principal figure will take. Shakespeare nods silently, reads, and in four different stage directions "doesn't react" (p. 3); he initiates no dialogue. The pattern of stasis and silence is established in the first scene. This pattern is formally resolved near the end of the play when Shakespeare mournfully asks, "How long have I been dead?" (p. 51). In between he recants a life divested of purposeful energy and meaningful action:

> I spent so much of my youth, my best energy . . . for this: New Place. Somewhere to be sane in. It was all a mistake. There's a taste of bitterness in my mouth. . . . I could have done so much. Absurd! Absurd! I howled when they suffered, but they were whipped and hanged so that I could be free. . . . I was a hangman's assistant . . . God made the elements but we inflict them on each other. (p. 48)

Shakespeare's self-conscious silence implies an unresolved tension. His daughter Judith says what her father knows: that reflection is insufficient, that "people in this town aren't so easily impressed . . . We can all sit and think" (p. 18). Shakespeare remains either cordoned off from feeling or numbed by too much of it. Yet his first words belie his apparent detachment: he offers money to an itinerant beggar woman. That Shakespeare is capable of a solicitous gesture is crucial to Bond's argument and is hinted in the subtitle of the play: *Scenes of Money and Death*. The subtitle suggests the primacy of money in culture; it implies that Shakespeare's gesture neither has any bearing on the woman's well-being nor requires any great sacrifice on his part.

Money in capitalist society has become a means to suppress individuality. It "destroys the effect of human values in . . . society because consumer demand can't grow fast enough to maintain profits and full employment while human values are effective. . . . When livelihood and dignity depend on money, human values are replaced by money values."[9] Instead of ridding itself of poverty, a consumer society creates it by depending on its "members [to be] avaricious, ostentatious, gluttonous, envious, wasteful, selfish and inhuman."[10] In *Bingo*, Bond relates our contemporary culture—"the most irrational society that's ever existed"—to its antecedent in Shakespeare's social order, on the basis of the dependence of each on the acquisition of capital:

> We live in a closed society where you need money to live. . . . We have no natural rights, only rights granted and protected by money. Money provides . . . the ground we walk on, the air we breathe, the bed we lie on. People come to think of these things as products of money, not of the earth or human relationships, and finally as the way of getting more money to get more things. Money has its own laws and conventions, and when you live by money you must live by these.[11]

Shakespeare's avoidance of conflict at the beginning of the play and his decision to evade reality reflect a social structure in which human values are replaced by money values. When Combe, the principal landowner and magistrate, arrives, Shakespeare fails to intercede for the Young Woman. His only relation to her has been through the money he has offered her. Similarly, he takes no initiative against Combe for the enclosure of the common fields, even though he realizes that this enclosure will destroy the rural community. In the course of the play he will learn that single gestures—isolated moments of charity—have no bearing on the life of the community. When Shakespeare begins speaking, his words betray his weariness and prepare us for his complicity with Combe: "I get tired" (p. 4), "I don't know anything" (p. 3), "There's plenty of time" (p. 3). A commercial culture, Bond explains, "must finally destroy most of our moral sensitivity because the struggle for profit is much more corroding than the struggle for survival in the old pre-civilized world."[12]

Perhaps Shakespeare's need for security is not quite dramatically convincing. But Bond is not concerned with Shakespeare's psychological motivation: "What are his motives for withdrawing? I don't know . . . He's old, he's tired, he wants security . . . I'm not really interested in his motives."[13] The ideas of art and money (security) merge when Shakespeare, the aging but prosperous burgher, describes his finances: "The rents. I bought my share years ago out of money I made by writing" (p. 5). Despite the dispossession of the poor and the renters who don't have leases, he convinces Combe to guarantee his tithe income. "You'll get increased profits," Shakespeare tells Combe, "—you can afford to guarantee me against loss . . . I invested a lot of money" (p. 6). Bond comments implicitly on Shakespeare's predicament in the introduction to the play: "To get money you must behave like money. I don't mean only that money creates certain attitudes or traits in people, it *forces* certain behaviour on them."[14] Shakespeare refuses to commit his sizable political power to any group and reveals his self-interest when he claims neutrality: "I'm protecting my own interests. Not supporting you or fighting the town . . . I want security. I can't provide for the future . . . My father went bankrupt when he was old. Too easy going" (p. 7). Such specious reasoning would be less transparent if this were not the figure whose plays

> . . . show this need for sanity and its political expression, justice. How did he live? His behaviour as a property-owner made him closer to Goneril than Lear. He supported and benefited from the Goneril-society—with its prisons, workhouses, whipping, starvation, multilation . . .[15]

Shakespeare's preeminence and moral force reside in his significance as a landowner with vested interests rather than in his artistic accomplishment. By making the arrangement with Combe, Shakespeare in effect accepts "certain laws, and a series of punishments to enforce those laws and a certain mythology to explain those laws."[16] By signing the new poor laws, he no longer functions as a symbol of culture or possesses a rational relationship with the world. By tacitly agreeing to Combe's plea —"Be noncommittal or say you think nothing will come of it. Stay in your garden" (p. 6)—he enmeshes himself in a system where capital is employed to satisfy artificial needs, foster consumption, increase profits, and promote further industrial activity. Greater unemployment and higher food prices result from the loss of corn as a marketable crop as well as from increased competition and aggressiveness. The politics of brutality and fascism are perpetuated; it is the function of the play to suggest the necessity for change:

> I think the contradictions in Shakespeare's life are similar to the contradictions in us. He was a 'corrupt seer' and we are a 'barbarous civilization'. Because of that our society could destroy itself. We believe in certain values but our society only works by destroying them, so that our lives are a denial of our hopes. That makes our world absurd and often it makes our own species hateful to us.[17]

In a process of de-mythification, *Bingo* reveals Shakespeare's self-loathing, how any man's moral life may become lost. Shakespeare is exposed as a petit bourgeois who aligns himself with a brutal regime that is dedicated to the subjugation of the lower-class and rural community. His compromises become acts of betrayal: they condemn the Young Woman, the Son, the Old Man, and the Old Woman to a life of confinement. "A rational and free culture," Bond contends, "is based on a classless society. . . . [And] the job . . . of writers, of dramatists [is] to . . . rationally argue for a just society, to state clearly the conditions under which we live and try to make everybody understand that they must bear the consequences of the sort of life they lead."[18] The opposite view is held by the chief magistrate, who insists that the only way men have discovered of running the world depends on "the long view," a dark and fatalistic estimate of man: "Men are donkeys and they need carrots and sticks. All the other ways: they come down to bigger sticks" (p. 6). This ruthless, dehumanizing judgment is tinged with class antagonism, and provides the kind of justice that Shakespeare witnesses when the Young Woman is denied his charity because "the law says it's an offense to give alms to anyone without a licence" (p. 17). The casual insensitivity of a society depleted of human value is concealed by a rhetoric that invokes slogans about personal responsibility, payment of one's debts, and protection of the public. This is a social order that defends *injustice*. "That's why," Bond asserts, "law-and-order societies are morally responsible for the terrorism and crime they provoke."[19]

Shakespeare's inability to act undermines his instinctive good will and results in a burden that he will be unable to bear. Ultimately, he neglects culture by avoiding the action that would implement rationality. Paradoxically, as Bond has pointed out, Shakespeare's plays show the need for sanity and its political expression, justice.[20] But he himself simply watches with discomfort as the Young Woman's persecution unfolds. In his Puritan extremism, the Son envisions bestiality being visited upon her; Judith, a naive moralist, projects her own dissatisfaction with her father on the situation; the Old Man, half-maddened at the sight of an axe-handle, lurches merrily around the grounds in revelry over his debauchery of the Young Woman. Shakespeare bears witness to the meagerness and hopelessness of their positions, but says nothing. Despite his silence, his mind is alive and perceptive. When the Young Woman is finally seized by a power structure without compassion, he sighs. He allows his final offer of mediation to be brushed aside too easily. He chooses to remain, as Combe had urged, in the quiet of his garden.

Alone, ensconced in silence, he speaks only in stripped-down, practical, monosyllabic prose. There is no need for a more complex syntax because Shakespeare has nothing more complex to say. His attempts to communicate with Judith are sheerly formal: his sentences are declarative, factual, and insensate. She is not without our sympathy. She pleads with her father, "People have feelings. They suffer. Life almost breaks them" (p. 18). Hers is part of the generalized disaffection that all the characters endure. Shakespeare's ailing wife, Judith tells him, "stays in bed. She hides from you. She doesn't know who she is, or what she's supposed to do, or who she married. She's bewildered—like so many of us!" (p. 18) When Shakespeare contemptuously replies, "You speak so badly. Such banalities. So stale and ugly" (p. 18), it is her form rather than her sentiments that he coldly reproves. He is not impervious to feeling, but he has detached himself from experience in order to be able to examine it aesthetically. His remarks are leveled against Judith's means of expression, as if she were uttering lines from an inferior play and uttering them poorly at that. Shakespeare's criticism here is an extension of his art in its tendency to formulate experience abstractly. Yet, as a type of communication, such criticism impedes feeling and resists human contact.

The issue that Bond addresses through the character of Shakespeare is how the artist, or any man of conscience, assimilates moral knowledge through experience. The execution and gibbeting of the Young Woman elicit different responses from different segments of a stratified society, and Bond uses these responses to anatomize a culture that resists any sense of community or mutual responsibility and that neglects human suffering. Two farm laborers conjecture, "She die summat slow" (p. 22); they are insulated from feeling by the hardship of their own lives. The Son's Puritan extremism is framed by an Old Testament religiosity that shrilly insists on its own righteousness: at the sight of the Young Woman's body, he declares, "Lord god is wherever there's justice" (p. 22). The Son interprets experience in terms of strict moral categories: "When a soul go satan-ways lord god come to'watch an' weep" (p. 22). Judith feels complicity in the Young Woman's death; she intuitively recognizes that her action, or inaction, has somehow widened the gap between her and her father: "Are you blaming me? Is that what I've done now?" (p. 24) The Old Man recalls the grotesque, riotous atmosphere that accompanies a public execution:

> (*He starts to cry.*) O dear, I do hate a hanging. People runnin' through the streets laughin' an' sportin'. Buyin' an' sellin'. I allus enjoyed the hangings when I were a boy. Now I can't abide 'em. The conjurors with red noses takin' animals out the air an' coloured things out their pockets. The soldier lads scare us. The parson an' 'is antics. (p. 19)

Rather than become personally involved in the spectacle of the Young Woman's death, each of these witnesses detaches himself from it either morally, intellectually, or emotionally, and thus reveals his own victimization by society.

After he has regarded the gibbeted Young Woman with an expressionless face, Shakespeare literally turns his back on the sight; yet, he is the only figure to attempt to acknowledge the reality of the scene and formulate a human response: "I thought I knew the questions. Have I forgotten them?" (p. 25) This is the first time he articulates self-doubt in the play. He talks deliberately, as if to reassure himself against his own worst fears. With the first glimmer of recognition come the guilt and self-reproach that had lain in wait at the borders of his consciousness. Up to now, Bond had cast Shakespeare's inexpressiveness as a kind of emasculated potential; still, the consciousness of the artist had always been at work—selecting, observing, registering—and what finally emerges is no longer neutrality or disengagement. Shakespeare transforms the world of the hanging into one of bear-baiting, and connects the victimization of the Young Woman with that of a bear:

> The baited bear. Tied to the stake. . . . Dried mud and spume. . . . Men bringing dogs through the gate. . . . Loose them and fight. The bear wanders round the stake. It knows it can't get away. . . . Flesh and blood. Strips of skin. Teeth scrapping bone. . . . Round the stake. On and on. . . . Howls. Roars. Men baiting their beast. . . . And later the bear raises its great arm. The paw with a broken razor. And it looks as if it's making a gesture—it wasn't: only weariness or pain . . . Asking for one sign of grace . . . And the crowd roars, for more blood, more pain . . . (p. 25)

Shakespeare recites this monologue of brutal persecution in an objective, reportorial manner; the sheer horror inheres in the facts themselves—they need not be embellished by the imagination. The artist himself seems a likely surrogate for the wounded bear: impotent, staked to a circumscribed lot of ground, unable to surmount the pain and weariness.

It is Judith's assertion, "You're only interested in your ideas" (p. 26), that impels Shakespeare to utter what Bond has prepared us for by means of the monologue on bear-baiting, the Old Man's account of a public execution, and the gibbeting itself: "What does it cost to stay alive? I'm stupefied at the suffering I've seen" (p. 26). The consciousness of the artist is the consciousness of any moral man in an immoral universe. Shakespeare has begun to exchange the inactivity and silence of the early scenes for movement and action, and so succumbs to recognition and culpability: "There's no wisdom beyond your own responsibility." This is the first draft of a line from the notebooks of Leonardo Da Vinci, the final version of which Shakespeare quotes: "There's no higher wisdom of silence" (p. 26). Bond comments:

> I thought it was very appropriate for someone like Shakespeare who has by far the most influence of any dramatist since the Greeks. And he would have said: Yes—but you see, I haven't really done anything, I haven't answered any of these problems and I haven't answered all those things that I want to, I haven't been able to set down solutions

that make sense to anybody.[21]

The artist who conceived King Lear is wrenched out of his fictive self-containment and is filled with bewilderment not unlike Lear's: "I quietened the storms inside me. But the storm breaks outside" (p. 27). It is the revelation of the play that Shakespeare acknowledges the efficacy of the artist in determining culture, yet still admits that he "usurped the place of god, and lied" (p. 27). There is a dichotomy between the artist who carries on an interior life and the responsible citizen who intercedes for the spiritual health of the community: a division between contemplation and action, art and activity, imagination and reality.

By the middle of the play, Shakespeare renounces his neutrality, but his split self is not so easily united. Bond purposely refashions him as a folk hero who is beset by the same doubts as other men. He is generous, but without endangering his own interests; he would have liked to aid the Young Woman, but he did not do so. Although his intentions remain unacted upon, his position as a landowning member of the gentry at least gives him the opportunity to pose the right questions. The Old Woman servant can only lament, "I yont afford arkst questions" (p. 27). Shakespeare has always acknowledged the importance of the issues but has suppressed them for the sake of self-interest. They resurface, transformed, in his metaphoric, epiphanic utterances. In a moment of outward calm he narrates his encounter with a swan:

> A swan flew by me up the river. On a straight line just over the water.
> A woman in a white dress running along an empty street. Its neck was
> rocking like a wave. I heard its breath when it flew by. Sighing. The
> white swan and the dark water. Straight down the middle of the river
> and round a curve out of sight. I could still hear its wings. God knows
> where it was going. . . . (*He goes to the gibbet.*) Still perfect. Still
> beautiful. (pp. 27-28)

For a moment art merges with reality, just as it did during Shakespeare's monologue on bear-baiting. The scene of the hanging is transformed and aestheticized. The flight of the swan becomes a metaphor for the pure, clean life of abstract art, which is created "automatically," without interference from the imagination. Shakespeare's swan glides noiselessly, unencumbered by the life below, the lazy curve of its flight like the slow withdrawal of a spirit from reality. The gibbeted woman, disfigured by a brutal death, remains in this way aesthetically intact. Shakespeare's imagination functions as a safety valve, an escape, a means somehow to temper reality by transforming its ugliness into beauty. Yet Shakespeare's words are counterpointed and at least partly called into doubt by the choric utterance of the Old Woman, whose hardheadedness enables her to penetrate the artificiality of his speech: "Her's ugly. Her face is all a-twist. . . . She smell" (p. 28).

* * *

The artistic process rather than the life of art is the subject of the confrontation between Shakespeare and Ben Jonson at the start of Part Two of *Bingo*. Shakespeare's acknowledgement that he writes nothing because he has nothing to say, partly indicates the disjuncture between his art and his experience. Jonson, by contrast, has had a continuous series of engagements with life. He unwittingly isolates the source of Shakespeare's discomfort when he asks, "What's your life been like? Any real blood . . .? . . . Life doesn't seem to touch you, I mean soil you. . . . You are serene" (pp. 31-32). Unsurprisingly, the artistic process seems to consume Jonson's powers without replenishing them. He shares Shakespeare's sense of impotence and articulates his more reknowned colleague's silent thoughts and hidden regrets: "I go on and on, why can't I stop? I even talk shit now. To know the seasons of life and death and walk quietly on the path between them" (p. 34). If he does not grasp Shakespeare's problem, he notices its symptoms when he adds, "Something's happening to your will. You're being sapped" (p. 32). As Shakespeare has said, he does not write because he has nothing to say. When he did have something to say, he expressed it in the context of his plays; the only thing that remains for him is to put his ideas into action and validate himself as a man of society as well as culture.

Jonson's notion of the artistic process echoes Shakespeare's vision of reality. Throughout the play, Shakespeare reflects on life like a merchant burdened by the exigencies of middle-class existence: "The garden's too big. Time goes. I'm surprised how old I've got" (p. 31). The tone is bourgeois and familiar to any middle-class household breaking apart because of internal stress. By emphasizing Shakespeare's relatedness to all men in this way, Bond suggests that any citizen should be prepared to act to change his society for the better—to bring his daily life in line with his aspirations, "the economic and political basis of society in line with our ethical propaganda."[22] Though Shakespeare and Jonson are both in despair, Bond implies that Jonson has in the past at least been passionately involved in life: he has been imprisoned four times, experienced several religious conversions, and has actually committed murder. Now he, like Shakespeare, grows desperate with thoughts of escape and solace, like any artist who has witnessed horror but stood passively aside.

Jonson's reverie, "To spend my life wandering through quiet fields. Charm fish from the water with a song. Gather simple eggs. Muse with my reflection in quiet water . . . And lie at last in some cool mossy grave . . ." (p. 36), is dramatically counterpointed by a central action in the play: the dispossession of the farm laborers. Combe confronts the rebellious peasants who refuse to be displaced by "rich thieves plunderin' the earth" (p. 35). The Son, the leader of the opposition, asks Combe, "Whose interest's that protectin'? Public or yourn?" (p. 36) As the two antithetical social classes in the play confront each other, the two writers resign themselves to positions that have no bearing on the life of the community. While Shakespeare is slumped over a table and filled with drink, Combe expounds his views of cultural evolution to the Son:

There'll always be real suffering, real stupidity and greed and violence.

> And there can be no civilization till you've learned to live with it. I live
> in the real world and try to make it work. There's nothing more moral
> than that. But you live in a world of dreams! Well, what happens
> when you have to wake up? You find that real people can't live in
> your dreams. They don't fit, they're not good or sane or noble enough.
> (p. 36)

This speech supports the idea that capitalism is founded "on the proposition that
men are by nature enemies and . . . works on the principle that it is natural for
the strong to exploit the weak, the powerful to shape the powerless."[23] Thus the
speech stands as an implied critique of Shakespeare's art, the art of an idealist
who believes that men can change the shape of events, can subvert a society that
prolongs itself through a distorted view of human nature. The realization that
his signature endorses an exploitative political system has become impossible to
endure, so Shakespeare has taken to rationalizing the system. His exhaustion in
this scene intimates less his decline as an artist than his death as a force in the
life of the community. The two authors, one drunk and the other unconscious,
inhabit a world of blunted possiblity.

Scene Five of Part Two follows the scene between Shakespeare and Ben
Jonson and begins with the stage directions, "Open space. Flat white crispy
empty. The fields, paths, roads, bushes and trees are covered with smooth,
clean snow" (p. 39). Shakespeare idly muses over this landscape: "How clean
and empty the snow is. A sea without life. An empty glass. Still smooth.
No footprints. No ruts. No marks of weapons or hoes dragged through the
ground. Only my footprints behind me—and they're white . . . white" (p. 39).
In effect, he creates here an image of his legacy to the world, which remains
"smooth" and "clean," untouched and unchanged by his powers. Bond's notes
for an earlier draft place another interpretation on these lines: "Snow = perfect
ideal. When it doesn't melt, WS lives in the perfect ideal. The perfect ideal is
false because it is unreal. An ideal is always a lie."[24]

When in the darkness the Son accidentally shoots his father,
"Shakespeare," says Bond, "ignores the wounded figure: this is the essence
of his situation. Here he is drawn into the discovery of self-knowledge, so
concentrated in his self-judgement, that you could probably set fire to his coat
and he wouldn't notice it."[25] For the first time, he is able to address Judith
with candor on a topic of intimacy:

> When I ran away from your mother and went to London—I was so
> bored, she's such a silly woman, obstinate, and you take after her.
> Forgive me, I know that's cruel, sordid, but it's such an effort to be
> polite any more. . . . I loved you with money. . . . But money always
> turns to hate. . . . I treated you so badly. I made you vulgar and ugly
> and cheap. I corrupted you. (pp. 41-42)

Though he finally acknowledges complicity in the corruption of his daughter
(with the same means that Combe used on him), even his contempt for her is

aestheticized and detached: "Don't be angry because I hate you, Judith. My hatred isn't angry. It's cold and formal. I wouldn't harm you. . . . There's no limit to my hate. It can't be satisfied by cruelty. It's destroyed too much to be satisfied so easily. Only truth can satisfy it now" (p. 42). Judith represents to Shakespeare (however unfairly) the irrationality of life, of society; the fact that this irrationality is of no relevance to her generates her father's hatred. His hatred is more likely a self-hatred, however, generated by the gulf between his humanistic intentions and the society that has eroded them. For Shakespeare, the impasse between a creative, searching interior life and the objective, peremptory world of action results in the artist's willed demise.

Shakespeare's political as well as artistic silence resolves itself in his suicide. Each of these silences has implied and complemented the other. Although creativity satisfies an inner need for expression and is necessary to sustain culture, it cannot thrive when sealed off from practical action. The result is the dispossession of the social self in addition to the artistic one. Nobody, not even Shakespeare, can create in a void. Our final image of him is of a limp figure helplessly twitching and jerking on the floor while Judith pronounces his legacy as she ransacks the room for a new will: "Nothing. Nothing. Nothing" (pp. 51-52).

Not surprisingly, it is Combe who presides over Shakespeare's demise as he casually hands him Jonson's poison bottle. Combe emerges "as the formidable enemy he is and neither Shakespeare nor the Son can oppose him."[26] In Combe's gesture of giving Shakespeare the poison tablets, Bond crystallizes the latter's confrontation with and capitulation to the ruling class. Yet Shakespeare's taking of his own life is a refusal, finally, to be part of the capitalist system. Rather than being the disillusioned words of a sterile aesthete, his refrain, "Was anything done?" (p. 51), acknowledges his altered vision as well as a measure of self-blame. Unlike the Son, Shakespeare refuses (however belatedly) to deceive himself. He has become self-critical, enough so that he can declare, "Every writer writes in other men's blood. There's nothing else to write in. But only a god or a devil can write in other men's blood and not ask why they spilt it and at what cost" (p. 43). Implicitly, Shakespeare has come to believe, like Bond, that "morality can exist only in a culture or be forged in the quest for one."[27]

NOTES

[1]Malcolm Hay and Philip Roberts, *Edward Bond: A Companion to the Plays* (London: Theatre Quarterly Publications, 1978), p. 198.
[2]Hay and Roberts, p. 59.
[3]Karl-Heinz Stoll, "Interviews with Edward Bond and Arnold Wesker," *Twentieth Century Literature*, 22, No. 4 (Dec. 1976), p. 418.
[4]Edward Bond, *Bingo* and *The Sea* (New York: Hill and Wang, 1975), p. 31. Hereafter cited by page number in the text.

[5]Stoll, pp. 418, 421.

[6]Stoll, p. 422.

[7]Hay and Roberts, pp. 18, 21; Stoll, p. 420 (from "It would be wrong
. . ." on).

[8]Hay and Roberts, p. 18.

[9]Bond, Intro., *Bingo*, p. xiii.

[10]Bond, Intro., *Bingo*, p. xiii.

[11]Bond, Intro., *Bingo*, pp. xii-xiii.

[12]Hay and Roberts, p. 46.

[13]Hay and Roberts, p. 62.

[14]Bond, Intro., *Bingo*, p. xiii.

[15]Bond, Intro., *Bingo*, p. xii.

[16]Hay and Roberts, p. 60.

[17]Bond, Intro., *Bingo*, p. xvi.

[18]Stoll, p. 418.

[19]Bond, Intro., *Bingo*, p. xv.

[20]Bond, Intro., *Bingo*, p. xvi.

[21]Hay and Roberts, p. 59.

[22]Hay and Roberts, p. 52.

[23]Hay and Roberts, p. 51.

[24]Hay and Roberts, p. 195.

[25]Hay and Roberts, p. 195.

[26]Hay and Roberts, p. 197.

[27]Edward Bond, *The Fool* and *We Come to the River* (London: Eyre
Methuen, 1976), p. viii.

Old Times: Pinter's Drama of the Invisible

Art Borreca

Yale Repertory Theatre

Much of the writing on *Old Times* exemplifies a disheartening aspect of Pinter criticism. The search for the "Pinteresque" turns every work into an experiment or game with a fixed set of techniques and themes: e.g., silence, ellipsis, menace, intrusion, dominance-subservience, memory. Seen as a manifestation of the "Pinteresque," *Old Times* is merely a recombination of such techniques and themes, and becomes interpreted in terms of the works that precede it in Pinter's *oeuvre* instead of for itself. Indeed, the usual view of the play is that it dramatizes Anna's irruption into Kate and Deeley's home and marriage; that the irruption causes a battle between Anna and Deeley for possession of Kate; that Anna and Deeley use their memories as weapons in this battle.[1] In other words, *Old Times = The Caretaker* or *The Homecoming* (intrusion, dominancesubservience) + *Landscape* and *Silence* (lyricism, memory).

To interpret the play in this way is to place it neatly into Pinter's development and to believe that we understand his dramatic method. But the power of *Old Times* is that it defies such understanding; to experience the play is to experience the method of this defiance. The mysteries of *Old Times*—the sustained poetic resonances not found in *The Homecoming*, for example, or the strangely conflicting memories not found in *Landscape* and *Silence*—cannot be explained (and thereby explained away) through reference to the "Pinteresque." They must be regarded on their own terms as aspects of the particular experience of *Old Times*.

A few critics—Martin Esslin and Benedict Nightingale, for example—have explored the play's mysteries, but even they finally try to explain too much when they spell out what the play's realistic context *might* be.[2] Stanley Kauffmann has written most incisively about *Old Times*: that it demonstrates Pinter's characteristic ability "to dramatize the invisible," that its "delicately modulated, chromatic, contradictory writing" constitutes "the mere surface index of a huge buried presence in us that has nothing to do with reason or explanation."[3] This inexplicable, invisible presence is so much the essence of *Old Times* that even the central conflict it generates defies description. Kauffmann claims that the conflict is sexual—that a battle for sexual possession of Kate manifests the invisible presence. Yet even the mysteries of sexual desire don't encompass the "huge, buried presence" in *Old Times*, and to call the presence "sexual" is to

clarify the stakes involved in Anna and Deeley's conflict, which are as elusive
as they are deeply felt (by both the characters and the audience).

The most recent significant American production of the play (directed by
Kenneth Frankel at the Roundabout in January, 1984, with Anthony Hopkins as
Deeley, Marsha Mason as Kate, and Jane Alexander as Anna) illustrated that
what defies critics also defies actors, who of course have the more difficult task
since they must find tangible means of intimating the invisible. This production
received a great deal of praise,[4] yet it merely demonstrated the corollary in
Pinter production to the disheartening aspect of Pinter criticism: a tendency to
play the "Pinteresque" and thereby eviscerate the play of its particular theatrical
force. Before exploring this production's problems and what they reveal about
Pinter production (and the production of *Old Times* in particular), I will defy
Old Times in turn by trying to describe its essence.

A major source of difficulty for both critics and actors is that Kate, Deeley,
and Anna reveal an ambiguous past while interacting in a setting that suggests
a real place:

A converted farmhouse.
A long window up centre. Bedroom door up left.
Front door up right.

Spare modern furniture.
Two sofas. An armchair.[5]

In this realistic setting we expect characters to provide substantial evidence of
their pasts and of their relationships to one another in the past and present.
Typically the past is ambiguous in Pinter's plays, so we may not expect to
get all the answers we get in, say, Ibsen. But the very dramatic procedure
of *Old Times* is that of unfolding the ambiguous past, and the play's subject
is memory. We find the procedure and the subject disconcerting because the
play's set is realistic. In *Landscape* the setting is "real" but Beth and Duff
do not converse with each other; we accept the past's ambiguity because we
can ascribe it to the play's lyricism. As we observe Deeley, Kate, and Anna
"merely" talk to one another in Deeley and Kate's living room (and, in the
second act, their bedroom), we want to piece together the information they
reveal into the story of their lives. Indeed, the contradictions between Anna's
and Deeley's memories heighten this tendency: we think we are working out a
kind of puzzle of character histories and relationships.

We think, in other words, that we are playing our correct part in a
"Pinteresque" game. To treat the play as a puzzle, however, is to try to resolve
a tension fundamental to the play's mysteries, a tension between real space and
other, figurative spaces that are the play's main concern: the space between self
and being, between being and being with others, between being and having been
with others. Pinter sustains this tension between real and what might be called
ontological space in order to fuel the interaction among Anna, Kate, and Deeley
and to transform them into figures in a drama about the essence of experience.
The "spare modern furniture" of Kate and Deeley's home incarnates life pared

down to that essence. *Old Times* is best served (as it was at the Roundabout) by a set that suggests an actual country home without seeming to *be* that home. Such a set intimates that what is being dramatized does indeed occur in such homes, is true to the actuality of our experience, and yet takes place in virtually imperceptible realms of that experience.

Something Bernard Beckerman has noted about Pinter's work has special relevance to our experience of this drama of essence or of the invisible: we must attend to "the motions and not the meanings"; we must observe the "figures of action" without supplying a "ground" that explains their motion.[6] We must stay with what emerges before us; we must remain *within* the play, allowing its tensions to work on us. The invisible drama of *Old Times* arises from the interaction of words and silences, which build upon one another to bring a heightened world into being. If we fill in information that we don't learn from what Anna, Deeley, and Kate say, we do so at the risk of deadening our capacity to respond to that world.

For Pinter has written the play as if it were a test for the *audience's* poetic imagination, for the kind of patience required to witness and experience fully a poem that creates itself word by word, line by line. He opens with silence and a visual image: in dim light, Kate and Deeley sit downstage as Anna stands upstage, her back to them, looking out the window. He adds a word ("Dark," Kate says, *"reflectively"* [p. 7]; Pinter's emphasis), then a pause. Only gradually can we recognize even the general subject of Kate and Deeley's conversation:

DEELEY. Fat or thin?

KATE. Fuller than me. I think.

Pause

DEELEY. She was then?

KATE. I think so.

DEELEY. She may not be now. (pp. 7-8)

It takes seven more lines for us to understand what Deeley is specifically asking Kate about: an old friend coming to visit. Yet before their conversation becomes clear to us on this literal level, it resonates far beyond the literal. As the dialogue and the opening image (sustained by Anna's continued presence) play against each other, Kate's uncertainty about what her friend looked like signifies more than simple failure of memory. In Pinter's emerging poetic world her friend is *there*, and her physical presence, in the light of Kate and Deeley's conversation, becomes symbolic of another kind of presence: the reality that memory both generates and tries to apprehend; a remnant of the past, what remains of another person after that person is no longer part of one's current experience.

Deeley asks, "Was she your best friend?" . . . "Can't you remember what you felt?" . . . "Why would she be coming here tonight?" (p. 8) . . . "Did you *think* of her as your best friend?" (p. 9) . . . "Is that what attracted you to her?" (p. 11) These questions are essentially the same: What is it that once bound you to each other? Fundamentally, Deeley is asking about the source of the "presence": "I'll be watching you," he tells Kate, ". . . To see if she's the same person" (pp. 11-12). Kate's responses are thin, both preceded and punctuated by pauses that are, in a sense, to be taken literally: as temporal spaces without words. In such spaces, the absence of speech implies either that Deeley's questions are unanswerable or that words are unavailable to answer them:

> *DEELEY.* Can't you remember what you felt?
>
> *Pause*
>
> *KATE.* It is a very long time.
>
> *DEELEY.* But you remember her. She remembers you. Or why would she be coming here tonight?
>
> *KATE.* I suppose because she remembers me.
>
> *Pause* (pp. 8-9)

In the theatre, the pauses in this dialogue heighten our awareness of Anna at the window: brief aural rests sharpen our focus on the visual image. Because our awareness of Anna is heightened, we sense, in each pause, Kate's inability to specify what generates the "presence" that Anna contains.

As silence recurs, it underscores a disjunction between Anna's physical presence (in Pinter's poetic world) and Kate's slight memories. In that disjunction, we sense the "huge, buried presence": experience that has given form to the self and bound it to others, yet that remains outside the attempt by consciousness to grasp fully what has been. What emerges from Kate's failure to answer Deeley's questions, in other words, is a profound gap between experience and memory. Pinter's pauses become metaphors for the gap. As memory works to fill it, language articulates the attempt and fills silence. Indeed, both in reading and on the stage, *Old Times* seems gradually molded out of silence, which is ever-present as a pressure behind words. As Deeley and Kate speak, the effect is that of a smooth surface forming to cover silence, to deny the gap.

Certain lines seem to jut from this emerging surface. For example, after having told Deeley that she doesn't know why Anna was her only friend, Kate has her first vivid recollection:

> *DEELEY.* Why her?

KATE. I don't know.

Pause

She was a thief. She used to steal things.

DEELEY. Who from?

KATE. Me.

DEELEY. What things?

KATE. Bits and pieces. Underwear. (p. 10)

Similarly, Deeley responds "abruptly" after a pause to the information that Kate and Anna once lived together: "You lived together?" (p. 16) This line and Kate's earlier one, "She was a thief. She used to steal things" (p. 10), give the impression that for an instant the gap between memory and experience has been filled. Because their specificity or abruptness contrasts sharply with the pauses that precede them, they seem to bear truths about Kate's and Deeley's lives. They do so, however, not only because they may be true to what actually was, but because they are clearly true to Kate's and Deeley's individual memories. Thus Deeley says, "I knew you had shared with someone at one time . . . But I didn't know it was her" (p. 17).

This kind of truth to the individual's understanding of what has been pervades the play, especially when Anna and Deeley speak their memories at length but do not receive confirmation of them from the other character they involve. When Anna suddenly turns from the window and speaks of "queuing all night" at Albert Hall and Covent Garden, "lunchtimes in Green Park," and afternoons at cafés "where artists and writers and sometimes actors collected" (pp. 17-18)—about all the excitement of her life with Kate—the fullness of her memory seems odd compared with Kate's almost silent responses to Deeley's questions. Yet the speech's fullness asserts its truth to *Anna's* sense of the past, even though silence sets in again when she finishes speaking:

ANNA. . . . does it still exist I wonder? do you know? can you tell me?

Slight pause

DEELEY. We rarely get to London.

KATE stands, goes to a small table and pours coffee from a pot.

KATE. Yes, I remember.

> *She adds milk and sugar to one cup and takes it to ANNA.*
> *She takes a black coffee to DEELEY and then sits with her*
> *own.*

DEELEY. (*to ANNA*) Do you drink brandy?

ANNA. I would love some brandy.

> *DEELEY pours brandy for all and hands the glasses. He*
> *remains standing with his own.*

ANNA. Listen. What silence. Is it always as silent?

DEELEY. It's quite silent here, yes. Normally.

> *Pause*

> You can hear the sea sometimes if you listen very carefully.
> (pp. 18-19)

The sense of silence setting in here recurs throughout the play, but especially when a long speech of memory by Anna or Deeley is followed by a pause-punctuated exchange among all three characters. Structurally, this alternation between long speeches and pause-punctuated dialogue is the play's fundamental rhythm, which repeatedly breaks the smooth surface of words that cover silence and thereby makes us aware of silence—the gap between experience and memory—as ever-present.

Such a "broken" rhythm is felt forcefully not only in our experience of the play's unfolding but also in our experience of the tensions among Anna's and Deeley's memories themselves: that is, not only in our experience of the play's forward dramatic movement but also of its "retrospective movement," as Anna's and Deeley's memories play against each other in *our* memory. Deeley recalls meeting Kate in a "fleapit" where he saw *Odd Man Out* and where she was the "only . . . other person in the cinema" (p. 29); soon after, Anna remembers a Sunday afternoon when Kate dragged her excitedly to the same film, which they saw "almost alone" (p. 38). In the second act, Deeley tells Anna that he remembers her "quite clearly" (p. 48) from a pub where he bought her drinks, and from a party at which he looked up her skirt; Anna denies having met him, but later says that she once borrowed Kate's underwear to go to a party, where a man spent the whole evening looking up her skirt.

The tensions among these memories arise not from outright contradiction—from one memory negating another—but from the way they "refract" each other, to use Stanley Kauffmann's term.[7] Anna's and Deeley's long speeches seem to present different versions of the same events; given a particular shape by one character's memory, an event later takes on a slightly different shape when it is passed through the other's memory. It's tempting to try to sort out the true from the false in Anna's and Deeley's speeches, since truth seems to rest in their areas of refraction, where different versions of the same event seem to overlap. To try to do this, however, is to seek a specific relationship between past and present in the play—the effect of one on the other, for example. This impulse is behind such gross misunderstandings as T. E. Kalem's, who wrote in *Time*: "The uses of the past are betrayed in *Old Times*. At the end of the play, nothing about the past has been clarified or illuminated."[8] The function of ambiguity in *Old Times* is to deny the notion that there is such a thing as an absolute past, a truth about what has been that makes discussion of the relationship between past and present meaningful. The ambiguity maintains the gap between memory and experience; it asserts that even though memories such as those in Anna's opening speech may be vivid and articulated with force, they, too, merely cover silence instead of replacing it.

This is not to deny that the memories refer to events that have taken place, but to say that Pinter does not center *Old Times* on an emerging past and its bearing on the present. He centers it instead on the condition of existing in time, on what it is to experience time's passage. That experience, he reveals, is a futile struggle: one can never say that the events one remembers have actually taken place at all. One may feel that something has been (one may feel its "presence") and assert that it has, but such assertions are fraught with a sense of loneliness and loss:

> ANNA. We weren't terribly elaborate in cooking, didn't have the time, but every so often dished up an incredibly enormous stew, guzzled the lot, and then more often than not sat up half the night reading Yeats.
>
> *Pause*
>
> (*To herself.*) Yes. Every so often. More often than not.
> (p. 22)

There's loneliness in the pause, in which Kate fails to confirm the memory; there's loss in the repetition of "more often than not," which implies Anna's fear that what she remembers actually took place more *not* than often—or not at all. "I was interested once in the arts," Kate says later, "but I can't remember now which ones they were" (p. 37). On a literal level her statement seems impossible to us. But Kate does not possess Anna's or Deeley's will to battle the uncertainty that time brings; she simply lets it stand. True to that will, which she manifests in her opening speech, Anna responds to Kate's remark with memories of "days at the Tate" (p. 38), of exploring old buildings, of theatres and concerts. But her speech, which ends with the recollection that she and Kate saw *Odd Man Out* together, is met with silence.

Soon after her opening speech, Anna makes a remark that captures perfectly the uncertainty she and Deeley battle:

> ANNA. No one who lived here would want to go far. I would not

want to go far, I would be afraid of going far, lest when I returned
the house would be gone. (p. 19)

Anna and Deeley are afraid to go far from their memories, for they might lose
a sense both of the past and of the self formed by that remembered past. The
alternative is to live somehow in the immediate present: to deal with each other
openly and now. But that present is charged with its own special uncertainty.
As silence threatens to set in after Anna's opening speech, for example, her
and Deeley's conversation grows frighteningly awkward:

> *DEELEY.* I wish I had known you both then.
>
> *ANNA.* Do you?
>
> *DEELEY.* Yes.
>
> > *DEELEY pours more brandy for himself.*
>
> *ANNA.* You have a wonderful casserole.
>
> *DEELEY.* What?
>
> *ANNA.* I mean wife. So sorry. A wonderful wife.
>
> *DEELEY.* Ah.
>
> *ANNA.* I was referring to the casserole. I was referring to your
> wife's cooking.
>
> *DEELEY.* You're not a vegetarian, then?
>
> *ANNA.* No. Oh no.
>
> *DEELEY.* Yes, you need good food in the country, substantial food,
> to keep you going, all the air . . . you know.
>
> > *Pause* (pp. 20-21)

In the view of the play as a battle for possession, the uneasiness here is understood as that of the emerging conflict between Anna and Deeley. Following as
it does Anna's long and effusive opening speech, however, the uneasiness is
in essence that of Anna's now actual presence, of Kate's continued quietness
(her failure, when confronted with Anna's memories of their life together, to
say more than she does in response to Deeley's questions in the opening scene),
and of Deeley's first (?) meeting with a woman who has come to visit for
reasons he could not establish in his conversation with Kate. There is a sense

that Anna, Kate, and Deeley, now physically present together, become aware of the "presence" dramatized in the first scene and deal with it by filling the silence in which it is felt.

Dramaturgically, Pinter sustains this impression of silence being filled by infusing the play with a sense of *presentness*: the sense that Deeley, Kate, and Anna deal with one another always in response to memories that have *just* emerged. Indeed, Pinter maintains focus on Anna's visit as an occasion for memory, and on the pattern of memory's emergence. Anna and Deeley move on from their awkward opening conversation to exchange, just as awkwardly, impressions and memories of Kate, what they find unique about her. This leads them to sing songs from the 1930s and 1940s—to play a game of "remember the lyrics" that becomes, in retrospect, a metaphor for their attempts to identify the experiences in which their individual bonds to Kate were born. Notably, when they finish singing there is a silence (the second silence Pinter designates), after which Deeley says, "What happened to me was this" (p. 29), as he begins to describe how he met his wife.

The speech that follows, like all such speeches of Deeley's and Anna's, seems to be both the slow articulation of a gradually forming memory and the forceful effusion of a singular image. This double quality reflects a significant aspect of the way memories emerge in the play: although the memories refract each other, Anna and Deeley seem unaware of this refraction as they speak; each seems as much to be creating a unique word-picture as to be remembering a common past. (Their apparent unawareness is important to the sense of "presentness.") In the *reader's* or *spectator's* experience, there is a sense that the memories collide with one another. There is also the sense that Anna and Deeley may feel this collision but cannot speak about it. Instead, they vent the frustrations it causes in their more awkward exchanges: for instance, when Anna explains at length that she was glad to hear that Kate married Deeley, and he responds by joking about a metaphor Anna uses to explain why she was glad. In another instance, after Deeley asserts that he and Anna have met before, they discuss who should dry Kate when she comes out of her bath:

> *ANNA*. Why don't you dry her yourself?
>
> *DEELEY*. Would you recommend that?
>
> *ANNA*. You'd do it properly.
>
> *DEELEY*. In her bath towel?
>
> *ANNA*. How out?
>
> *DEELEY*. How out?
>
> *ANNA*. How could you dry her out? Out of her bath towel?
>
> *DEELEY*. I don't know.

ANNA. Well, dry her yourself, in her bath towel.

Pause

. . .

DEELEY. I've got a brilliant idea. Why don't we do it with powder?

ANNA. Is that a brilliant idea?

DEELEY. Isn't it?

ANNA. It's quite common to powder yourself after a bath.

DEELEY. It's quite common to powder yourself after a bath but it's quite uncommon to be powdered. Or is it? It's not common where I come from, I can tell you. My mother would have a fit.

Pause

Listen. I'll tell you what. I'll do it. I'll do the whole lot. The towel and the powder. After all, I am her husband. But you can supervise the whole thing. And give me some hot tips while you're at it. That'll kill two birds with one stone.

Pause

(*To himself.*) Christ.

He looks at her slowly.

You must be about forty, I should think, by now.

Pause

If I walked into The Wayfarers Tavern now, and saw you sitting in the corner, I wouldn't recognize you. (pp. 55-57)

In exchanges such as these, it's important to distinguish the sense of collision from competition. Although the collision centers on Kate, she is not the object of a battle for possession. She is, rather, the visible locus of Anna's and Deeley's desperate need to possess the experiences they remember: in a sense, to possess aspects of their selves formed by those experiences and to feel some control over time, which is constantly passing, carrying experience out of memory's reach.

However one may wish to interpret the substance of Anna's and Deeley's memories, it is this sense of struggling to possess what cannot be possessed, to control something invisible, that is the essence of *Old Times*. The play closes with two events unlike anything that precedes them. Kate, who has no other long speeches, gives the longest speech in the play: she remembers Anna "lying dead" with her "face scrawled with dirt" and her "bones breaking through [her] face" (p. 72); she remembers bringing Deeley into her room and trying to plaster his face with dirt, which "he resisted . . . with force" (p. 73); she remembers Deeley suggesting "a wedding instead, and a change of environment" (p. 73). Then, in *silence*, the three characters physically go through what seems to be a reenactment of one of Anna's memories. In that memory, she returned home one night to her and Kate's room to find a man crumpled in an armchair, crying; she went to bed; he stood in the center of the room, came slowly over to her bed, and bent over her; he went away, but she later saw him lying across Kate's lap on her bed.

Kate's speech cannot be called a memory. It does not try, like Anna's and Deeley's speeches, to close the gap between memory and experience; it transforms what seems to have been a series of painful experiences into a dream vision. It expresses not recollections, but only feelings about them; it tries to articulate *directly* the "presence" that memory generates. The silence that follows Kate's speech differs from the kind that pervades the rest of the play: it is not the silence of the gap between experience and memory, but the silence left after the ultimate effort to deny that gap by articulating part of the "huge, buried presence" itself.

Significantly, the apparent reenactment doesn't match Anna's memory event by event: Anna and Deeley both turn towards the door but do not leave; at the end, Deeley has not left but sits again in the armchair. The reenactment thus reminds us of Anna's memory but collides with it. Ultimately, we must leave Anna's memory behind—in experience of the play *and* in interpretation. What Anna remembers can be expressed in language; what is enacted at the end of the play cannot. To express Anna, Deeley, and Kate's bond to one another, Pinter lets words fall away. The invisible tie that cannot be spoken—because of the gap between memory and experience—is made visible in the closing image:

> *Silence*

> *Lights up full sharply. Very bright.*

> *DEELEY in armchair.*
> *ANNA lying on divan.*
> *KATE sitting on divan.* (pp. 74-75)

The play returns, in a sense, to its opening: to a visual intimation of what Kate could not express in the first scene. At the same time as the play circles back to its opening, however, it moves far beyond that opening: to a visual intimation of the bond among Anna, Kate, and Deeley, not only of the "presence" in which they feel that bond.

The difference between the silence with which *Old Times* closes and the silence pervading the rest of the play is the difference between silence at the limits of speech and what might be called the silence *beneath* speech. And yet, although Pinter ultimately lets language fall away, it would be wrong to say that the invisible in *Old Times* is communicated only—and ironically—visually. Indeed, one of the remarkable aspects of the play is Pinter's expression, in the language of the memories, of the invisible's inaccessibility. The sheer lyricism of his language makes us aware of words briefly living and then dying, momentarily taking possession of the time in which they move:

> ANNA. Queuing all night, the rain, do you remember? my goodness, the Albert Hall, Covent Garden, what did we eat? to look back half the night, to do things we loved, we were young then of course, but what stamina, and to work in the morning, and to a concert, or the opera, or the ballet, that night, you haven't forgotten? and then riding on top of the bus down Kensington High Street, and the bus conductors, and then dashing for the matches for the gasfire and then I suppose scrambled eggs, or did we? (p. 17)

Even though the memories cannot be verified, even though what Anna says may not connect wholly with what has been, words have a force to create a vision of what has been that will suffice, powerfully, for the time being.

Having thus returned to the beginning of the play (from silence to speech, as it were), the question of the Roundabout production remains. For it is in Pinter's delicate balance between speech and silence that any production of the play succeeds or fails. The essential question: How is an actor to convey that sense of words living and dying, of the awkwardness of filling silence with speech that tries to connect with the past—and the sense of the invisible that all this intimates? The tendency, in playing the "Pinteresque," is to show either too much (to intimate more than the play reveals) or too little (for example, to expect an entire character to be created out of only slight bits of evidence).

At the Roundabout, three markedly different kinds of actor—with markedly different senses of how much to show—shared the stage. The result was a production without a center, without a vision of the play and the way it *emerges* before an audience. Marsha Mason took her image of Kate from Anna's and Deeley's remarks that she exudes "a kind of floating" (p. 54) and that she is a dreamer. She gave a one-note performance for the most part: she gazed into space to make it clear that she was dreaming, and she spoke dreamily. Mason seemed so far removed from the stage reality, in fact, that it was impossible to believe she was the object of Anna's and Deeley's memories. (She suggested no sense at all of at least this basic function of Kate's character.) Oddly, she played Kate's closing speech as if, line by line, it described a single, actual event; she seemed suddenly to shift into a realistic conception of her character, as if she had made up a character past to help her get through the speech.

Mason's singular dreaminess and sudden realism had this consistency: they each turned Pinter's language on its head, if from different angles of attack. Anthony Hopkins' performance, by contrast, was consistent in its manner of attack. He so much wanted his Deeley to be real that he seemed to create another play, one with a logical story, around Pinter's. In fact, in a *New York Times* article Hopkins remarked that, to play the role, he had to ground it in reality by imagining a full biography of Deeley.[9] There is nothing wrong in itself with doing this, of course. The problem was that Hopkins carried the weight of his biography onto the stage. He overplayed Deeley's memories by pushing hard on their words; he gave them an edge that obscured the natural resonance of Pinter's language. In the latter half of the first act, he had Deeley grow drunk quickly, abruptly, following a standard model for acting in a "living-room-and-drinks" play. He based his performance so much on a naturalistic interpolation into the play that he forced subtext into many lines: he turned Pinter's poetic language of memory into a hard, pointed language of threatening but indirect confrontation.

Jane Alexander's Anna did not respond to Deeley's confrontations—the effect being that Deeley seemed often to be forcing a conflict that Anna did not acknowledge. Alexander's performance was the best of the three. While she never sank to Hopkins' level of alcohol-induced threat, she played within his naturalistic limits; at the same time, she never lost awareness of the play's heightened reality. She spoke Anna's memories with sensitivity to their poetry, infusing them with life as actual, concrete recollections; she sustained a naturalistic surface that emanated from a poetic core. The main problem with her performance was that the naturalism finally delimited the poetry: she did not let her poetic instinct break the surface enough, enabling us to see the core directly. It seemed as if she happened upon the naturalistic-poetic fusion because she was trapped between Hopkins' and Mason's modes: between justifying the play in realistic terms and acting *narrowly* within the text.

Paradoxically, both these approaches—that of Hopkins, who showed too much, and that of Mason, who showed too little—spring from an actor's sense of the "Pinteresque." Realistic or naturalistic interpolation gives the actor a basis for "playing the pauses"; acting one or two dominant traits creates the impression of a singular, "Pinteresque" character. In both cases, the actor finds comfortable ground on which to deal with unknowns and ambiguities in the text, and consequently obscures its peculiar force. Both approaches seek a consistency that makes sense of the play, rather than the means dramatically to embody its ambiguities. *Old Times* needs actors who can infuse it with the sense of "presentness," who are not afraid to leave questions about their characters unanswered. Indeed, it needs actors who see the process of acting the play as that of laying out those unanswered questions, who move comfortably from speech to silence and through the shock and surprise that what they just said is the opposite of what they said earlier. For actors, then, the most difficult requirement of Pinter's drama is that they find the means to *let* and not *make* it live. From this point of view, there is no tangible method of conveying the invisible; there is only (what was missing from the Roundabout production) the skill of not searching for meanings in the spaces between words, and of allowing Pinter's words themselves, containers of the invisible, to release what they contain.

NOTES

[1]See, for example, Ronald Bryden, "Pinter's New Pacemaker," *The Observer* (London), 6 June 1971, p. 27; Bernard F. Dukore, *Harold Pinter* (New York: Grove Press, 1982), pp. 89-98; Arnold Hinchcliffe, *Harold Pinter* (Boston: Twayne, 1981), pp. 144-146; Stephen Martineau, "Pinter's *Old Times*: The Memory Game," *Modern Drama*, XVI (1973), pp. 287-297; Kristin Morrison, *Canters and Chronicles: The Use of Narrative in the Plays of Samuel Beckett and Harold Pinter* (Chicago: University of Chicago Press, 1983), pp. 190-205.

[2]Martin Esslin, *Pinter the Playwright* (London: Methuen, 1984), pp. 187-193; Benedict Nightingale, "Three's a Crowd," *The New Statesman*, 11 June 1971, p. 817.

[3]Stanley Kauffmann, "Pinter and Sexuality: Notes, Mostly on *Old Times*," in his *Persons of the Drama* (New York: Harper and Row, 1976), pp. 346-347.

[4]See, for example, Benedict Nightingale, "Back to Pinterland, Where the Living is Uneasy," *New York Times*, 22 Jan. 1984, Sec. 2, pp. 3, 6; Edith Oliver, "The Theatre Off Broadway," *The New Yorker*, 23 Jan. 1984, pp. 86-87; Frank Rich, "Pinter's 'Old Times'," *New York Times*, 13 Jan. 1984, in *New York Theater Critics' Reviews*, XXXXV, No. 3, p. 369; Richard Schickel, "Connections," *Time*, 23 Jan. 1984, in *New York Theater Critics' Reviews*, XXXXV, No. 3, p. 372.

[5]Harold Pinter, *Old Times* (London: Methuen, 1971), p. 6. All further citations refer to this edition and are noted in the text.

[6]Bernard Beckerman, "The Artifice of 'Reality' in Chekhov and Pinter," *Modern Drama*, XXI (1978), p. 158.

[7]Kauffmann, p. 343.

[8]T. E. Kalem, "Is Memory a Cat or a Mouse?," *Time*, 29 Nov. 1971, in *New York Theater Critics' Reviews*, XXXII, No. 20, p. 182.

[9]Leslie Bennetts, "The Clockwork of 'Old Times': Three Actors Keep Balance in Pinter Play," *New York Times*, 9 Feb. 1984, Sec. 3, p. 19.

II. PERFORMANCE CRITICISMS

Denaturalizing Ibsen/Denaturing Hedda: A Polemical Sketch in Three Parts

Alisa Solomon

The Village Voice

After Nora dances her liberating tarantella at the party in *A Doll House*, Torvald criticizes it for being "a bit too naturalistic—I mean it rather over-stepped the properties of art."[1] Torvald doesn't mean that he believes his wife had really been bitten by a tarantula and was trying desperately to shake death off (though we know how much her "life depended on it"). Unable to contain her passions in a more decorous form, she danced as wildly, we assume, as in the rehearsal we saw when "she seems not to hear [Torvald's directions], her hair loosens and falls over her shoulders; she does not notice, but goes on dancing." Her dance is "naturalistic" not because Torvald mistakes it for the real thing on which it is based, but because it depicts the deepest, most mysterious essence of a real life in a way that breaks the conventions Torvald accepts. Alarmingly, Nora has exceeded expectations, just as Ibsen did when he burst the seams of the well-made play and perfected the form of naturalist realism.

Though there hasn't been a great naturalistic play since *The Cherry Orchard*, by which time the style had reached a fulfillment, naturalism remains the standard of mainstream contemporary American drama. But this drama is in no way tarantellian—not because it's no longer shocking for a woman to walk out on her husband, or because penicillin can cure syphillis, or because we are so overrun with kitchen sink plays that we wouldn't be impressed by the presence of a washbasin on stage, as were the first audiences of *The Wild Duck*. Today's naturalism remains entirely within the "proprieties of art" because it lacks explosive meanings that must erupt.

Like a paradigm in Thomas Kuhn's scientific theory,[2] naturalism reached, with Ibsen and Chekhov, what Kuhn calls a state of crisis; it could no longer supply dramatic solutions for the problems it encouraged. Contemporary naturalists, then, are like physicists who, in the age of relativity, insist on Newtonian perspectives. Yet their plays are less exciting than those of the original "Newtonians" because they lack not only the perfection of their predecessors' work, but also its forward-looking tension.

Prevalent American dramaturgy presents enormous obstacles for producers of Ibsen. Sitting through a naturalistic American play is like riding a commuter

85

train for the zillionth time. Even when the people might seem curious or the scenery beautiful, the journey is tedious and predictable, and the destination rarely worth the trip. These plays, trundling through the same familiar terrain, have worn out the vehicle. As mainstream theatre and television have co-opted the simplest and least evocative aspects of naturalism, the genre has been belittled into exhaustion.

One need only compare Arthur Miller's dramatically eviscerating version of *An Enemy of the People* to the original (one of Ibsen's most schematic prose plays) to see how his form was reduced to a simplistic strategy for platitudes. A generation later, Miller's flat dramaturgy—Newtonian in a different sense with its emphasis on causality—has become normative. Plays by dramatists such as Beth Henley, August Wilson, James Duff, Marsha Norman, Michael Cristofer, David Rabe, and by almost anyone produced at New York's Circle Repertory Theatre, may claim some heritage from the great modern playwrights; nonetheless, they depend on everything Ibsen abhorred.

A quick list of oppositions (a few of them over-generalized, I admit) will demonstrate the impoverishment of American dramaturgy. Ibsen is full of mystery; ours is a theatre of explanation, of effect and revealed cause. Where Ibsen created plots, contemporary playwrights offer situations. They have replaced dramatic action with psychological excavations that produce artifacts of suffering, and that cast the audience as liberal pop psychologists who must both understand the protagonist's unacceptable behavior and feel guilty about it, as they see that the Catastrophe this behavior brings has been caused by Circumstance. In Ibsen, characters create catastrophe through acts of will we are never to comprehend. In American drama, explanation comes from exposition that merely describes the past; in Ibsen, exposition creates an anticipated future.

Similarly, our settings simply depict environments in tediously realistic detail; in Ibsen, everything on stage is pregnant with meaning—not only the obvious symbols like General Gabler's portrait or pistols, but the room itself. Secretary Falk's house has windows so that Hedda can soften the sunlight that's "just flooding in." There is a fireplace so that she can burn Løvborg's manuscript. Perhaps Ibsen's symbolic use of setting is why Eric Bentley finds in him such a strong "sense of fate."[3] For Ibsen, in sum, naturalism is a set of conventions; in our day, it is considered a lack of artifice.

Under these conditions, Ibsen seems impossible. How can his work be presented for audiences conditioned by our formulaic theatre? Do we inevitably expect sitcoms or simple guilt dramas every time we see a box set, and therefore influence what we perceive?

Nowhere are these issues more pressing than at the two-year-old American Ibsen Theater in Pittsburgh. This serious, ambitious theater is certainly not alone in taking up the challenge of breathing new life into Ibsen, but because I was disturbed by the way the AIT's artistic staff described their mission when I visited last summer, I want to focus on it as an instance of the problems a theater can have producing Ibsen in America today.

*   *   *

"Don't look for teacups and wallpaper at the American Ibsen Theater," proclaimed the artistic director, Michael Zelenak, in his opening address for the National Ibsen Symposium that the theater sponsored in August, 1984. It's as if the scenery itself must cry out, "Hey! This is Art, not a Lanford Wilson play or, God forbid, television!" Indeed, Travis Preston's 1984 AIT production of *Little Eyolf*, with its presentational acting, side lighting, nonrealistic set (a boat stood vertically on end throughout Act III), and lack of walls, created an evocative and chilling tone. Denuding the play of the integuments of naturalistic detail curiously heightened its human issues. Yet the AIT's artistic staff expounded a theory behind Preston's work and behind its "film noir" production of *Hedda Gabler* (also 1984), with Charles Ludlam in the title role, that seemed largely at odds with the actual effects of the production. Zelenak and his army of dramaturgs, employing some trendy deconstructionist jargon, deny some of the fundamental mechanisms of illusionistic drama. They must be careful not to throw out the dishwater with the china.

In their zeal to counteract the conditions of TV dramaturgy, AIT theorists are jumping exultantly onto a post-modern bandwagon and promoting an abstract way of looking at Ibsen. This view is productive both as a corrective and as an element of a larger perspective. But when wielded as an overriding principle, it is misleading and, ultimately, breeds a drama just as empty as what it means to redress.

In post-production discussions, on Symposium panels, and in the AIT "Repertory Reader," Zelenak and other spokesmen—Rick Davis, Brian Johnston, and Leon Katz among them—promoted a vision of Ibsen that denies audience identification with characters, emphasizes the metatheatrical aspects of the plays, encourages little discussion of meaning and even less of its simpler cousin, relevance. If one didn't know that Ibsen was the subject at hand, one could have thought at times that these men were talking about Richard Foreman, Ping Chong, or the Wooster Group, theater artists who, in Elinor Fuchs's words, "seem to perceive that they are in a new kind of world in which there is no longer anything 'out there,' or anyone 'in here,' to imitate or to represent."[4]

Davis, for instance, disparages audience identification as "the shallowest and least implicative of all the possible aesthetic responses," and proposes that Hedda's problem is that she is trapped inside the wrong kind of play. All the other characters, he suggests, are acting like figures in a well-made melodrama, but Hedda belongs to a higher art. A similar argument is often make about Hamlet: he is the only one who does not subscribe to the rules of a standard revenge tragedy. This attractive reading rebounds in the spiralling self-referentiality of Elizabethan non-illusionistic dramaturgy; in the case of Ibsen, such a reading leads nowhere. We can smile at the cleverness of this characterization of Hedda's predicament and easily be persuaded of its plausibility. But so what? That can't be all the AIT wants its audiences to get from *Hedda*.

But who knows what, or if, the AIT wants its audiences to think. Echoing Johnston, an AIT mentor, Davis claims that "watching an Ibsen play should be like listening to a symphony." Though one immediately grasps and applauds the impulse to aesthetic appreciation of such a statement, one also worries about the dismissal of some of the humanistic energies of drama that it implies. A play written under the conditions of naturalist realism never is and never should be as abstract as music.

Johnston's formulation is not quite as extreme. Unlike Davis, Johnston doesn't seek to banish more standard literary interpretation—how could he with his insistence on Hegelian issues and mythopoetic structures?—but one can see how his arguments lead to the "post-modern" conclusions of his young disciples. In his "Repertory Reader" essay "Text and Supertext in Ibsen's Drama: Or, How to Read a Play," Johnston writes, "While responding intensely to the human situation presented before us, we yet rise to a perception of the aesthetic beauty of the presentation, and the ever-expanding significances of its total metaphor." He adds that "this is possible when the emphasis is not on the story being told, but on the terms of the performance itself." Johnston thus separates "responding intensely to the human situation" from the complex totality of theatrical perception, and considers it a lowlier activity than recognizing beauty.

Furthermore, despite the way AIT actors and directors approach their work (in a "Repertory Reader" interview, Mel Shapiro, the director of *Hedda*, speaks only the language of subtext, and submits that "Hedda is trapped in the wrong body"), Johnston declares that it is "as absurd to psychoanalyze a character in a play as to psychoanalyze a figure in a painting." Of course that's true insofar as it is always preposterous to mistake any artistic creation for a real person. Yet one reason we go to plays and read novels is to understand characters' actions as somehow richly emblematic. Though we never forget that characters are fictitious creations, we confer on them the power to tell us something about our own lives. We don't make one-to-one emotional correspondences with characters, but we do allow for delicate implications in their words and actions. In naturalism, as Mary McCarthy puts it, "the audience must believe that the people on the stage are more or less like themselves,"[5] not in order to be duped into thinking that they are real, but to accept that they are sufficiently *like* real people to be complexly meaningful.

In his newsletter essay "Seeing Hedda Whole," Richard Gilman writes that "the seeming naturalism of *Hedda Gabler* is . . . a ground for the play's true action: its movement into a realm of existential, or ontological being and its vision of crucial values at stake and at war." In *To the Third Empire* Johnston goes further in seeing naturalistic conventions merely as conduits to Ibsen's more important matters. He writes: "Only by inserting such details can Ibsen cunningly infiltrate the full content of his dramatic concept into the play and adequately present his full dramatic 'argument.' " Johnston thus makes it sound as if dramatic style were something a playwright inserted at the end, like the symbols Mary McCarthy's famous student needed to go back and put in after she was all done with her writing.

Gilman's and Johnston's views contain astute truths, of course, but they also convey subtle and dangerous judgments about the involvement of an audience with a dramatic work. These views suggest that Ibsen, perhaps grudgingly, used a base form, naturalism, and elevated it to higher purposes. In a sense he did, but that form was not merely the sole, nasty one available to him; it is an integral, and itself beautiful, aspect of his tarantellian dramaturgy. The "dramatic argument" is in fact what happens in the theater. A spectator's getting caught up in the fictional lives of characters is not the means to a loftier end, but part of Ibsen's dramatic design. An audience never *merely* empathizes; this kind of emotional engagement combines with other, simultaneous experiences to create complicated responses. Naturalist realism can be as aesthetically pleasing as any other set of artistic conventions; Johnston, Gilman, and the AIT seem to consider the style an embarrassment.

When AIT aestheticism demolishes the conditions of Ibsen's dramaturgy and disparages the particular kind of imaginative complicity that makes his plays wonderfully thrilling, it also makes the social and thematic levels of his plays irrelevant. No wonder these theorists are left with a reading of *Hedda* that is only "about" performance. If Ibsen could witness the AIT's tendency toward abstraction, he might remind Zelenak and company that he was *something* of a social philosopher. The dangers of wisping Ibsen into the stratosphere were most glaring in Symposium discussions of *Hedda*.

* * *

A featured panel was titled "Ibsen: Humanist or Feminist?" (as if anybody could be one without being the other). This panel only thickened the old morass of strident claims for the play as a woman's liberation tract versus equally strident denials of its feminist impulse, and never proposed any resolution. The one woman on the panel of six, Patricia Montley, offered a most inelegant argument for the feminism of Ibsen's play, trotting out a schematic definition of feminist drama and then applying its criteria successfully to *Hedda*. On the panel, which was moderated by Davis and also included Katz, Johnston, Phillip Larson, and Julius Novick, her remarks served as a straw argument that Katz and Johnston could readily dismiss as reductive. (Novick and Larson didn't get involved.)

Hedda is certainly not a feminist tract; if it were, Hedda would kill everyone else instead of herself. But it plays on a feminist field; it has a feminist aspect simply by virtue of its being realistic. There would be no play if Hedda were a man. "A woman cannot be herself in the society of the present day, which is an exclusively masculine society," Ibsen wrote.[6] He used this fact as the condition of his play, the fertile ground out of which more general ideas would issue. Similarly, Athol Fugard's plays are not anti-apartheid statements or revolutionary works. South Africa is the necessary background for their exploration of human actions. Apartheid may be implicitly indicted in works like *A Lesson From Aloes* and *Master Harold . . . and the Boys,* but such indictment is not their endpoint. Just as racist South Africa is the context of Fugard's psychological dramas, sexist bourgeois values provide the fateful background for Ibsen's mythic work. If these plays were making rebellious points, they would demand that the background conditions be changed; if they are in some sense tragic, it is because those conditions, though not deterministically fixed, define characters by limiting them. The socio-political context is powerful, but never the focus. (As it is not in *Death of a Salesman*. Thus it seems funny that China produces *Salesman* because it considers the play an exemplary indictment of capitalism.)

If it is an error to confuse background with foreground, as Montley has, it is equally misleading to do away with *Hedda*'s circumstantial realm, as Johnston, Katz, and Davis do by proclaiming the play's "higher" concerns. "Hedda is not a woman," panelists were fond of repeating (sometimes with the variation, "Hedda is not *merely* a woman"), "but a human being." In *The Second Sex* Simone de Beauvoir explains that this cover of human-beingness simply hides the way "human being" is entirely male-defined. By making this abstraction about Hedda, white male critics simply redefine the character into terms they can most easily identify with themselves, into the dominant notion of the "everyman." Whenever a protagonist is not a white man, white male critics tend to say that his or her identity is metaphorical.

Words, props, and characters certainly can and do have metaphoric and mythic meanings; but first, because they are on a stage, they have *literal* meanings, especially within illusionistic conventions. Flowers may stand for death or nature. First, however, they are flowers. Hedda may be a tragic or mythic figure. But first she is a woman. And she can have tragic and mythic resonances *because* she is a woman.

If women respond to *Hedda* with a sense of universality that derives directly from their understanding of Hedda's womanhood, it's certainly arrogant to tell them that they're missing something if they do not leap directly to an all-embracing "humanistic" response. Women have accepted the rich dimensions and resonances of Oedipus, Hamlet, or, for that matter, Solness, without having to jump to rhetorical justifications. No one says, "But Hamlet's not a man, he's a human being," in order to make us understand that his actions in the world of the play can reveal something about human thought and behavior in general. It is not women's artistic naiveté or "over-identification" that leads us to insist on Hedda's gender; it *is* a deficiency of the men in our culture that they cannot take the same valuable insights from a female protagonist that they do from a male one without turning her into an abstraction.

If the American Ibsen Theater wants to rescue Ibsen from the influence of the prevailing "proprieties of art," it will have to examine the passions that drove Ibsen to expand contemporary forms, and it will have to embrace the aspects of audience response that it now holds in contempt. The overwhelming fervor and commitment of Zelenak and his staff promise the possiblity of Ibsen production that is at once true to Ibsen and true to our own age. For now, they must keep rehearsing the tarantella.

NOTES

[1]This quotation and all subsequent ones from Ibsen's plays are taken from Rolf Fjelde, trans., *Ibsen: The Complete Major Prose Plays* (New York: Signet, 1965).

[2]Thomas S. Kuhn, *The Structure of Scientific Revolutions* (Chicago: University of Chicago Press, 1962).

[3]Eric Bentley, "Taking Ibsen Personally," in his *Theater of Commitment* (New York: Atheneum, 1967).

[4]Elinor Fuchs, "The Death of Character," *Theater Communications*, 5, No. 3 (March 1983).

[5]Mary McCarthy, "The Will and Testament of Ibsen," in her *Theatre Chronicles 1937-1962* (New York: Farrar, Straus and Co., 1963).

[6]Ibsen quoted by Leo Lowenthal in his "Henrik Ibsen: Motifs in the Realistic Plays," in *Ibsen: A Collection of Critical Essays*, ed. Rolf Fjelde (Englewood Cliffs, New Jersey: Prentice-Hall, 1965).

Squat: Nature Theatre of New York

Gautam Dasgupta
Performing Arts Journal

"They give birth astride of a grave, the light gleams an instant, then it's night once more."

—Pozzo in *Waiting for Godot*

THE CITY AND THE THEATRE #1

The year was 1975, the city Budapest. Somewhere in the inner city, at the farthest limit of an intricate grid of winding streets, stood an unappealing façade of forgotten masonry graced by an oversized wooden double door. Cut into one half of the door was a smaller entrance way, a frame within a frame, so characteristic of old European architecture. Inside, the vista broadened out to encompass a sprawling courtyard, the surface of its rough-hewn, pebbled bed overgrown with weeds. Rising along its perimeter were four or five stories of apartment units, each floor girded by a wrought-iron balcony overlooking the courtyard.

To the right of the entrance way stood a wide marble staircase, its former grandeur now a faint memory, but its haunting beauty captured forever in the writings of Kafka. The apartment complex itself seemed a relic of days gone by, of pleasanter times perhaps. But on that day in 1975, the cruel silence locked behind the individual doors to each residential unit bespoke the despair and anguish of a nation tucked away, incommunicado, behind the Iron Curtain. Those individual pockets of fear and secrecy—households wracked by uncertainty, people deformed by the hypocrisies of social, political, and cultural forms—were the landscape of the Hungarian novelist George Konrad's "fictions," the very same Konrad who had befriended a family of artists that lived behind one of those closed doors.

If in those days this intrepid band of theatre artists had a name, I was not told of it. In Hungary, as in many East European countries, it is better to remain nameless. To retain one's essential freedom, it becomes necessary to shed exterior forms, if not altogether to erase or blur the contours of one's self. One does so not to blend in unobtrusively with the flock, but to define one's self as supremely alone, to will a nothingness, to create an antiform (a non-

93

form, if you will) that is impervious to the designs of power. It was only later, in 1977, when this troupe of theatrical artists in search of fertile artistic ground left in exile—much like the Gypsies of their native Hungary—that they were given a name: "Squat."

There were no announcements in the local dailies about their performances that night in Budapest. The faithful knew, the way one knows the truth. As in the Biblical story of the shepherds who had a dream telling them where to go, so too was it that night in 1975. A silent voice, a message from the unknown, directed the chosen few to the cramped quarters of Squat's abode. Since no one could congregate outside on the balcony for fear of being reported to the authorities (revolutionary modes of artistic practice have little to do with the revolutionary fervor of socialist or communist partisans), members of the audience—mostly young, unkempt, and smoking American brand-name cigarettes—were herded into a tiny room adjoining the slightly larger living/performance room. We were asked to keep silent and not to applaud at any time during or after the performances. In a world where the living die a slow death, strangled by the life-denying forms of a repressive order, walls seem to take on an existence of their own: they sprout ears.

And then, standing shoulder to shoulder with that audience, unable to utter a sound, I realized how introspective the mind gets. All of reality is played out on the stages of the inner mind. Objects and gestures picked out by the eye become protagonists in the inner drama of the mind. Surrealism becomes the sole artistic mode in which the mind functions if it is to fulfill the dictates of its conscience. As walls usurp auditory functions, the visual and tactile senses gain prominence. Theatre, derived from the Greek *theatron*, a place for viewing, here regains its original status in the history of myth and etymology. To engage in theatrical activity means to reflect on the nature of visual perception itself, on what constitutes the visible and the invisible.

And who can deny the potency of theatre when it has dared to exist at the extreme limits of the visible and the invisible? Oedipus blinds himself so that we may see better, we who shield our eyes from the horrifying spectacle on stage only to turn our gaze inward and contemplate the knowledge we have gained in the process. From blindness to vision, from external perception to inner wisdom, such is the road to interiority that the theatre charts for us. On the stage of history, Squat, proclaiming its invisibility within the cultural life of Budapest, its desire to see but not to be seen, reveals to us the nature and intent of the powerful forces that control its destiny. Seeking concealment, it leads us to an essential revelation.

To move along this path where the visible and the invisible circumscribe the boundaries of theatre is also to contemplate the hold of the irreal on the material world. Think of Oedipus facing the Sphinx, of Hamlet goaded to action by the vision of a "questionable shape," of the Prince of Homburg visited by a dream—in each instance a union of two disparate realities underpins a great dramatic invention. What these plays remind us of is a willingness to confront that which is hidden, mysterious, to see with the "mind's eye," to accept the surreal juxtaposition of two differing orders of reality.

A DIGRESSION: THEATRE AND SURREALISM

In the age of realistic drama, which had no use for myth, the mythic theatrical encounters of the past were given new life instead in the paintings of the surrealists. These artists not only introduced a radical reworking of the nature of visual perception, but wrestled with the idea of theatre itself in their canvases. Through devices of framing (a retooling of the theatrical proscenium) and through a disjunctive approach to the world, the surrealists isolated segments of reality, only to regroup them later according to the dictates of their imagination. The procedure implied the ability to make invisible, to conceal the contiguous reality surrounding an object, and through this process of negation to restore to the object itself its "material supremacy," a phrase used by Artaud in a letter to Breton.

But not only is the visible made manifest through the process of making all else invisible; by having its essential materiality evoked, the visible is also transformed into an object of contemplation. Paradoxically, by virtue of its density, its material supremacy, and not unlike the black holes of outer space, the perceived object sheds its substantiality, turning itself into an abstraction or an essence that can then be appropriated by the inner stages of our mind. To see with wisdom is to see well. As Vladimir says to the Boy in *Waiting for Godot*, "Tell him . . . (*he hesitates*) . . . tell him you saw me and that . . . (*he hesitates*) . . . that you saw me." To be seen is to have restored to the self the truth of sensuous existence. And so the theatre, the place for viewing, returns us to our bodies and our minds, to our innate sensuality, mirroring not reality but life, the surreal, not the real, the mythic, not the prosaic.

SEEING

And saw we did—"surrealistically"—that night in Budapest as two tableaux revealed themselves in all their haunting power and beauty. In the first, a sedentary, ashen-faced Anna Koós sat on a wooden platform, her feet encased in oversized, heavy cement boots, her hair done in long and numerous braids that were tied to a galaxy of miniature household objects and tiny plaster-cast human replicas scattered about her feet. Some of these objects she could stretch out to and touch, others were beyond her reach. At times, the image would come to life as Koós shuffled her feet, threatening to crush the figures beneath her, or strained her arms to caress these very same figures. Tiring of such actions quickly, she would return to a state of benign disinterest, head lowered, body stooped, as if she were about to disappear into those cavernous boots. Before long, a figure appeared under the platform—we could see his silhouette on the white tablecloth covering it. Hastily setting lighted matches to the cloth, this figure (Peter Berg), together with Koós and her world, disappeared behind a cloud of smoke.

In the second tableau, a bare-bodied Péter Halász sat regally on a high-backed chair. While Halász was being gently washed and scrubbed, then wrapped in wide, gauze bandages, a performer alongside him read from a text having to do with the Don Juan legend. (Apparently Squat was working on *Don Juan* at the time; a textual segment derived from their research was appended to this performance.) The tableau came to a close with Halász's disappearance behind yards of linen.

REFLECTIONS

What was I to make of these mysterious, ruminative figures in stately poses, defying me to pry open whatever secrets they may have possessed? My initial bewilderment, coupled with the obvious impact these images had on me, becomes comprehensible partly as a function of the historical circumstances in which I found myself. In a country where the deliberate losing of one's self turns into the most progressive, radical act, the most resonant, poetic gesture is the one that consciously refuses to define itself through the structure of a message. Messages must always be coded in a form, a terrible fixity that defies imaginative, surrealistic playfulness. The only true messages—and I think back to Oedipus and the Sphinx, Hamlet and the ghost of his father, the Prince of Homburg and his dream—are those that originate from undefinable realms. These are the messages that must be taken on faith, and it was this faith in the presence of Squat's artistic courage that I felt in that room, a faith, and a courage, shared by others in the audience.

It would be unfair of me to deny that many in the audience, including myself, saw in these chained, mummified presences a sad reminder of the history of a nation. But such symbolism, perhaps unintentional on Squat's part, is a small component of their theatrical aesthetic. Their theatre is no mere "fictional reality" that allows us a vicarious glimpse into the real world. Both tableaux, concentrated in their imagery, intense in the performers' commitment to the task at hand, and yet somehow incomplete because of their refusal to yield up an overt message, gripped us all with an uncompromising beauty born of the rhythms of life itself.

"To be a man means never to be oneself," wrote Gombrowicz. But man, as this eccentric Polish genius of our century understood all too well, is not only the product of powerful, external, "higher forms," he is also the "producer of forms." Thus, to be true to one's essence as a man is to find oneself in a perpetual state of creating and destroying, of denying the very forms one has created at the moment of their crystallization. To employ reality only to demolish the autonomy and contours of that reality, to make visible and invisible at the same instant in a relentless mirroring of the very process of life—this is the divining rod of Squat's artistic practice.

The images of Koós and Halász inhabit an eerie space betwen the living and the dead, their multiplex messages forever contradicted and nullified by other opposing messages. Koós's constricted gestures, delicate and fragile, seemed to belie the suprahuman power of this figure towering over the tiny world spread out at her feet. Her gracefulness was grounded by her imposing presence; by contrast, the weighted objects surrounding her were rendered insubstantial by virtue of their miniaturization. And then what was I to make of her gray make-up, its dull coloration blending in with the objects around her? The impression was that of a live presence relegated to the realm of the inanimate. Was this another version of the disappearing act, a manifestation of the urge to become invisible and tangible at the same time? Or was it, with Koós's tresses converging atop her head, the world of objects seeking invisible status within the contours of her mind? And inversely, was the radiation of those tresses outward perhaps a suggestion that the world itself is but a product of the human mind, of the mind's infinite capacity to imagine the real?

At the other extreme there is Halász, whose masculinity, though bereft of clothing, is still enveloped by a light, airy realm. Paradoxically, his very passivity or immobility betrays his naked, human presence. Then, as he is scrupulously washed and bandaged, coming vaguely to resemble an Egyptian mummy or a statue cast in marble, he once more returns to the realm of the dead. During this time the text about Don Juan is being read aloud, in which a statue's coming to life results in Don Juan's being burnt in the fires of hell.

Both of these brief, intense images seemed to relish the contradictions implicit in the minute range of gestures of which they were comprised. Each gesture led to its opposite, as if a mirror were throwing back a reversed image; but here, another mirror caught the other's reflection in an endless game of abstraction. This relentless mirroring, set into motion by a precisely modulated theatrical reality that is transformed into "pure form" (the phrase is Witkiewicz's), marks Squat's theatrical practice as an ontological quest for the very nature and significance of the theatrical in our lives. Is not the act of mirroring synonymous with the act of reflection, of being seen and contemplating that which is seen? Is it not in a mirror's reflection that we first catch a glimpse of ourselves as the other to be reflected upon? Here is the mirror as stage, and in its reflection, in the intangible presence of an image, we are born again.

So Squat's mirroring act in continually positing and denying experience would be something like continually raising and lowering the theatrical curtain (or doing the same to the eyelids in everyday life). Kafka ends his short story "At Night" with these words: "Someone must watch, it is said. Someone must be there." And it is this elevation to theatrical status of all experience, to the status of something that must be watched, that becomes the operative mode of Squat's aesthetics. Their way of being is a theatrical one—to be is to be seen, that is, to be on stage—a fact that became self-evident as I sat watching these performances in their living room, their private space made public.

To reflect on all of reality as if it is by nature theatrical is also to seek out the theatrical in the tiniest aspect of reality. Perhaps that is why both performances exist on a highly obsessive and precise level of theatrical activity. Every single gesture is deliberately made visible, not for the purpose of retelling a fiction as in the realistic theatre (where gestures, however precise, are made to serve the purposes of a preformed narrative), but to implant its objecthood as an indelible construct on our consciousness so that we may reflect upon it. To appropriate the gesture's materiality as an idea in itself demands that the gesture be situated in an uncluttered space, one where there is enough room for contemplation and that allows us to focus in on that single gesture. Perhaps for this very reason—the desire to appropriate the gesture's materiality as an idea in itself—the performances I saw that evening in Budapest were short and intense, employing concentrated imagery and little, if any, movement. This may well also have been the reason for the performances' use of miniaturization and fragmentation (both spectacles seemed deliberately incomplete, unformed, snippets of a whole). These two reductive practices serve to make the visible more dense by capturing in a smaller form the essence of a much larger whole.

In both these performances I felt the urgent need to make the performers themselves attain the same objecthood as their gestures. Their impassive, blank faces ultimately reveal both Koós and Halász to be reflective figures and figures to be reflected upon. Their impassivity is not that of performers aloof from their tasks; it is that of individuals who romantically martyr themselves to each act they commit on stage. They exist so beautifully, so radiantly before us that what remains are traces of their essences as live presences, which we then replay in our minds. It is, I soon realized, the exquisite mastery of Squat that whatever they create on stage turns into matter for reflection, for reverie, for dreaming. (Perhaps this is why the image of fire plays such a prominent role in these two performances. As Gaston Bachelard put it, fire was the "*first phenomenon* on which the human mind *reflected*." And to go back to the dawn of reflection, was it not Heraclitus who saw in fire the energy that embraces regeneration as well as destruction, and Paracelsus who claimed that fire was like life itself, feeding on others to stay alive?)

To dream along with Squat and their surreal, unformed, fragmented visions in Budapest was, for me, to capture anew the magic and power of theatre that treats the quintessential issues of life and death, of vision and blindness—mysteries to be contemplated. After Kafka's "An Imperial Message," could we have expected more than the drama of an incomplete message sent out by an illusive Godot? And as in *Godot* ("We always find something, eh Didi, to give us the impression we exist?"), so too in Squat is life in its most intense and captivating form paraded before our eyes. There is no message, Squat seems to be telling us; living (or rather, doing so aesthetically) is all. As Kafka's parable reminds us, living is ". . . to sit at your window when evening falls and dream it [life] to yourself." And like all dreamers, we wake up before the dream—unformed, a fragment—completes itself, so strangely satisfied are we at having glimpsed the mysteries of our larger existence. To reflect on my experiences in Squat's Budapest apartment is to recall the lines by the Polish poet and playwright Tadeusz Różewicz:

> unborn
> it fills the emptiness
> of a disintegrating world
> with unknown speech

But Różewicz's "unborn," endowed "with unknown speech," is yet another manifestation of the "regressive" tendencies that underlie so much of what Squat does—in this case, of their impulse to make invisible the visible. These childlike, "regressive" tendencies take various other forms in the group's approach to theatre. By emphasizing the dream quality of their visions and allowing us to dream with them, they force the hard-edged, determinate contours of reality to give way to a formless, surreal landscape where reality is reshaped as if it were clay in a man's hands. And by their mirroring, they reintroduce the narcissistic joy of contemplating the self in all its sensuality and abandon. But their artistic innocence and grace derive most of all from their reflecting on those "inadmissible passions" of which Gombrowicz wrote so eloquently:

> We are "infantilized" by all "higher" forms. Man, tortured by his mask, fabricates secretly, for his own usage, a sort of "subculture": a world made out of the refuse of a higher world of culture, a domain of trash, immature myths, inadmissible passions . . . a secondary domain of compensation. That is where a certain shameful poetry is born . . .

It was this infantile poetry created by artists living marginally on the fringes of Hungarian society that I witnessed for the first time in Budapest. Two images of playfulness did I see, two spectacles that dared, with childlike abandon, to make public two mysterious, private rituals.

And then, in 1977, Squat's marginality became permanent. Exiled by decree, the group achieved forever their goal of invisibility within Hungary, resurfacing in America where they settled in New York, like children in a new home.

THE CITY AND THE THEATRE #2

Their new home was on 23rd Street in Manhattan. A ground-level space, fronted by a large window overlooking the street, was converted into a theatre, while the upper floors were taken over as living quarters by the group's members. The playing area, situated between the street and the seating space for the spectators, is visible to passersby on the outside. This architectonic openness, so unlike the closure of the Budapest apartment, put Squat in the midst of the *polis*. The window not only allows the outside spectators to peer in and look at the theatrical action inside, it also reduces the inside audience to an entity that is itself placed on stage to be watched. But the people on the street, by either consciously or unconsciously entering the window frame, are themselves in turn transformed into "performers." Here, through an ingenious transformation of the mirroring aspect of Squat's dramaturgy, one audience sees itself mirrored in the other, just as that same audience, as "performers," see themselves mirrored in the other-audience-become-performers. In new surroundings, Squat once again plays games of narcissistic abandon, of incestuous mirroring.

And this very same window, which acts as a proscenium, isolates the indeterminate flow of life on the street outside, rendering it visible and imbuing it with theatrical materiality. This inventive use of space is related to Squat's earlier, preeminently surrealistic, use of space in Budapest. But here, unlike in Hungary, the group's rituals spill out into the street, where a considerable amount of action takes place, and this very theatricality in a "natural" space transmogrifies the real into the surreal. Nothing seems to escape the magic touch of Squat's surrealistic wand, which creates at every instance a dream world where we, the audience, sit at the window and dream it to ourselves.

Squat's 1983 retrospective in New York was comprised of the three shows on which their reputation, at least in the West, rests—the three shows that have been said to make up their "Golden Age": *Pig, Child, Fire!*, *Andy Warhol's Last Love*, and *Mr. Dead and Mrs. Free*. Given the visual abundance of these pieces and the endless reflection that each, as a result, can provoke, I think that detailing all that transpires in them would be an unnecessarily elaborate undertaking. What I prefer to do is select various images and themes from them that either continue Squat's artistic explorations begun in Budapest or never been treated by the group before.

In *Pig, Child, Fire!*, Squat's first piece outside Hungary, the title itself proved to be revealing. Fire is conceived of as creator and destroyer; the child as dreamer; and the pig (in performance it was replaced by a goat) as representative of the far end of the spectrum of sensuous life, of being without consciousness, like the animals in Kafka's fables (and Kafka, more than anyone else, is the guiding spirit of Squat's art). To admit the cosmos in all its variegated forms, as Squat does here, is to embrace "a secondary domain of compensation." Nothing is precluded from the group's reflections on the world. Human heads grow in surreal fashion out of the anus of a puppet hanging upside down in *Pig*, and in the other two pieces respectively, Ulrike Meinhof appears from the dead and a robotized toy comes on stage to emcee a cabaret skit.

But perhaps the most significant aspect of *Pig, Child, Fire!* was Squat's use of filmic images (video, and later film). It is worth remembering here that, after surrealism had exhausted its original drive in the pictorial image, it continued to make gains in film, where reality could so easily be fragmented and edited back into whatever form the imagination desired. But for Squat, the image on the video monitor or screen was yet another device for mirroring reality, for making visible that which was hidden (that is, for superimposing another order of reality on the theatrical one being presented before our eyes on stage), or else for making insubstantial through the medium of the filmed image that which was visible and tangible. This interaction between film and theatre, between two contrasting orders of artistic representation, each one at the same time affirming and denying the other's autonomy, is another manifestation of Squat's ability to embrace opposites, of their prodigious transformative vision.

Theirs is a continual denial of the fixity of experience, a denial captured partly by their uncompromising will to work with fragmentary forms. Each of the three larger parts of *Pig, Child, Fire!* is comprised of short segments subsumed in their entirety—some of these are transplants from their earlier works in Hungary (for example, the glass-cutting sequence in *Pig*, and the moment in *Andy Warhol* when there's a fire under the transmitters). Here once more, the principle of the surrealistic collage applies, as does that of the mirroring of earlier work. In this theatre of the mind, memory plays a significant role. Nothing is ever lost to this theatre; all experience is stored up in the expansive stage of the mind, to be replayed forever and ever. No wonder, then, that Squat performances seem to end and begin all over again; there are no finite parameters within which their performances lie. And rightly so, since there are no limits to seeing, particularly when one is given to dreaming.

One instance of their incessant dreaming is the opening sequence of *Pig*. Dostoevsky's *Possessed* (Stavrogin's Confession) is being read aloud in the presence of a little girl and a hanging puppet with an erection (in Dostoevsky, it is a little girl who hangs herself). One recalls Vladimir's hope in *Godot* that hanging would lead to an erection. The puppet is finally revealed to be an actual performer with a fake penis; the performer then simulates masturbation—life and death are embraced in one imagistic stroke.

The act of seeing itself is made equivocal in Squat's theatre. To use a hanging puppet with multiple facial masks, all alike, and an actor (Istvan Balint) with an uncanny resemblance to the title figure in *Andy Warhol's Last Love*, is to play with the illusory aspect of perception. The stepping out from film of various performers onto the stage (and vice versa) is another visual strategy on which they rely. All that remains of this confusion of realms is our knowledge that we have been in the presence of a consummate group of artists who have created an elaborate edifice of "theatricalness," which they have embossed with a sure sense of engagement and style. And it is this sure sense of style and engagement that I take away from all my experiences with the Squat theatre. Digging deep into the infantile recesses of their minds, they dare to dream the impossible, to dream through "lesser forms" to create a "shameful poetry," but poetry nonetheless. They have sought out radical and marginal experiences for their theatre of mixed forms (the punk and new wave scenes, old Hollywood films and musicals, popular songs, rap sessions, fashion shows, electronic media displays, etc.). At the same time they have borrowed texts from Dostoevsky, Artaud, Karl Kraus (the "Dear John" letter in *Mr. Dead and Mrs. Free* is from Kraus's *Last Days of Mankind*, that play of limitless theatricality), Edgar Allan Poe, and Kafka to engage us in a reflection on the nature of interiority—of private confessions made public—and the nature of communication. They have also shown us what the theatre can do when it is "revisioned" to the point that it shows us publicly all that can be rightfully (and tastefully) imagined. They make public their private lives (in *Pig*, Koós goes so far as to train the camera on her vagina, which then appears on the video screen while a family watches the evening news and eats supper—an innocuous image compared to the scenes of violence on the news), their "inadmissible passions" (a child puts on false breasts, two young girls talk like adults about sex), their real-life vocations (the actual witch in *Andy Warhol*), and finally their theatre, which at times terrorizes the public outside (two performers draw guns on the street as passersby duck in fear of their lives).

And so, even as Ulrike Meinhof commands us to make public our deaths in *Andy Warhol's Last Love*, Squat commands us to make public our lives through their visions. This "making public," they remind us, is designed to teach us to see better, to see with inner wisdom: to be free (Mrs. Free) to behold a world in which nothing is hidden, where everything, through the transformative powers of art and beauty, leads us to the truth of vital, sensuous existence. Our path takes us to the "Nature Theatre" of Kafka's *Amerika*, that " 'almost limitless' theatre" where, as Max Brod noted in his diaries, Kafka felt that his hero "was going to find again a profession, a stand-by, his freedom, even his parents, as if by some celestial witchery." We find the same at Squat's "Nature Theatre of New York," their 23rd-Street space from which and in which we can embrace the world. I think back again to Oedipus blinded, then to Mr. Dead's oversized doll's eyes pierced by video monitors: two theatrical blindings that frame not only the history of the theatre, but also the concept of human life itself, the light that gleamed only an instant.

"Riding on a Smile and a Shoeshine": The Broadway *Salesman*

Michael Bertin

Temple University

Dustin Hoffman, as Willy Loman, enters the office of Howard Wagner, his former employer's son now running the firm. "Riding on a smile and a shoeshine," Hoffman is all back-slapping bluff and timorous cheer. Howard (capably performed by Jon Polito) is, you will recall, listening to the taped recording of his children's inanities. Loman, here to fight for his job, is progressively humiliated as Howard persists in listening to the tape of human voices while ignoring the man before him. If you overlook for a moment the melodramatic underpinning, the scene is a telling image of an alienation that has acquired for our society the status of an archetype. Hoffman is sharp. Stooped in deference, he patiently endures the stripping of his pride. He swallows hard and is fired. As his mask falls, the frenzy begins.

When we ask what in Arthur Miller's *Death of a Salesman* still holds and urges respect, the answer that immediately occurs is its compassion. In today's political climate we discount that emotion at our risk. Miller has known the despair of sudden poverty, and our streets are littered with the poor, who are dismissed as so much nuisance by rulers with mentalities on a par with Ronald Reagan's. The depression aura of *Death of a Salesman* still surrounds many unfortunate men and women; they remind us all of the callousness that prevails at the highest reaches of power. A play that recapitulates the shape of private economic ruin is bound to touch us where it counts, in our hidden fear: there but for the grace of an education and some luck go I.

This review of the 1984 Broadway revival of *Death of a Salesman* will not belabor once again the arguments against the play. They are known and for the most part just: Miller's plot and his perspective on Loman are confused, his stance towards capitalism is ambiguous, and his ethnic painting is blurred at best. But given that the play still provokes an ache, it is pertinent to ask if compassion on stage is enough today. Among other things, *Death of a Salesman* purports to examine a gritty social case, and in an age that knows Brecht and Bond, to name two, it is legitimate to challenge Miller for being as unaware as his protagonist. Miller fails to extend compassion into insight, but his play is good enough to allow creative actors the chance of transcending it through specific performances of revelatory force. Granting this, however, there are still flaws that no staging can amend.

The production's strategy begins by taking the historical criticism into account. Whether inspired by Hoffman, Miller, the producers (Roger Stevens and Robert Whitehead), or, as I suspect, the director (Michael Rudman), an effort is apparently under way to counter the drama's temporality. In effect this means that Hoffman and Rudman impose an interpretation on Loman that is merely hinted at in the play: the alienation induced by the marketplace is translated into Willy's self-alienation, which ultimately forces him from his family and mankind.

The company assembled to provide the context for this action is good and performs, by Broadway standards, with the air of an ensemble. Kate Reid fulfills the image of Linda. Her assurance to Willy is kind, her denunciation of her sons is acute, and her overall demeanor of ravaged care for her crippled spouse is right. David Huddleston, as Charley, issues through the play a sane presence deflecting his friend's distortions. A large and rollicking man with an expressive belly, Huddleston adds humor to Willy's otherwise sorry decline. David Chandler renders Charley's son, Bernard, with an ingratiating gawkiness growing into mature sympathy. Louis Zorich grapples with Miller's metaphorical Uncle Ben. Forced to pass lines such as the pseudo-Ibsenite, "One must go in to fetch a diamond out," he is hindered by Ruth Morley's one mistake in costuming: a white Panama suit topped by a white fedora that has him preening like a banana-republic martinet. Stephen Lang is adequate as the more immediate, concrete, and sexually panting brother, Happy.

Much has been written about the inauthenticity of the play's ethnic milieu. The present company goes far in silencing that criticism by playing the language for all the ethnic allowance we can grant it. Such middle-class Jews, their acting implies, often speak like this, straining for utterance, their awkwardness becoming part of a rhythm of life and joke of existence rather than being revealed for what it is: Miller's failure of conception. The only glaring flaw in the production, in fact, is Alex North's bloated score with its resounding climactic chords that are reminiscent of *On the Waterfront*. When all is said, the revival's prime achievement is its fulfillment of the drama's spine: the match between father and son, Willy and Biff.

Dustin Hoffman is a small man. Physically, he is the smallest actor on stage. But this is all that's small in his attack on Willy Loman. From his initial entrance, we sense that we are in the grip of a metabolism different from Lee J. Cobb's (the original 1949 salesman). Where Cobb lumbered into view, pausing to be framed in a door, a photograph of grief, Hoffman walks in fast, favoring feet creased with pain. Dropping his huge sample cases, he seems puny, an appendage to business. His wincing relief is suffering we receive as a shock. Despairing, he hides in a pallid gray suit set off by an exuberant tie that is as wrong as a wish in a negligent world. His glasses are thick and dehumanizing; his hair offsets them in its thinness, its suggestion of the passing of a life. I know this man; our century knows him, too. "I'm a human being," he screams. Miller's Jew has arrived.

We are in a house designed by Ben Edwards. Wider and a bit more unwieldy than the original Mielziner set, it is still the skeleton of a home that reveals the enclosing tenements behind: monoliths oblivious to the petty sufferings below. On the second story are the sons still sleeping their lives away. The wife frets a dream to the side. Here is a family set against bricks like a collaboration of spirits set against necessity. The scene is held in Thomas Skelton's purple city haze, the accomplished lighting design of an artist. Rudman allows the mood to settle.

Hoffman is engaged in a ferocious war with Willy's destiny. Rarely has our stage witnessed the heights of passion he brings to bear here. Though it is initially hard to accept him as a 63-year-old, his is a risky and brave performance with dividends. Not an unhandsome man, Hoffman has recalibrated his face and physique into something mean, cratered, almost repellent. He is under the misconception that he is being asked to play Oedipus, and he *is* playing him with Greek passion. His movement alone is astounding as he bounds about the stage, expanding its borders within our minds. He explodes *into* the play. When left weeping by Biff on the hotel room floor, Willy is described in Miller's stage direction as "left on the floor on his knees." No question of knees here. Hoffman is prone on the floor, pounding it in rage and desperation. Biff's discovery of the assignation becomes not only proof of Willy's flayed mortality, but also a stupid cause for final severance between father and son. Felt passion at this level implies tragedy; Miller's melodramatic meanderings are enlarged into reality by Hoffman. At other times, Hoffman displays a puckishness that escapes Miller's more sober vein. Willy is a veritable jokester: a husband nudging his wife into acceptance, a father poking his sons in the ribs, a man rocking on the balls of his feet anticipating a better day.

The peripheral characters float through the porous scene, fragments of a fragmenting mind. Willy has but to look to the wings to beckon his reconstructed phantoms from the past. When he does so, the concrete city set recedes with delirious speed, changing into a superimposed projection of verdancy, the recalled vestment of youth and hope.

The other performance of note is given by John Malkovich as Biff. (The only other time that I've seen this Chicago-based actor was on a television broadcast of Sam Shepard's *True West.* Playing Lee, he invested the role with a menace that deepened the character's potential instability. What I took then to be a flavor determined by Shepard's sure skill was, as I now see it, as much attributable to the actor's poetry.) Biff has been out West playing at cowboys and Indians, avoiding responsibility for his life by escaping as a ranchhand. Malkovich convinces us that the return is motivated by an unconscious drive to face his father and become a man. He and Happy hear Willy fumbling downstairs at the play's opening. His Biff is an uncomfortable and tentative boy (in his mid-thirties) twitching for his manhood, his father's rhythm inciting his own. When he speaks, it's with the wrested sweetness of the fundamentally vulnerable and shy. A big man, Malkovich flows easily into the galloping glee of the adolescent athlete of the flashbacks.

The drama's second act is stronger than its first. The transitions between dream and reality are surer on Miller's part (notice how well he gets from

Howard's office to Charley's office to the New York restaurant through the
Boston hotel). Rudman realizes Willy's infantile fantasy of success as a dark
destiny strangling Biff. Living his father's dream, Biff comes to see it as a
disaster: "I realized what a ridiculous lie my whole life has been! We've been
talking in a dream for fifteen years"; and later to Willy: "Listen, will you let
me out of it, will you just let me out of it!" Rudman rarely misses a beat. His
direction has the virtue of a solid conventionality, suggesting that this is how
these scenes *must* be staged. In the restaurant, for example, he has the conflict
between father and sons resolve itself in a downstage triangle with Willy at the
upstage apex—this hints at primary things.

Rudman guides the drama to a cathartic climax. Act I ends with an aborted
union between Willy and Biff. After a severe argument, Biff refuses to befriend
his father; he cannot bring himself to hug him. The second-act climax proceeds
through a gnarled fight that points to another potential hug of reconciliation. Biff
is on his knees resting his head on Willy's breast; Miller's stage direction has
Willy fumbling with his son's face. But instead, Hoffman *imposes a recognition*
on this moment. With Biff sobbing on him, Hoffman's hands are suspended just
above his son's back. We wait for physical contact. It never comes. The hands
do not descend. Willy cannot touch and comfort Biff. The moment is clear
and strong as Hoffman shows that Willy at last understands. The alienated
salesman sees himself alienated from his son, from humanity. "Riding on a
smile and a shoeshine," he has indeed been on a ride. Willy has become the
imprisoned, eternal, egotistic child. When Willy comes to his conclusion, after
the family has dispersed, Hoffman yanks him out, running him into the wings
as if he were pulled by invisible wires. Listening to the dictates of his inner
voice, Willy commits suicide from the knowledge that he is beyond love.

And so we arrive at the grave. There is a palpable hush in the house as
the company proceeds through its stark summation of a life. Arrayed on the
apron in a signifying tableau, the family, attired in autumnal shades, meets for
the last time. Behind them, radiating through the dark, the light from tenement
windows speaks of other lives. Underplaying with a quiet elegance to choke
any hint of cheapness, Kate Reid whispers the last rite. Happy, obliviously
happy still, leaves carrying his father's dream like a disease. Biff departs with
the possibility of life. And Willy? Willy is just gone. Miller's play—granite-
like, flawed and awkward, yet oddly moving—has cried its dirge.

*   *   *

Willy Loman responds to the callousness of his time with a singular
selfishness of his own. His ever asserted "ME" prevents him from confronting
the world. Miller's *Death of A Salesman* is thus less a tragedy—for tragedy
implies maturity—than a play about the failure of man to live tragically, with
awareness. It is melodramatic in that it merely raises issues without sounding
their depths. Though Biff has become disenchanted with his father's dream,
it is unclear if that disenchantment encompasses the American Dream. And
Willy remains an unfocused and pathetic victim to the end. As a protagonist,

he doesn't challenge the tragic, economic destiny of his society. In this light, it is significant that we never learn what Willy sells. Peter Holland has written that "for Bond, as for Brecht, it is the transactions over the *object* that define the articulation of relationship" (my emphasis).[1] Miller leaves the object out, and his fuzziness on so elementary yet crucial a level indicts the vagueness of the play as a whole. In *Death of a Salesman*, we do not so much *see* social transactions taking place (with all the consciousness that this implies) as respond to their emotional heat. Once we admit Miller's general theme that in America you sell yourself, what is left?

Compassion is not enough. Without awareness it is an empty gesture. It's the tip our Broadway theater pays to assuage its guilt. We can imagine an alienated staging of *Death of a Salesman* in the Brechtian sense. The placard would descend to announce the scene: "Willy Loman gets the axe." While being axed by Howard Wagner, the actor playing Loman would step out of character as if to ask us for a loan. He would reveal himself as aware, and we would be forced to face the implication of our compassion: would we afford the vagrant on the street corner of America the inflated price of our ticket? The play would thus not simply reflect the moment unthinkingly, it would attack it critically with a cool wink. In gaining a historical perspective on the great American play of mid-century, we would at the same time be "tipped off" to the nature of our own evasive tips. "Riding on a smile and a shoeshine," for us as well as for Willy, would no longer be *riding blind*.

NOTES

[1] Peter Holland, "Brecht, Bond, Gaskill, and the Practice of Political Theater," *Theatre Quarterly*, 8, No. 30 (Summer 1978), p. 30.

Southern Theatre Chronicle*

> Dramatic criticism is or should be concerned solely with
> dramatic art even at the expense of bankrupting every
> theater in the country.
>
> —George Jean Nathan

Robert James

Tulane University

    I am sorry to say that I have only bad news to report on theatre in the South. When I conceived the idea of a "Southern Theatre Chronicle," I planned to cover the seasons of the major as well as the up-and-coming Southern regional theatres. What I have discovered is that, for the most part, those seasons are not worth covering. In these inflationary days when mere survival, let alone artistic growth, in the professional theatre is a magic trick, most of our regional theatres have turned to commercial fare—musical comedies; recent New York hit productions, usually of strainedly or sappily serious new plays; "updated" or "adapted" classics; vapid, unambitious new plays of their own discovery— to attract large numbers (and donors) to the theatre. So that leaves a critic like me with very little to write about. I will go ahead and discuss the one bad new play and two butchered classics I saw this fall, in addition to a new, now recycled play I saw three years ago, in order to get some of my venom out. But I promise in the future to search out theatre about which I can write well: that of some of the smaller, lesser known, but bolder theatres of cities like Dallas and Atlanta, and that of univerity theatres from Austin to Athens.

    Land of Fire is a new play that the Dallas Theater Center produced from 28 October–22 November 1980. I do not know any of the other plays of its author, Glen Allen Smith—he is something of an institution at the Dallas Theater

---

*Editor's note: This was the first and last "Southern Theatre Chronicle" that James wrote for the *New Orleans Review*. It was never published, since, shortly after approving the idea for the column, the journal decided against any coverage of the theatre in its pages. I include the chronicle here for two reasons: Professor Kauffmann often prodded James to write more theatre criticism when the latter was at Yale; and Kauffmann himself has often spoken of, and written about, the unfortunate incompatibility of art and (much of) the regional theatre in this country.

Center, where he has had no fewer than four "world premieres"—but I can say, on the evidence of this play, that this is a man who has mastered the craft of playwriting while paying little attention to its art. That is, he knows how to construct a play, to keep it moving; he can even turn a nice phrase every now and then amidst all the workmanlike dialogue. But he is not an artist. He does not understand the uniqueness and the complexities of character. He is not honest. And he has no ideas, no vision: it is not clear that he sees the world in any way but through the eyes of an unreconstructed sentimentalist. Of course I am assuming, again on the evidence of *Land of Fire* alone, that Mr. Smith wants to be thought of as an artist, otherwise I would have no grounds to criticize him. This is a serious play, or what passes for serious in a society that has lost all connection with the great drama of the past yet would create a great drama of its own. I am assuming, along with this, that it is the business of regional theaters in this country to foster the continued growth of a truly serious native drama, not to manufacture hits to export to New York in return for those hits it has imported from the Great White Way.

    Land of Fire is the story of Bill and Irene, a seemingly happily married middle-aged, middle-class couple in Southern California. The plot revolves around Irene's taking an old, vagrant Latin American into her home and keeping him in her cellar. He plays the flute, they dance, she gazes into his sad, knowing eyes. Bill, a harried furniture-store manager, wants to get rid of the old man. Irene, incredibly, says that if he goes, she goes. The dissection of Bill and Irene's marriage begins, and what we learn is that Bill has always made Irene's decisions for her; he hasn't spent enough time with his wife and son; Bill and Irene seem to be sexually incompatible; etc. So she is ostensibly trying to assert her independence by bringing the old man into her home for his benefit and her entertainment. But what she is really trying to do, we learn much latter, is replace her son, Andy, with the old man, Emilio. Andy has run away from home at age 15, and the detective whom Bill has hired has not been able to find him.

    Mr. Smith, cleverly, does not even let us know that Andy has run away until about midway in the play; Irene has spoken so wistfully of her son that we began to presume he had been dead for some time—that he might have died young of illness or of an accident. Because we were wondering so much about Andy, we were almost distracted from the lifeless characterization and action onstage. Toward the end of *Land of Fire*, Bill reveals that in fact Andy is dead—he died, apparently, of drug addiction or a drug overdose in a Taos, New Mexico, hospital—and that he has kept this from Irene so she could always live with the hope of her son's return some day. This revelation neatly exonerates Bill of the heartlessness and selfishness of which he has been accused by Irene for not pressing the investigation into Andy's whereabouts. It also makes for the tearful reunion of the couple as they resolve to make the best of their lives without Andy—but *with* Emilio, whose real worth Bill, predictably, has come to see, and whom he has ensconced in Andy's room upstairs. Bill's acceptance of Emilio into his home is kept from us until the very end, so that the former can be turned from bad guy into good guy once again: Irene thinks that he has thrown Emilio out or handed him over to the police as an illegal alien. That's it. That's the whole play: we find out what's happened to Andy. Along the way, we get echoes of *Who's Afraid of Virginia Woolf?*: the absent son, lots of booze, much argument and accusation, the visitor to whom the wife is attracted. But whereas the subject of Albee's play is George and Martha's relationship and, by implication, how they might have destroyed their son had they been able to have one, the subject of *Land of Fire* isn't a subject at all: it's simply the protracted revelation of a single piece of information, the fate of Andy. The real focus of Mr. Smith's play should have been *Bill and Irene* and what in their behavior as well as their son's character drove the boy to run away and begin using drugs. I said earlier that Mr. Smith is not honest. He isn't, because he does not permit his characters to speak for themselves; he is too interested in getting to the end of the play, which is where *Land of Fire* began in his mind. He knew how he was going to end it before he wrote it, so it became more or less a matter of marking time until he got to the finish. Knowing the ending in advance can be dangerous for a good playwright; it is fatal for a struggling one like Mr. Smith. It robs his play of life, of guts, if you will. Bill and Irene are not characters, they're clichés. Character comes from detail, nuance building up finally to action or resolution. Did Irene pay too much attention to Andy and did her husband not pay enough? Why did they act in this manner and what are some specific examples of their behavior toward their son? How responsible was Andy for his own problems? Do the father and the mother recognize their guilt and, if so, how do they propose to move on from it? The question of Andy aside for the moment, what kind of past did each partner bring to the marriage and what sort of marriage do Bill and Irene have? What type of person was Andy away from his parents? These are questions Mr. Smith has chosen not to explore, or not to explore in depth, and his play suffers greatly for it.

He should have left the Latin American "houseguest," Emilio, out of the play completely. Emilio is the playwright's excuse for avoiding the questions I have just posed; the question of whether he stays or goes becomes almost the only one. Emilio superficially substitutes for Andy in a play that sorely needs to *evoke* Andy through the confrontation of his mother and father. And what a miserable stereotype of the Latin American male Emilio is: he is idle and fun-loving, with a talent for making music, drinking, and charming women. We never see him. I guess that his absence is meant to be evocative in itself, but it isn't. For reasons unknown to me, the title of the play comes from the name of his homeland: Tierra del Fuego, or land of fire.

John Logan, the director, does his best to enhance the idea of confrontation in his staging by physically opposing, and distancing, Bill and Irene where the playwright has failed them Hwith language. But I am long past believing that a director can give life to a script already dead on the page. Mr. Logan proves no exception, and neither do his designers in their attempt to serve the play. You can dress characters up, you can light them as realistically as the stage will allow, and you can place them on a set where no detail has been spared (this set is a kitchen, so we get as a bonus the preparation of food and its ingestion

on stage), but it is through their words and actions, finally, that they live. If
the play does not begin with Glen Allen Smith's writing, it doesn't begin at
all. Good acting can help, but it can't do the work of the playwright, just as
directing cannot. Jacque Thomas as Irene and Christopher Pennywitt as Bill,
alas, are not good. They seem to think that the play is written well enough to
carry their mediocrity; they bring no life to their characters beyond the paltry one
furnished by the playwright. Miss Thomas is the more interesting of the two—
she at least knows how to "act," to decorate a moment emotionally. Would
that her technique were at the service of some inner truth. I can say no more
for Mr. Pennywitt than that he is sincere in his dullness and passivity. This is
a man made to act on television, and television only.

Well, the reader might legitimately ask at this point, if the play is as bad
as you say, why has so much interest been shown in it by regional theatres
in America (*Land of Fire* was originally produced as a staged reading at the
Pittsburgh Public Theatre)? Perhaps because there is a dearth of fine dramatic
writing in this country at present; perhaps because the people who choose new
plays for production at the regional theatres don't know good writing when they
see it, or are afraid such writing will overtax the minds of their subscribers.
One thing is certain: together, two theatres have spent a lot of time and money
on this play, and their efforts have been wasted. It will not survive as dramatic
literature. I don't know how to improve the state of playwriting in America,
except to say that standards must be raised and writers goaded to meet those
standards, to stretch their abilities as far as they can, by discerning artistic
directors and literary managers. A critic can, of course, only tell the truth
about each play as he encounters it, be a sort of watchdog, and hope that in the
long run this will have a salutary effect on the work of playwrights and their
producers.

I was unable to make it to Actors' Theatre of Louisville for the production
of Ted Tally's "new" play *Terra Nova* (2-26 October 1980), but I can tell you
that the play is not new at all, and that the praise it has garnered is one more
example of the American theatre's propensity for making a mountain out of a
molehill (for reasons conjectured above, and most certainly in areas other than
playwriting). *Terra Nova* had its world premiere 18 November 1977 at Yale
Repertory Theatre in New Haven, Connecticut. It has since been produced at
the Mark Taper Forum in Los Angeles, at Alaska Repertory Theatre, now in
Louisville, and this spring it will appear at the Asolo State Theatre in Sarasota
and the Hippodrome in Gainesville, Florida. These are the productions *I* know
of; there are probably more. I saw it at Yale and remember it well (I made
extensive notes on it at the time). It is not a good play. It does not even contain
the idea for a good play, I'm afraid. Like its protagonist, Capt. Robert Falcon
Scott, it is doomed from the start: he by his decision—his obsession—to race
Roald Amundsen to Antarctica without dogs; the play by its very choice of him
as subject matter, or, shall I say, by its determination to give Scott's point of
view of the journey.

Terra Nova is not Ted Tally's first play, but its "errors of enthusiasm"
are clearly those of a young playwright finding his way. Mr. Tally is 28 and

a graduate of the Yale School of Drama. He remarked in the *New York Times* at the time of the Yale production that he found Scott's story, as recorded in a journal that the Captain kept until he perished along with his men, "irresistible." And indeed it is: five explorers braving the worst weather conditions on earth for months just to be the first human beings at the South Pole and coming in second. Scott himself, however, is of limited interest as a protagonist. A fortyish captain who tells us that he should at least be a commodore by now, like his comrades of similar age, he has already failed in one attempt to reach the South Pole. A figure whose name is known, nevertheless, by all schoolchildren in the Britain of the time (ca. 1912), he can only be concerned about a permanent place in history and a sizable pension to retire on. (I assume that this is the truth about Scott. If the real Scott was a nobler man, I am hard pressed to decipher why Mr. Tally reduced him to this.)

Scott is hardly a tragic figure, then. He is too flawed, too petty, and, it appears, completely responsible for his own, and *his men's*, destruction. If there was pressure from his countrymen to make the journey, surely it was not pressure to go it *without dogs*; his wife begged him not to go. I suspect that Scott chose to forego using huskies not for humanitarian reasons, as everyone at Yale seemed to think (the Norwegian "barbarian," Amundsen, used dogs to pull his load *and* for food, when provisions became scarce), but because he thought his victory would seem all the greater for having been accomplished against greater odds. We have here the case of a man who simply bit off more than he could chew. He was overambitious, and maybe even a little stupid.

The very structure of *Terra Nova* emphasizes the man's overriding self-concern. The Yale program note said that "the play consists of a series of scenes from Scott's expedition, from his earlier life, and from his fantasies," all taking place in his mind. Ah, sweet platitude! His life flashes before him as he slowly freezes to death, and his biggest discovery is that man can be truly alive only at the moment of his destruction. So much for the four men who died with him. Several times during the play Scott proudly claims responsibility for his men, but, curiously, nothing is ever said of his *prior* responsibility, of the part he has played in putting them where they are in the first place. And nowhere is the lameness of his pride and his lack of self-awareness more apparent than when he learns, upon arrival at the South Pole, that Amundsen has beaten his team there by a whole month.

Earlier, Scott had declined repeatedly to leave the fatally injured Evans behind in order to make better time. (Tally makes much of this, too much, as an example of Scott's clinging to "personal values in a world where such values are despised for their impracticality" [the playwright's words]. There's only one other such example. Scott refuses to take a lethal does of opium once it becomes certain that there is no hope for survival, but only after ceremoniously allowing that his men have the right to make this choice for themselves.) When he and his party finally arrive at the Pole, only to find the Norwegian flag staring them in the face, Oates goes berserk and blames their failure on Evans, who, for fear he would be sent back to base camp, hid his severely cut hand until it was too late. Then a letter left on the spot by Amundsen reveals that, even had

Evans not been injured and not caused his group to lose time as a result, the Englishmen would still have lost the race. Incredibly, so stunned is Scott by defeat at this point and so absorbed with its meaning for himself that he barely responds to this information, even though it resoundingly confirms the high value he supposedly places on human life. (How the "play" of his own mind comes back in this way to discredit him!) Further, the facts notwithstanding, he does not once consider blaming himself for what has happened. Mr. Tally could have salvaged a measure of pathos for his character here and let him face death self-knowing, self-accusing, but this was not to be. We have to follow this "hero," unenlightened, to the end.

Still, the fact remains that four men more than willingly went along with him (he chose them, it seems, from among many volunteers). The question is, why? Mr. Tally and Scott never really answer it to my satisfaction. We are led to believe that Wilson, Bowers, Evans, and Oates are as taken with the glory of the expedition as Scott; also, and especially, that they are very taken with him as a leader of superior ability and immense appeal. It is in particular on the characterization of Scott as such a leader that the script falters. But even if the real Robert Falcon Scott had great charisma, it is difficult to believe that there was no serious questioning of his authority by his men, no private doubts and anxieties, at the very least, about his motivations and competence. Dr. Wilson is vehemently against Scott's decision to permit Bowers to end his life quickly with opium (Evans and Oates are dead by this time), but Wilson's is a moral or "academic" rebellion that is not intended in any way to challenge the Captain's leadership. Oates, it is true, disagrees with Scott's decision not to sacrifice Evans for the good of the group, but, significantly, he never does so to the Captain's face. (Oates later sacrifices *himself* for the welfare of his fellows, but this moment was lost on me for its being completely lost on him *and* them. Half out of his mind with pain, he at least had a partial excuse for not noting the consistency of his behavior.)

In the *New York Times* article Mr. Tally spoke of his desire to create "impressionistic poetry" in *Terra Nova* as opposed to "documentary drama." That is why, he claimed, he set the play in Scott's mind. For his information, true poetry would have taken the time and the risk to probe, first, the reasons Wilson, Bowers, Evans, and Oates went along on the expedition, and second, what they were thinking at its key moments. Why assume that Scott's point of view, simply because it is in print, is the only one, or the truest one? Why not speculate for truth's sake instead of playing it safe in the name of art? The better moments in the play were those from which Scott was excluded as a direct participant, those among his men: the cameraderie between Bowers and Oates, for instance, or the confrontation between these two in the matter of Seaman Evans. Such scenes only strengthened my conviction that *Terra Nova* should have been their play and Wilson's and Evans' as much as Scott's.

In between the objectivity or literalness of "documentary drama" and the subjectivity—here, the artiness—of the single point of view, there is the middle ground of multiple focus, of several points of view, which is the turf of the vast majority of good plays. The playwright does not side with or project himself completely into any one character; he permits each to speak for himself, perhaps even one to speak for him directly, knowing that in variety, in complexity and ambiguity, is born the truth of art. Certainly it is possible to achieve this "infinite variety" in the drama of one man's mind (Strindberg, for example, does it in his Expressionistic plays), but that man (often the playwright himself, or the playwright's alter ego) must be infinitely worthy of our attention, our scrutiny. And, to my mind, Robert Falcon Scott is not.

If Mr. Tally's "poetic rendering" of his story did not go so far as to bore, it was because of the tension this rendering set up between what we knew would happen at the end and what was happening before our eyes. That is, knowing we would "get" something at the end of the play (the death of Scott), we felt sure we'd get at least a few more things in between (besides the death of his four men): we were disappointed. *Terra Nova* was also less than boring because of the sheer daring of its attempt to simulate on stage what film can do much more easily. Not necessarily better, though, since a film about Scott would—or should—have a different aim than a play about him. The wide, bleak expanses of Antarctica would be a "character" in such a film, and the depiction of man's small place in them could take precedence over the depiction of his relations with his fellow men and his struggle to carry out everyday activities.

Mr. Tally might have turned to better use the so-called limitations of the stage, however. Rather than shifting around in time and place so much, sometimes awkwardly, sometimes a bit too patly, he could have concentrated more on the "clinical presentation of a segment of life as it is, without alteration or embellishment or contrivances" (this is a definition of absolute naturalism, as reported by Stanley Kauffmann). The aesthetic pleasure or theatrical excitement in watching such a presentation would be in seeing temporal requirements met: stage time would have to coincide, or seem to, with the real time involved in moving, camping, eating, even talking in the heavy snow and severe cold. In other words, maybe it wouldn't have been such a bad idea, as Mr. Tally thought it was, to have "actors walking around, blowing on their hands and saying, 'Gee it's cold!' "

That reminds me: the language in this play left something to be desired. What is the actress who plays Kathleen, Scott's wife, supposed to do when, in response to, "I have to be alone," she is made to say, "Poor Con [Scott's nickname, after Fal-con], can you be anything else?" Mr. Tally tries to fill nearly every utterance with Significance, and as a result his characters come away appearing wooden. Especially Amundsen, who doubles as the symbol of Death or Conscience. Need I say more?

I saw Ted Tally in Atlanta during the summer. Believe it or not, on the strength of this one forgettable play and a second play, *Hooters*, which opened at Playwrights' Horizons in New York to poor notices, he was invited to be a playwright-in-residence at the Alliance Theatre Festival of New Works and give other young playwrights advice! Appropriately, the night I attended the festival, he said nothing when asked to comment on a play by Mark Berman (who is not so young, but who is more talented than Mr. Tally and is beginning to get the recognition he deserves): with his inexperience and small talent, he wasn't *able* to say anything. Now his *Terra Nova* is playing regional theatres all over the country—because directors are fascinated, I think, with the idea of making actors behave as if it's cold when it's really quite hot under those lights—and he's getting an undeserved reputation. What a shame. Mr. Tally just might have grown a little artistically if he had been left alone. Now he doesn't have to grow: he's a success.

And the Hippodrome Theatre of Gainesville, Florida, is also a success, to judge by its own assessment of itself, its list of patrons, and the federal as well as state funding it has received. More on this later. First to a discussion of the Shakespeare play that the Hippodrome butchered—*As You Like It*, produced from 31 October-29 November 1980 on its Warehouse stage (the theatre is about to move to a new, large and lavish facility, so successful has it been).

As You Like It criticism, if it is keen, focuses not on the idyllic quality of the play alone, but on the way in which Shakespeare contrasts court and country, human vice and human virtue, man's wisdom and his folly (especially in matters of love). The playwright does not take one side or the other; he knows the truth or rationale of both. But is this all *As You Like It* adds up to, finally, an "as you like it" where one truth is as good as another, everything is relative, and all the men and women are merely players in the great, elusive, and illusory game of life? I think that there is more to the play than this, and that its enormous charm, the spell it can cast over an audience when it is produced well, has never been fully accounted for.

As You Like It is, of course, a comedy, but its charm does not consist merely in our knowledge that, despite everything that may go wrong in the play, matters will turn out happily in the end. The charm of *As You Like It* is richer than this. The characters act happily *along the way*, despite all that goes wrong and with no knowledge that events will end happily. This is not a play about the (comic) conflict of character—Orlando versus Oliver (except for their initial argument or disagreement), Duke Senior versus Duke Frederick (we never discover how Duke Senior came to lose his kingdom, and the two men are never even on stage together), etc. Reconciliation or restitution in *As You Like It* comes through miraculous conversion, not through the ironing out of differences or the defeat of the villains. I would call the play less an endorsement of romantic love (the happy unions of Rosalind and Orlando, Celia and Oliver, Phebe and Silvius, Audrey and Touchstone at the end), as some have labeled it, than an endorsement of whatever life one happens to be living, wherever; further, an endorsement of the *acceptance* of whatever road down which one is led by life, of whatever is sent one's way during existence.

Thus, we find Rosalind living at the court of her uncle, Duke Frederick, who has usurped power from her father, Duke Senior, and banished him. When we first meet her, she is sad to be apart from her father, but within ten lines resolves to rejoice in her love for her cousin Celia and Celia's love for her, and to forget her father (without ceasing to love *him*). She is separated from her father and living at the court of the man who has defeated him, yet she can be happy! Shakespeare does not mock her or her situation: he sends in Touchstone for "sport" and comfort. When Frederick then banishes Rosalind herself from his court, she does not scheme to stay; she goes quickly, disguising herself as the young man Ganymede to discourage attack by highwaymen. She is as content in her new role as she was in her role as Celia's cousin at court: once in the forest of Arden, where her father has sought refuge, she will not give up her disguise. She does not seek reunion with her father, though she knows that he is there. She does not reveal herself to Orlando, though she can very soon be sure that he loves her (she tests him in various ways through her disguise). She seems unwilling or unable to give up her man's attire and the new relationship to people it has brought, until she absolutely must—in order to secure Orlando's affections forever. She has so accepted the role life or "fortune" has pressed on her that she cannot change back to her old role. When she finally does at the end of the play, no one realizes that she was previously disguised as Ganymede or makes much of it if he does: it is as if Ganymede were one person and Rosalind another. It is as if Ganymede really existed.

What is true for Rosalind, who is at the center of the play, is true for the other characters. Orlando is deprived of his inheritance by his brother Oliver and goes into exile in the forest of Arden, ready to kill anyone who will not give him food, but what we remember most about him is his love for Rosalind. It is his love for her that dominates his thoughts once he is in Arden, not his poverty or his desire for revenge on Frederick and Oliver, even though he can have little hope he will see Rosalind again soon, since he does not know that she, too, has been banished from Frederick's court. Orlando lives his poverty, lives his exile, lives his unrequited love, though each of these states might make anyone else miserable. But not anyone in *As You Like It*: Silvius' love for Phebe goes unrequited until the very end of the play, but this does not stop him from loving her absolutely and deriving pleasure from that love along the way. And despite the fact that she does not love Silvius, Phebe agrees to marry him, because he loves her and because she cannot have "Ganymede." She accepts the truth about herself, that she is "not for all markets," and settles happily for marriage to Silvius. Duke Senior, his throne and wealth usurped by his *brother*, his daughter residing at his brother's court, can only sing the praises of life in the forest; he never says that he misses his daughter and he does not condemn his brother. Once Frederick returns the crown to him, Duke Senior does not think twice about going back to court: he embraces his good fortune even as he embraced the bad. He will go back, and he will make the most of life at court.

So will Celia, who abandoned her father, Frederick, to accompany Rosalind in her exile, and who will join Duke Senior's court as Oliver's wife. She has cheerfully accepted her dull looks (as opposed to Rosalind's good ones) and her separation from her father, and she will just as cheerfully accept Oliver's love. Touchstone will also return to the court, with the country girl Audrey as his wife, whereas he had originally left the court for the country with the "city" girls Rosalind and Celia as his companions. As fast as he fell in with Rosalind and Celia, just as fast does he fall in with Audrey. He does not seem bothered that, once in Arden, Rosalind and Celia have less need for his jesting; he quickly finds a woman who may not understand any of his jokes, but with whom he is nevertheless happy.

There is one character in *As You Like It* by whom to measure all the rest, for he experiences neither calamity nor great fortune: he neither relinquishes land nor gains it, neither loses love nor wins it. This is Corin, the old shepherd of Arden. He loves his life as it is and knows (and says) that no life is better or worse. To him, life is simply what you make of it, and throughout the play we see characters unconsciously imitating him, making the most of bad situations and the best of good. This view of the play—that it is an endorsement of "pure living," of taking advantage of opportunities as life presents them and not living in the past or for the future—makes it easier to accept Oliver's, Duke Frederick's, and Jaques' "conversions." Their characters don't suddenly change; rather, Shakespeare places them in new and different situations to which they quickly adapt.

Duke Frederick is behaving in character when he gives up the throne to follow a religious man. As impetuously as he seized power from his brother, just as impetuously does he seek the "power" of religion and the ascetic life. In both cases he pursues his own mind, acts in his own interests, divorcing himself from his family (Celia and Duke Senior). Oliver's "conversion" can be similarly understood. He, too, is acting somewhat in his own interests when he declares his love for Orlando after the latter saves him from a lioness. Oliver no longer has Duke Frederick's favor—the Duke thinks that he helped Orlando escape the court and has seized his land and money until Oliver can find Orlando—so he sincerely accepts his brother's favor. He does not consider going back with Orlando to get what is theirs from Frederick; he is content to remain in the forest, secure in his brother's love, his love for his brother, and what that love has brought him: the added love of Celia. He completely accepts the new situation in which he finds himself and he exploits it, in a manner of speaking, never looking back and never looking beyond his present happiness.

The melancholy Jaques, although he is not unhappy in his melancholy at court and in the forest (this is no contradiction: in the Arden edition of *As You Like It*, Agnes Latham writes that "towards the end of the sixteenth century a temperamental hypersensitivity and thoughtfulness, often a genuine response to the stresses of an age of transition, was high fashion"), wants to "get away" and ply his melancholy elsewhere, with the same religious man to whom Frederick has apprenticed himself. He reacts in a melancholic way to the happiness of the marriage ceremony and to the restoration of Duke Senior to power: he'll have none of it. He is contemplative and curious, and he has run out of subjects in Duke Senior's company (Touchstone and Orlando have been his latest ones). His character remains the same; the company he keeps will change.

As you like your life, then, to the degree that you take what life offers and live it, so will you be happy and prosperous. All the characters in this play are, and one can construe its happy ending as Shakespeare's reward to them for simply being as they are. A large source of tension or suspense in *As You Like It* comes from our knowing, on the one hand, that, once the characters are in Arden, they are fairly content or settled in their roles—I am thinking here particularly of Rosalind in disguise as Ganymede—and our knowing, on the other hand, that matters will change, that Rosalind will marry Orlando, that there will be some resolution of the differences between Duke Frederick and Duke Senior, that Jaques de Boys, the brother of Orlando and Oliver, will be heard from, etc.

If the reader is wondering why I have gone to so much trouble to elucidate an idea that I see at the heart of *As You Like It*, it is because there are no ideas in Bruce Cornwell's production of the play at the Hippodrome, and I had to go back to the text to decide what the play meant to me. In addition, I have been reluctant to talk about the production because, on the whole, it was embarrassing. The embarrassment begins with the setting of the play in "a somewhat rural part of Italy during an earlier part of the twentieth century." Mr. Cornwell tries to explain why he did this in a program note, but he explains nothing. In order artistically to justify such a movement of the play in time and place, you have to make some *idea* in the text relevant to rural Italy in the early twentieth century or vice versa. Mr. Cornwell's Italy, moreover, is the one out of television commercials for wine and pasta, the stereotype of tough-talking (but passionate) men, lusty women, and alternately lively and sentimental music. He calls it "the world's most romantic culture" and concludes that, since *As You Like It* is a "romantic" play, it can be set in his Italy.

This is a founding artistic co-director of "one of America's best regional theatres" speaking, believe it or not. He, too, is not an artist—he has little more than a choreographer's eye for arresting movement and a hack's hand for "business"—and the Hippodrome is far from being one of the best even of the bad lot of American regional theatres. It is more like a community theatre with artistic pretensions taking advantage of the government's affirmative-action program in the arts, according to which money is given to self-proclaimed artists throughout the country on the condition that they do not work for profit and attempt to reach the "general public." Well, I have news for everybody. There are very few true artists to be found anywhere, and the "general public" is interested in entertainment, not art. And that is exactly what the Hippodrome, and most other regional theatres, are giving them, in the name of art: the "relevant" revivals of classics such as *As You Like It*, vapid new works, musical comedies, and restagings of recent New York hits that I talked about in my introduction to this chronicle. The problem is, if you want your theatre to be "experimental" and "innovative"—and the Hippodrome wanted it this way when it opened in 1973, if it never had the personnel capable of real experiment and innovation in the theatre—you have to forget about drawing a nice weekly salary and appealing to a wide audience (at least in the United States). You can't have it both ways, you can't be dedicated to an artistic ideal in this country at the same time you get the public to subscribe en masse to your theatre. Catering to the public is commerce, not art, and commerce is what the Hippodrome is engaged in at present. They seem to be fooling people, since their "reputation" is spreading far and wide. Let their betrayal of their original ideals and inferior work stand exposed here.

Mr. Cornwell himself must be held responsible for this inferior production of *As You Like It*, because he shows no understanding of the play and no ability to work with actors, to make them work as a unit. This play calls for ensemble acting more than others since, as a comedy, its emphasis is less on the individual character (his "psychology") than on the society that has produced him; and as a pastoral comedy, its emphasis is less on the individual character than on a group of characters exhibiting a particular attitude toward life. Part of Mr. Cornwell's problem is that he is not directing a resident company of actors (good actors in most cases don't stay with a regional theatre; they go to New York to lose their art and get rich), but a hodgepodge of college students, housewives, frustrated professors and professionals, and Equity actors jobbed in from New York. Another part of his problem is that he is attempting to appeal to the lowest common denominator in his audience, to "sell" his show, and this doesn't call for ensemble acting: it calls for tricks, some (mocking) homosexual suggestiveness here and there, and the eating of spaghetti on stage as well as the playing of taped music from *The Godfather*.

Most of the acting is bad, or just wrong. Corin and Adam are condescending caricatures of old men. (Andrew Gordon, who plays Adam, should be advised never to act again. He is the epitome of the terrible community theatre actor with aspirations.) Silvius is a sniveling fool and Phebe a silly flirt. Oliver and Duke Frederick are mere villains, as opposed to villains in the service of the play, which is something altogether different. It has to do with comic acting, with somehow being aware of the character you are playing, commenting on him, at the same time you *play* him, give him credibility. Only Stephen Root, as Touchstone, was able to succeed at this, but his performance, for all that was good about it, stood out in another, not-so-good way. Mr. Root has toured in *As You Like It* with The National Shakespeare Company, and his performance here looked "used," as if he were running it by us, repeating it from previous work, on his way to another job. Laura Copland, who played Rosalind, is intelligent but uninteresting. If Rosalind is to succeed, and the play along with her, she must capture our interest *of herself* at the same time she does so with her ardent love for Orlando.

Two other actors were passable: Daniel Jesse as Jaques and Mark Sexton as Orlando. Mr. Jesse has charm, wit, and verve, but he misses some big moments, and he seems at times to perform his Jaques in a vacuum, without relation to the other players and the play of which they are all a part. The character Jaques is of course by definition somewhat removed from the action, but I am talking about something quite different from this. Mark Sexton is not a robust and wise enough Orlando for me. His face impassive and his body too erect, he seems statue-like, asking to be adored all the time. He might have made the proper Silvius. Orlando loves himself, but he loves his community, family, and Rosalind more. Mr. Sexton has good concentration and some presence, in addition to a certain friendliness or vulnerability in his vanity, but none of that was enough here.

Obviously nothing was "enough" in the Hippodrome's production of *As You Like It*, and I fear that I am one of the few to have said so. I'll hope against hope that this theatre will return some day to its original goals and ideals— perhaps when its state and federal funding are cut off as a result of inflation— and stop trying to "go national." Localism alone can lead to culture, it has been said. But that means true localism or regionalism, not the kind attached to federal funding and fat cats' pocketbooks, with one eye forever looking to New York and the other blind to everything but the desire for its own survival.

After all that I've said about *As You Like It*, I have nothing to say about the Alley Theatre's (Houston) production of Bertolt Brecht's *Threepenny Opera* (27 November 1980-11 January 1981), because it wasn't Brecht's work they produced, but rather Marc Blitzstein's adaptation—a better word would be distortion—of it. (At least the Hippodrome was faithful to Shakespeare's text.) Brecht wrote a satire on the bourgeois society of post-World War I Germany (he was himself adapting John Gay's *Beggar's Opera*, written in 1728), equating the bourgeoisie with criminals. Blitzstein turned it into a cute, harmless musical comedy that just happened to contain greedy, murderous characters; he didn't bother to consider why, and neither did the New York audiences who made it a great success. (A recent frivolous exploitation of this same paradox was the musical *Sweeney Todd*.) The Alley, being itself engaged in commerce, not art, chose to use Blitzstein's version, and the result is beneath criticism.

As for Brecht's own work, it can be said that *The Threepenny Opera* is not the great play some have cracked it up to be, but neither is it negligible in the author's canon, a "potboiler" written just to turn a quick buck. The important aspects of it to recall are that, as Eric Bentley has pointed out, it is Brecht's first fully developed "epic" play, and that it is designed not only to satirize the bourgeoisie but also, through its songs/poems, to suggest that before the bourgeoisie can change, the society that produced it must change. Many would question the need for such change; they are precisely those at whom Brecht aimed his play.

Like all the epic plays to come, *The Threepenny Opera* is didactic, but it does not preach: in the end, it indicts all segments of society, not just the bourgeoisie. Life is tough, and man is fallible. Brecht was too intelligent to think that the world's problems could be solved by dismantling the middle class. But he did think that this was a good place to start. If his largely middle-class German audience didn't agree and made *The Threepenny Opera* a huge commercial success in its original version, this was less the fault of Brecht's writing than of middle-class masochism. Ideally, Brecht wanted the bourgeoisie to see the error of its ways and join the forces of revolution. Instead, it embraced its own greed and callousness, proving that there was a need for a dramatist of social change like Brecht and, ironically, giving him the success that enabled him to continue one form or another of attack on the bourgeoisie.

If the play loses much of its effect in (faithful) production today, this is because everyone in this country is bourgeois or aspires to be: to be bourgeois is no longer to be a member of a privileged class, privileged to laugh at itself. We are classless in that we are all essentially the same, or want to be. And many of us will go to any lengths to achieve what we want or keep what we have, in the face of heavy, endless competition. So we don't laugh or aren't particularly surprised or appalled when we learn that Tiger Brown, the chief of police, is on the take from Macheath: we accept corruption in police departments as a way of life, as one more way (however shady) for people to get ahead. Similarly, we don't find the merchant Peachum's outfitting of beggars to "arouse human pity" and thereby get more money (most of it for himself) shocking/funny. We don't find the *fact* of his exploiting the poor shocking/funny; we are merely amused at the *manner* in which he exploits them, the lengths to which he will go to do so. We accept and practice economic exploitation as a way of life. Only occasionally will its more bizarre manifestations cause us to raise our heads (but that is all). At the other end of the spectrum, we don't laugh when the criminal Macheath criticizes his cronies' taste in furniture: we take it for granted that big-time criminals aspire to the "good life" and are often status-conscious, if not in fact intelligent men. And we don't laugh when Macheath is raised to the nobility at the end of the play: we think that it's corny. To be raised to the nobility was the dream of the German bourgeois of the time; to be bourgeois is the ultimate for us. Brecht would not approve in either case, and, to his credit, his play goes on reminding us that he would not.

How to produce *The Threepenny Opera* for a modern audience is a good question, and there have been various acceptable answers to it from various countries in the past few years. It's too bad that one of those answers did not come from Houston, among cities in the United States, in 1980. Gay satirized the London aristocracy in 1728, Brecht the German bourgeoisie in 1923. Perhaps the play should be done today, or re-adapted, as a satire on the American working class, which apes the bourgeoisie in the same way that the German middle class aped the nobility, and whose members exploit one another in the race to get ahead.

That brings an end to the bad news; my venom is spent. I go in search of good theatre.

The Theater of Satire, or Politicians and the Arts

Joel Schechter
Theater *Magazine*

I.   How Political Satire Forced Richard Nixon to Resign the Presidency

Commenting in April, 1975 on the comedy of David Frye and other mimics, Albert Goldman observed that their take-offs on Nixon were

> . . . annihilating—primitive, insulting, savage, and yet enormously popular with the Las Vegas crowds. Perhaps because Americans harbor so much suppressed rage towards Nixon . . . they're hungry to see him no less than symbolically destroyed before their eyes . . . destroyed, too, with his own voice, mannerisms, and look—stolen from him and thrown back in his face.

Depriving Nixon of his own voice, mannerisms, and look, nightclub mimics intimated that the Chief Executive was not only counterfeitable, but also counterfeit; he was more a set of jowls than a president. Every night in Las Vegas the presidency of the United States was usurped by an impostor other than the one elected. There was only one way for Richard Nixon to stop that anarchic nonsense: resign. And so he did.

Perhaps the former President now takes pleasure in knowing that, while he may have a small following, David Frye's audience is infinitely smaller. Frye had to leave Las Vegas or become a waiter there, or so Nixon suspects. In fact, Frye simply had to learn how to chew gum, which, some say, is all that Gerald Ford ever did.

Unfortunately, no satire drove Nixon to resignation. Neither David Frye's jowl movements nor Philip Roth's parodic novel, but rather a transcript of his own words forced the President to seek asylum in San Clemente.

His expletives had been deleted from the Watergate transcript, of course, but the deletions simply increased national awareness of Nixon's hypocrisy. In public he pretended to deplore foul politics and foul language, but privately he swore with frequency. Nixon's abusive language damaged his reputation. He was exposed as being no more moderate in temper than his wife was modest in dress. (She secretly wore a shah's jewels, not content with a plain cloth, Republican coat, it was revealed late in the Watergate scandal). How could a country founded by Puritans forgive the President his four-letter vocabulary, or let a Republican Lenny Bruce (humor deleted) stay in the White House?

Nixon himself was ashamed of his expletives. Now a sense of shame in a politician is a wonderful thing—for his opponents. Shame instills a fear of public disapproval. Ideally, every politician should promise to have a sense of shame if elected.

Actually, President Nixon's shame had less to do with the loss of public support than with the loss of honor that was to accompany his secret peace plan and also accompany his name in history books. Historians and publishers who agree that Nixon deserves no honor ought to delete his name from their books, or, better yet, turn "N***n" into an expletive. (Unfortunately, one television network paid him half a million dollars to clear his name in a series of interviews.)

II.   How Political Satire Forced Robert Walpole to Applaud *The Beggar's Opera*

N***n has not been the only president to suffer from mimicry and verbal abuse over the past few decades. Carter had four years, and Lyndon Johnson had his term. But Johnson was not so easily shamed by satire or abusive language. He knew how to dry up the pens of satirists: ask them for autographed cartoons. Jules Feiffer was invited to send an autographed cartoon critical of Johnson to the White House. If LBJ had been extremely shrewd, he also would have visited *Macbird*, to disarm his Off-Broadway critics. Emerging from the play, he would have said of the actor caricaturing him: "That Stacy Keach is quite a card. Even funnier than Walter Kerr said he was. I've asked Stacy to stand in for me at the next White House Press Conference."

The embracing of satirists by satirized politicians—call it "satirical chic" if you will—was most notably practiced by Sir Robert Walpole, Prime Minister of England. Walpole attended *The Beggar's Opera* in 1728, and while there he applauded at least one of the verses written to ridicule him. According to an eyewitness account of the incident, an actor sang these lyrics by John Gay:

> When you censure the age
>   Be cautious and sage,
>   Lest the courtiers offended should be.
> If you mention vice or bribe,
>   'Tis so pat to all the tribe
>   Each cries—That was levelled at me,

at which time the greater part of the audience

. . . threw their eyes on the stage-box, where the Minister was sitting, and loudly *encored* it. Sir Robert saw this stroke instantly, and saw it with good humor and discretion; for no sooner was the song finished, than he encored it a second time himself, joined in the general applause, and by this means brought the audience into so much good humor with him, that they gave him a general huzza from all parts of the house.

Despite the Augustan stateman's embrace of Gay's satire, Walpole apparently was offended by *The Beggar's Opera* to the extent that months later he arranged the banning of Gay's next play, *Polly*. Perhaps the ban on stage productions of *Polly* was merely an expression of Walpole's gratitude to Gay, for the ensuing controversy insured the playwright enormous profits from sales of *Polly* in book form.

The satirical chic that Walpole displayed toward *The Beggar's Opera* when he saw it was shared by many wealthy Londoners in 1728. The upper classes, whose manners whores and thieves parodied in Gay's opera, printed *Beggar's Opera* lyrics on playing cards, fire screens, women's fans, and silk handkerchiefs that permitted gentlemen to blow their noses at the satire.

Not until 1737, nine years after Walpole saw *The Beggar's Opera*, and after Henry Fielding had also satirized Walpole on stage, did the Prime Minister confess that such theatre "not only wounded his feelings as a man, but very materially injured him as a Minister in the estimation of the people." Injurious though it may have been, *The Beggar's Opera* benefited Walpole in a manner best described by William Hazlitt. Discussing the impact of Gay's opera on later prime ministers, Hazlitt observed:

The very wit . . . takes off from the offensiveness of the satire; and I have seen great statesmen, very great statesmen, heartily enjoying the joke, laughing most immoderately at the compliments paid to them as not much worse than pickpockets and cut-throats in a different line, and pleased, as it were, to see themselves humanised by some sort of fellowship with their kind.

III.   Reagan and the Arts

Radio and film not only affect the function of the professional actor but likewise the function of those who also exhibit themselves before this mechanical equipment, those who govern. . . . This results in a new selection, a selection before the equipment from which the star and dictator emerge victorious.

—Walter Benjamin.

No other president has proven his comic gifts more ably than Ronald

Reagan. He performed opposite Bonzo, a chimpanzee, and managed to hold his own against the zany, lovable behavior of his feral companion. He delivered hilarious one-liners ("I'd rather be in Philadelphia") from a hospital bed after an assassin failed to quell his sense of humor. (At least the line was hilarious when W. C. Fields said it). "I forgot to duck," Reagan's quip after the bullet hit him, testifies to almost immortal wit. No doubt he has already asked aides to prepare some humorous remarks suitable for broadcast before a nuclear war. ("We begin the bombing in five minutes" was a joke he tested off the air—unaware that his radio microphone was on—in 1984.)

Jonathan Swift noted, in reference to *The Beggar's Opera*, that politicians "of all ranks, parties and denominations" attend political plays "from a consciousness of their own innocence, and to convince the world how unjust a parallel malice, envy, and disaffection to the government have made." Ronald Reagan may be one of the first politicians who has no need of other actors to prove his innocence.

IV. Dario Fo, Twice-Banned Satirist

No one has proven the ability of an actor to advance political causes better than Ronald Reagan. He is no comedian, however, and it may have been fear of other, funnier actors stealing his show that led the Reagan administration to keep two of Europe's finest political satirists out of America prior to Reagan's re-election. When the U.S. State Department denied entry visas to Dario Fo and his wife, Franca Rame, in 1980 and 1983, the American public lost an opportunity to see the couple perform comic monologues already applauded by hundreds of thousands of spectators in Italy, France, Germany, England, China, even Peru.

The two political satirists were finally permitted to enter the United States the day after the 1984 elections. The occasion of their visit was the Broadway opening of Fo's most popular satire, *Accidental Death of an Anarchist*. This farce about police repression of dissent had over 130 other productions around the world, including a year's run on London's West End, before it and its author arrived in New York.

Evidently the Italian pair's political activism and leftist satire, welcome in so many other countries, had earlier posed a threat to national security. John Caufield of the State Department claimed (inaccurately) that Fo and Rame "had done fund-raising and other activities for Italian terrorist groups." In fact, the actors have condemned terrorism. "Terrorism never destabilizes the established rule; rather it strengthens it," Fo has noted, and the State Department's seizing on terrorist activity as an excuse for visa denials bears this theory out. Fo and Rame have engaged in campaigns to prevent the torture of prisoners in Italy and to insure that fair trials are given to political prisoners, but this hardly amounts to support of terrorism. It places them slightly to the left of Amnesty International. (They are not members of any political party, incidentally. In Fo's words, the couple prefers to remain "unchained dogs," free to attack anyone in power.)

The first time they were denied entry visas, by the Carter Administration in 1980, Franca Rame thought that "it was the Italian government who didn't want us to go to the States. . . . Italian political leaders weren't happy that we do political satire and were going to represent Italy [at a festival in New York]." Rumor had it that during his 1980 visit, Fo was planning to impersonate Jimmy Carter on stage. When he arrived in 1984, Fo's first act at a press conference was to thank Ronald Reagan for making Franca and Dario better known, by denying them visas and giving them publicity. The gift of publicity was the "gesture of a colleague," Fo said about his fellow actor's behavior. He also said that Reagan called him personally to plan the publicity campaign. Reagan would probably deny this.

Over the past 35 years (he is now 58), Fo's satirical targets have included such venerable institutions as the Catholic Church, the Mafia, the CIA, and Christopher Columbus. The Italian Communist Party (PCI) ended a two-year sponsorship of Fo and Rame's tours in 1970, when the couple started ridiculing the party bureaucracy. Their humor knows few boundaries; it falls somewhere between the ribaldry of Boccaccio and Lenny Bruce, and the political wit of Brecht and Mayakovsky, with occasional borrowings from Marx, medieval jesters, and *commedia dell'arte*.

Fo and Rame's plays, created with a theater collective in Milan, have become increasingly popular in America since the first visa denial in 1980. Perhaps the "publicity campaign" coordinated by the State Department in 1983 has helped theaters such as New York's Public, Arena Stage, the Mark Taper Forum, Yale Repertory, and the San Francisco Mime Troupe to recognize Fo's importance as a playwright. (If so, the State Department should have helped a little more in New York—to counteract the negative *New York Times* reviews of Fo's first Broadway production, *Accidental Death of an Anarchist*.)

Dario Fo is fond of quoting another persecuted satirist, the Russian poet and playwright Vladimir Mayakovsky, to the effect that "the end of satire is the first alarm bell signaling the end of real democracy." The first alarm bell rang twice, in 1980 and 1983, when Presidents Carter and Reagan chose not to let Fo and Rame enter America. Have our presidents become too protective of their own acting talent not to let in the competition until after the election? Only time, and a presidential visit to one of Fo's plays, will tell.

Beyond *Verfremdung*: Notes Toward a Brecht "Theaterturgy"

Michael Evenden

Allegheny College

1.   The State of the Brecht Stage: An American Impression

"Montrously delicate" is how Brecht described his poetry to Eric Bentley[1]; the same might be said of Brecht's plays—and of the task of staging them. In the United States particularly, directing Brecht is a process that never seems to go right; one reads or hears of rather frequent Brecht productions in the network of university and regional theaters, but seldom do they spur much enthusiasm, seldom is a real Brechtian satisfied. The cliché persists with few rebuttals: American artists don't seem to know what to do with Brecht's plays.

Given the elusiveness of the Echt Brecht (in production or in production style), one is naturally tempted to idealize Brecht's own stagings at the Berliner Ensemble. Those stagings, now legendary, have browbeaten a generation of theater artists and set a standard that is ineradicable, yet indecipherable: we sense the superiority of the original stagings without being able to reproduce it. Dutiful imitation is the height of our achievement, and it is poor imitation at that: we manage to bypass the famous power, clarity, and humanity of the original, and reproduce only the grayness, the monotony of the *Modellbuch* photos in dispiritingly familiar, derivative, and hollow revivals.

Clearly, we have fallen into a trap, albeit one set by Brecht himself. We idealize his stage direction uncritically, failing to discriminate between letter and spirit in the "law" of the *Modellbücher*. Further, because a theatrical style is the most fragile and impermanent of artistic codes, we court the clear and present danger of confining Brecht's plays in what are now overfamiliar and dated theatrical practices, practices that have fossilized at the Ensemble since the playwright's death a generation ago.

On the other hand, one cannot ignore the international acclaim for Brecht's own productions when they were first seen, nor avoid the impression that those plays became something greater under the playwright's direction. This wayward genius' eccentric, elusive way with actors and with mise-en-scène seems to have added new ranges of signification, a new fullness of import and meaning to his texts. There can be no complete understanding of the plays that does not consider these celebrated productions.

These notes are intended as a beginning effort in a much-needed analysis of Brecht's directing style—both as a dramaturgy of texts and a "theaterturgy" of stagings, aimed at discovering some of the principles which underlie the distracting plenitude of discussable details that Brecht crowded onto the Schiffbauerdamm stage. It is an axiom of this study that Brecht's direction tapped the power of his own scripts through a precise, organic connection between play and production. If this is true, analysis of the plays and of their stagings must interpenetrate: the play as written becomes a guide to understanding Brecht's staging, and the staging reveals the play. One hopes that, when this project is finally and fully addressed (as can only be done tentatively and in the way of foundations here), it will facilitate new productions that can incorporate new theatrical environments, vocabularies, and conventions without betraying a play's structure, techniques, and dramatic identity.

2.   Issues in Brechtian Style: *Verfremdung* and the Lifelike

2.1   Brechtian Realism: The "Lifelike"

Brecht's criticism must be read critically; only then can it help to deepen our understanding of his dramaturgical procedures. This is particularly true of his persistent inveighing against the tradition of naturalism, and of his sometimes hyperbolic claims for having utterly rejected its techniques.

In fact, if one were to say outright that Brecht was a naturalistic director, the error would be only partial. The textural aspects of naturalism appealed to Brecht's taste a great deal. His careful attention to realistic stage "business," the use of real objects bought in markets rather than stage property simulations, the love of the unadorned textures of real wood, metal, leather, and rough fabric—all these manifest a personal visual and tactile sensitivity that brought a number of naturalistic surfaces onto Brecht's stage, and in so doing insured an appearance of realism, a particular kind of verisimilitude.

Of course, outside of its sensual value, verisimilitude was tonally and ideationally important to Brecht: it manifested his yearning for a proletarian authenticity. That is why, although he was a great (and self-promoting) theatrical stylist, Brecht was nevertheless suspicious of the impulse toward style. (I am consciously using the word in the customary, if somewhat imprecise way that comes readily to hand in a mimetic age: "style" as anything that differs from photographic realism.) He wanted to encourage an audience to peer beneath familiar surfaces so as to discover the political and moral truths that are often undetected in daily living—yet he wanted to leave those surfaces, those outward appearances and manifestations of reality, as undisturbed and undistorted as possible. It is a fundamental ambiguity: a naturalistic and anti-naturalistic impulse mated.

This opposition of impulses yields a kind of Brechtian hermaneutics, in which the audience is impelled to recognize, and more, to penetrate and pass through familiar appearances in order to seek out a truth that is implied but never explicitly stated. The audience proceeds imaginatively from its own time and space through a fictional realm of more or less realistically rendered events, until they come to a plane of partially-defined causes and suggestions of insight, a plane beyond common appearances, beyond customary ways of seeing.

This implicit progression changes the nature of the natural, making it both an oracle and a veil. The term "naturalism" will not do here. Brecht opposed the "natural" ways of seeing that the word implies. He tried to appropriate the word "realism" from the socialist realists, but this, too, has the wrong connotations. For this essay, I will call Brecht's peculiar verisimilitude "the likelike," insofar as the word can imply both a similarity to and a difference from the "life" of apparent reality. To study Brecht's dramaturgy and/or staging must necessarily be to study the lifelike—and the half-disguised, half-exposed techniques with which Brecht violated lifelikeness, shaping experience to his ideas without too severely disturbing its familiar appearance.

2.2 Violation of the Lifelike: *Verfremdung* as Principle and as Catch-All Term

For all its incorporation of lifelike elements, however, Brecht's practice clearly differed from any strictly mimetic drama, and Brecht liked to make much of that difference. Unfortunately, he tended to state the matter in somewhat confusing terms, centering on the loosely-deployed word *Verfremdung*.

In the larger sense, *Verfremdung* is the key concept in Brecht's aesthetic, the umbrella term that covers all his methods of alerting the audience into a special critical awareness of the dramatic action. In this full sense, the term covers a great many different features of Brecht's work: the exotic settings, for example; the use of verse or song to heighten a point in the dramatic argument; an instance of dramaturgic juxtaposition in which a character's most earnest statement is made ironic by an unexpected context.

This is *Verfremdung,* then, as a general or categorical term, covering a number of dramatic and theatrical devices—but only when those devices are used for the specific purpose of surprising the audience into a higher, and more critical, awareness. No device is inherently a *V-Effekt*.

And it was on this point that Brecht himself created confusion, by applying the general term to a smaller and more specific instance of itself, blurring principle and example. That is, Brecht came to use the general term *Verfremdung* as a synonym for what a theater historian would more rightly call theatricalism— meaning nothing more than the use of frankly theatrical devices, such as masks, non-illusionary settings, visible scene changes, and the like. Brecht assumed that dressing the mise-en-scène with theatricalist elements—which in a loose sense could mean anything non-mimetic—will naturally lead the audience to the elusive wakefulness of *Verfremdung*.

This is, inferrably, related to Brecht's misreading of Shklovsky, whose *ostrannenie* was a direct ancestor of Brecht's neologistic *Verfremdung*: where Shklovsky proposed an artistic practice that made one aware of the artist's materials, Brecht added an assumption that this attention to the (dramatic) medium would necessarily draw an audience into contemplating the larger outlines of the dramatic argument.

Any good Prague semiologist could have shown Brecht that theatricalism doesn't always work that way; many august Brechtians have made the same argument; Daphna Ben Chaim wrote a book on the subject[2]; and Brecht himself acknowledged the problem, as if on the sly, in the *Short Organum*.[3] Yet Brecht continued to function as if on faith, on a willed belief that with the use of theatricalist decoration, he could solve the extremely subtle problem of controlling his audience's sympathy with push-button ease. It became a kind of never-ending refrain in Brecht's self-explanations: every sharply-defined stylistic touch became not itself but another *V-Effekt*, and the *Verfremdung* was supposed to suit and explain virtually everything Brecht did.

The result is an imprecise and reductive vision of Brecht's writing and staging, although a vision that Brecht himself engineered. It suggests that every non-mimetic device in Brecht's extremely heterogeneous staging style is equivalent to every other in intention and effect; worse, it fosters the belief that theatricalist mannerisms are what makes Brecht Brecht—so that any production, of any kind of play, that uses a visible scene change is suddenly understood to be "Brechtian."[4] Words like "Brechtian" and "defamiliarization" (or its less adequate synonym "alienation") are drained of meaning this way, and any precise perceiving of Brecht's work and methods dissolves into a blurred understanding.

If we were to reverse this distorted vision, we would come closer to the truth. Brecht's non-realistic passages and elements are not synonymous and uniform, but diverse, and directed toward discrete, separable effects (thus, an exposed lighting instrument is not the equivalent of a mask, and an ironic song is not a non-realistic setting). Moreover, theatricalism in itself is not some Quintessence of Brechtism. On the contrary, some of his theatricalist habits are inessential and decorative, while others are indispensable manifestations of central traits in his playwriting. Such distinctions have to be made before the relations between play, production, and theoretical criticism can yield a useful understanding.

3.   First Principles of Brecht's Staging Techniques

The following notes will offer initial explanations of a number of the non-realistic elements in Brecht's stagings, attempting a kind of anatomy or phenomenology of style. That these are "first" principles is true in a double sense: in that this analysis is only a beginning that will leave a great deal still to be explored, and in that these principles operate on a primary level, one of deep structure, giving order and predicating dramaturgical patterns.

It is important that the incompleteness of these notes be kept in mind, for there is a risk of falling into Brecht's own trap of analyzing his work too narrowly, or of assumptively categorizing every element of the Brecht stage as if it were only another interchangeable element in an abstruse intellectual design. Brecht's work is only partly susceptible to systematic analysis; there is an impulsive, improvisational quality to the writing and the staging, and an eccentric beauty to both that, while they are important, can only be peripherally addressed here, since my investigation is aimed at what I've called the "hermaneutics"—the significations—of the Brecht stage.

3.1 Principles of Directed Attention

Stage naturalism—in theory—presumes an accidental quality, a sense of dispersed focus and a prizing of each available locus for the viewer's attention. There is at least a pretense of a minimal distortion of experience, a renouncing of manipulation and artifice. (That theatrical naturalism promised this, yet tended to include frankly melodramatic contrivances, was part of what spurred Brecht's disgust for the form—and his preference for relaxed tonalities and disjointed structures.)

Brecht's distinctive staging style begins with a rejection of dispersed focus: he specialized in subtly directing his audience's attention so as to arouse a special, penetrating awareness that might not withstand distraction.

3.1.1 Heightened Detail

Characteristically, Brecht loved the suggestive detail, the small, barely noticeable gesture that bears a huge meaning. This is the vision that sees importance in a general's handling of a bar of soap, draws proud attention to Weigel's way of biting a coin, finds an important hidden meaning in Weigel's accentuation of a single word in Courage's lullaby to the dead Kattrin, and insists that a fugitive aristocrat in *Caucasian Chalk Circle* would be unable to copy a poor man's way of eating.

Accordingly, staging methods for Brecht's plays need to include a way of drawing the audience's attention to selected, significant details. This is a principle that shapes not only the performance, but the writing of the plays as well.

For instance, characterization tends to be built through selective emphasis. With most of his secondary characters, there are only a few traits that are important to Brecht, and accordingly, he highlights them. Consider the photographs of the *Puntila* masks in *Theaterarbeit*, where one can see the "typicality" of characters—the absurdity and obtuseness of the judge, the strangely cold and almost brutal quality Brecht sought to bring out in Puntila[5]; we learn about these characters only what we need to know for them to fill their place in the drama, but we learn it in a striking, theatrical way.

Significantly, these masks are only very subtly distortive. It would be possible to glance at these figures and see them not as masked "types," but only as unusually vivid characterizations in costume, bearing, and makeup. Always reluctant to stretch the lifelike too far, Brecht saw to it that such physical distortion remained subtle, a matter of stressed detail that moves us immediately into the realm of his idiosyncratic, mannerist realism. With somewhat less subtlety, but with a similar process, characters are simplified into an exaggerated essence by the cruder and more obviously theatrical masks of *Caucasian Chalk Circle*. Even without masks, one can see traces of the same thing in the clearly defined postures of the actors in each of their many characterizations as they are shown in *Theaterarbeit*[6]; perhaps this was the essence of the never-too-clear doctrine of "gestic" acting—a distinctive, if slight, exaggeration of bodily gesture that makes the essential (and for Brecht that means social) traits of the character unusually readable and clear.

The same kind of selectivity and reliance on detail can be found in Brecht's language. One example might be a phrase in the rubric of the first scene of *Mother Courage*, which is usually translated "Mother Courage loses a son," but more precisely would be "Mother Courage comes to lose a son"—a subtle difference that makes a point, since Brecht's effort with this linguistic detail seems to be to draw our attention, not to the fact that Courage loses Eilif, but to the way (that is, the reason) that she comes to lose him, which is the essence of the play in miniature.

In short, Brecht's "realism" is colored and subtly reshaped into something cryptic, suggestive, delicately distorted, a quietly formalized version of reality not unlike the Barlach sculptures that Brecht admired. Brecht wanted to essentialize experience by carefully directing his viewer's eye, without, perhaps, seeming to do so.

3.1.2   Selective Abstraction

The second principle of focusing the audience's attention is nearly inseparable from the first: that the carefully selected details to which Brecht draws attention are displayed against a ground of great spareness. Conciseness and concentration are the signal virtues of Brecht's poetry; this is the same quality in theatrical terms: precisely realized details on a nearly blank stage.

This principle has proved a major stumbling block for many American designers and directors of Brecht's plays. For those who choose to find some route other than simple imitation of the Neher or Otto designs, the invitation to use theatricalist techniques often provokes a blinding flurry of mad "creativity," endless elaborations of simple ideas, luxuriation in unnecessary invention. What these enthusiasts fail to realize is that Brecht's technique is one of precisely calculated abstraction in which all unnecessary matters are expunged.

This is most clearly exercised in the design of the settings that Brecht supervised and later glossed in his notes. Brecht adored the spareness of Neher's designs for *Mother Courage*, their functional quality of providing the actors with exactly the objects needed to carry out their theatrical tasks, but beyond that only the sketchiest indications of place and physical conditions. Rough screens and a flat stage floor were for Brecht a beautiful aesthetic economy; he exulted in the refusal to fill in the empty spaces, preferring the fragmentary, suggestive, brisk look of a quick sketch.

The same spareness is present in Brecht's distinctive control of stage movement. The movements of actors under Brecht's direction have been described as bold, purposeful, never random, never indecisive or hesitant, but organized, clear, and uncluttered. Clearly, Brecht's habit of working from Neher's sketches to create the "grouping" of actors created a continuity of technique from scenic design to mise-en-scène; but more important, Brecht and Neher shared an exclusive and spare compositional style that linked not only groupings to scenic design, but all the visual elements to the writing itself.

The same principle enters Brecht's writing in a number of ways. It is there in the conflation of time in *Caucasian Chalk Circle*, when, with a narrator's help, a few minutes' pantomime enacts Grusche's night-long vigil over the child in the first act, or when, without any intrusive devices, a single unbroken conversation stretches from midwinter through the spring thaw in the shed at Lavrenti's farm.

Perhaps most important, this radical selectivity affected the way of writing characters, for Brecht did not write psychologized personalities, but cautionary figures whose psyches were dictated and shaped by their given social roles. Brecht politicized the self and expunged purely psychological motivations: there is no libidinous subtext, there are no hidden obsessions; even when Gutschen copulates with Lauffer as a substitute for her absent fiancé, the substitution is more or less conscious and excites no horror in the girl. Her motivations are not a Freudian tangle of unbidden urges; for Brecht, desire is concrete and unmysterious.

The real mystery that shapes Brecht's dramaturgy is not that of unconscious desires, but of irreconcilable roles, contradictory social pulls acting on a single character. Inner conflict comes from without. In accordance with Brecht's methods of abstraction, these conflicting needs are generalized, assumed, freed from biographical particularization: there is no point at which Mother Courage came to love her bastard brood, because her loyalty to them is a given; similarly, Shen Te's affection for her flier arrives at an appropriate point in the dramatic action and is not particularized—Brecht is not Marivaux. He was interested in the *results* of a generous impulse, and typically drew attention away from that impulse's wellsprings or its character-bound idiosyncrasies. Brecht's characters are all to some degree ideational emblems; they are all stylized.

Just as designers are tempted to fill in the Brechtian blanks—those areas of the stage that he deliberately left in rough outline—actors will be tempted to fill in the characters' broadly outlined motivations with psychological additives that shift us onto the wrong sort of dramatic ground. Brecht put certain characters into masks for a reason—their *roles* were masks, simplified, essentialized, sharply defined theatrical beings that must be played by imaginative actors who can match the thrust and precision of the minor characters' incarnations (as well as those of the more specifically realized central characters), while still keeping the performance "clean," free of extraneous additions that only muddle the characterizations Brecht devised.

This means that actors and directors in Brecht must be critical of their own impulses, able to select from their random impressions those elements that accord with what Brecht has given. Brecht wanted richly detailed acting in his plays: he could wax rhapsodic over the minutiae of a good actor's performance, but those elements that he praised were all relevant to the Brechtian world—the bitten coin, the increasingly servile bow of a frustrated student out of work, the lust of a prostitute's protector—all are what Brecht called "social gests," small, realistic actions that reveal the underlying social and economic relations of the characters involved. The psychological and the quaint are irrelevant here and are best excluded; beneath all its theatrical richness and subtlety, Brecht's is a rigorous aesthetic.

3.2   The Principle of Visual Contrast

Brecht's dramaturgy is founded on carefully designed contradictions. He stated that explicitly in any number of his working notes. Here follow some of the ways that this ground of calculated contradictions found expression on Brecht's stage.

3.2.1   Contrast Over Time

The clearest example is Brecht's immediate juxtaposition, between Scenes 6 and 7, of Mother Courage's "God damn the war!" with her fierce defense of that war ("Stop running down the war. I won't have it")—an opposition that clarifies the "merchant-mother's" contradictory roles and displays her moral discontinuity. By the starkness of the contrast, eliminating all gradation between her opposed positions, Brecht clarifies a striking incongruity that impels his audience toward a critical view of the character.

More common to Brecht's dramaturgy—and less obvious—were the more gradual reversals that shape his construction of scenes. Brecht described this principle—a fundamental structural principle for him—in the *Messingkauf*:

> Suppose you've a play where the first scene shows A bringing B to justice, then the process is reversed in the last scene and, after all kinds of incidents have been shown, B brings A to justice, so that there's one and the same process (bringing to justice) with A and B exchanging their respective roles (executioner and victim). In such a case you'll undoubtedly arrange the first scene so as to give the maximum possible effectiveness to the last. You'll ensure that on seeing the last scene the audience will immediately be reminded of the first; that the similarity will be striking; and at the same time that the differences will not be overlooked.[7]

It was this principle of writing that determined a naturally corresponding principle of staging: reversal of the mise-en-scène in the course of a scene, so that the final stage image altered and commented on the first. Thus the famous scene in *Galileo* of the Pope whose attitudes toward Galileo change with his social role—with the donning of his clerical robes.[8] Like Saint Joan's change of costume after her confession in *The Trial of Joan of Arc at Rouen*, the Pope's scene gives a theatrical extension to a change of political roles and their accompanying attitudinal reversals. One man exits, and—both externally and internally—another enters, a transformation of the first.

These examples function within a single scene. Others function over a span of scenes as a progression in the plot and in the mise-en-scène. For example, the changes in Courage's financial status are linked to her choices of action; thus, the changing appearance of her wagon and wares and the decreasing number of her family and followers are calculated, theatrically expressed criticisms of her decisions. Shen Te's self-division into generous and selfish halves becomes a sequence of costume changes—a division that is echoed in a similar, but more gradually and realistically rendered, change in her lover, who begins as a careless but visionary pilot, only to become a vicious capitalist lackey.

The same principle can extend across whole plays from beginning to end. In this way, the final image of Mother Courage dragging her own wagon is made more outrageous and telling by our memory of her first entrance with three children and with her own greater youth and strength. Similar are *Galileo*'s closing scenes, when his lifelong student leaves him to his food. Or the gods' unheeding exit at the end of *Good Person of Setzuan*, amid cries for help—the exact obverse of their richly anticipated arrival in the first scene. *The Mother*'s concluding posture, with the titular character marching, flag in hand and part of a revolutionary band, is strengthened by our memory of her initial appearance alone, homebound, and helpless. In each case the stage picture clarifies the single "ground-reversal" upon which Brecht structured every one of his mature plays.

3.2.2 Contrast Across Space

Brecht loved stage settings divided into two adjoining sections: he wrote them into *The Mother*, *Mother Courage*, *Caucasian Chalk Circle*, and *Galileo*, either for the sake of allowing one half of the stage to comment on the other (as when Courage sings "The Wise Woman and the Soldier" to disrupt Eilif's dance in the next tent), or else simply because Brecht so enjoyed juxtaposition that he would put dissimilar things next to each other onstage simply for the sake of gratifying his own taste, no more—as in the wedding scene in *Caucasian Chalk Circle*. But at his best, he could combine this taste for laterally registered contrasts with an eye to clarifying the ideational contradictions in a scene.

Often he would make his points simply by movement and positioning, that is, by "blocking" patterns within the mise-en-scène: in the scene outside the devastated village, Mother Courage's acquiring a coat is visually contrasted to Kattrin's rescue of a baby; at the end of the scene, each raises her own booty into the air, and the audience is tacitly encouraged to compare the two kinds of acquisition. Later, during the "drum scene," Kattrin climbs a roof and risks her life to sound a warning of an impending attack to nearby villagers; on the opposite side of the stage, an old peasant woman, helplessly and unhelpfully, kneels and prays for the village's deliverance.

Brecht had a way of using this lateral opposition to suggest moral opposites and temptations: there is scarcely a scene in *Galileo* in which the representatives of Church and science do not position themselves on opposite sides of Galileo in order to sway him each to his or her own side—it is particularly true of the last scene between Andrea, Virginia, and Galileo, but works throughout the drama in an unusually direct way,[9] almost as if Brecht were recalling the good and bad angels arguing with Faustus. Similarly, the playwright specified in his notes the meaning of a tableau in *The Tutor*: "It is here, at the university, that the young store up experiences, both on the intellectual and the physical plane. We see our man Fritz von Berg poised between sacred and profane lovers, between Pātus and Bollwerk."[10] When Courage loses Eilif, she is divided in space between a soldier, who tries to distract her, and Kattrin, who tries to alert her to the danger. Courage's choice, and her priorities, are made into something physical, kinetic—both realistically credible and symbolic at a high level of abstraction.

3.3   The Principle of Layered Discourse: The Composite Brecht Stage

This intellectual progression from the imagined reality of fictional characters to the issues that their existence implies—what I have called Brechtian hermaneutics—is a journey through three realms of thought. Tacitly Brecht's audience is addressed on three different levels: in terms of its own historical time and place, in terms of a fictional world (a different, conventionally given time and place), and in terms of an awareness of the issues that unite the fictional and contemporary worlds.

In a theatrical realization, these three steps of an intellectual process become spaces on the stage, each keyed to a different mode in Brecht's writing. Brecht's theatrical practice and his dramaturgical techniques can be said to coalesce into a general pattern: the composite Brecht stage, an ideal division of theatrical space that can theoretically house the fullness of Brecht's theatrical discourse by separating it into its constitutive elements.

3.3.1   Center Stage: Dramatic Time and Space

Of Brecht's three realms of dramatic/theatrical expression, we can begin with the one that Brecht's drama shares with any other dramatic form: the fictional realm of depicted action, what Susanne Langer calls "virtual space"— the principal stage space behind the proscenium arch, where actors represent characters, and the stage a place and time outside of itself.

What distinguishes Brecht's treatment of the enacted events in this fictionalized space is his desire to endow them with a special, implicative significance. As noted above, Brecht organizes the fictional events through carefully planned juxtapositions in the mise-en-scène, and through stylistic heightening of selected details and de-emphasizing of extraneous matters: he attempts in these more or less subtle ways to clarify patterns and significances within the dramatic action.

He also has recourse to other ways of attacking the audience's customary, possibly uncritical, ways of seeing. Two other realms of thought are recruited by Brecht and physically attached to the action, so that the surrounding stage becomes a commentator on the conventional dramatic sphere.

3.3.2 Downstage: The Audience's Time and Space

The first of these extensional realms is one that expressly mediates between the fictional world of the drama and the time and space occupied by the audience: it is a sphere of explanation and exhortation, a perlocutionary element in Brecht's writing. In the texts, it is the realm of the prologues that are always addressed expressly to the audience and suggest an understanding of the play in terms of the audience's own current concerns. In the theater, it is a space located just downstage of the famous half-curtain—a space literally between the fictional action and the audience, figuratively joining the same time and space as the audience itself.

It is the place for the prologue to *Antigone*, which relates Sophocles' story precisely to postwar Berlin's situation; it is the realm of the scene-titles for *Arturo Ui*, citing the precise events in German history that the "parable" was to illustrate by analogy. The prologue to *Caucasian Chalk Circle* is similar in principle, explicitly connecting the ancient myth that is about to be enacted to the problems of postwar reconstruction under socialist principles; *Puntila* and *The Tutor* both have verse prologues that delineate the present usefulness of their stories. The function of this realm is almost anti-imaginative, anti-fictional; if the relation between the fictional realm and the audience's circumstances is one of analogy (as it always is with Brecht), then the intervening realm of the prologue demystifies that analogy by explaining it.

Even when this element of Brecht's thought is not used in so blunt a way, the same impulse can be felt in his writing; this is the impulse to address contemporary concerns through scarcely concealed references in the fictional action and dialogue: for example, Galileo's attention-getting observations on the need to hide the truth while traveling through Germany, or the rather sentimental remarks he makes about the skeptical intelligence of the proletariat, are clearly directed to a particular audience's self-awareness. When Brecht's dialogue strains for this kind of undisguised relevance (in the middle of a fictionalized, "defamiliarized" action), it is language straining to break out into this downstage sphere of discourse, this direct mode of address.

3.3.3 Behind the Scenes: The Obscured Plane

The third realm of expression in Brecht's plays is the physical and tactical opposite of the prologues and similar references to the audience's immediate circumstances. This is the quintessentially Brechtian realm of obscured realities, of the invisible causes of the dramatic situation. If Brecht's direct address to the audience is comparatively crude, this third sphere is refined enough to be difficult to express in any concrete theatrical way. It is a sphere of implications, of what lies "behind" the enacted events—and its stage space is that of the backdrop or even the backstage upstage of the drop, literally "behind" the fictional action.

For this reason, it is fitting that the final chorus of soldiers that comes closest to stating the playwright's "message" in *Mother Courage* is heard singing behind the scene. The enormous political forces that govern the action of *The Mother* are embodied in the huge, hovering political portraits projected on the backdrop and peering down at the fictional action. And *Puntila*'s reality is shaped by a hermetically sealed bourgeois family situation that cannot tolerate the presence of the proletariat—so Brecht has a portrait of the family and friends, smiling and undisturbed, placed upstage to clarify the tensions that take over when the chauffeur Matti enters; the assumption of bourgeois hegemony is embodied on the backdrop, the better to be put into question by the contrasting tableau beneath it. The stage directions of *Galileo* suggest a frankly symbolic use of light—including a pair of astronomical projections on the backdrop that openly symbolize the allure and challenge of the truth and give a motivic unity to a long and complex dramatic action.

Even when it is not manifested as a literal backdrop, the same impulse to imply or to express in symbols the larger social issues "behind" the dramatic action can be detected. In one scene in *Galileo*, when the conflict between the state and the new science is most clearly introduced, the formal cordialities of Galileo and the elder statesman are juxtaposed against the image of Galileo's pupil and the young duke grappling and, in the process, breaking a Ptolemaic model of the universe: the symbolism could hardly be more obvious, but is effectively displayed, like the backdrop projections, as a simultaneous illustration of the underlying tension in the accompanying, lifelike scene.

This assemblage of impulses, which I have called the composite Brecht stage, is another example of Brecht's way of balancing an unblinkingly specific realism with calculated abstraction: the drama moves from direct audience address in the most specific terms through a more or less realistically rendered story set in a more remote reality, and from there into a shadowy, symbolically rendered, incomplete and implicative sphere of inquiry, inquiry into implied causes, into the very assumptions of social life that must be addressed and changed. As one imaginatively moves away from the audience into the back reaches of the stage, one traverses fissures in Brecht's language and rhetoric, moving from the almost importunately concrete to the teasingly unexpressed. Working in tandem, Brecht's three modes of address form a complex, suggestive totality. They also create an unusually rich, original use of the stage's opportunities for and means of expression.

3.4   The Poetic Principle: Motifs of Imagery and Symbol

I want only to mention briefly a matter that is extremely important in an appreciation of Brecht, but one that has been given only scattered attention. This is Brecht's theatrical poetry, his poetry *of* the theater, in Fergusson's phrase, a poetry of theatrical elements and effects rather than words. Beyond the symbolic use of mise-en-scène, there are symbolic tropes and patterns of reference, some of which echo from one play to the next and reinforce each other's meaning. Fuegi points out most helpfully the recurring images of the cross and crucifixion in *Mother Courage*[11]; the image returns in the flier's scene in *Good Person of Setzuan* and in the Christ imagery that surrounds the beaten and bloody Azdak in the final scene of *Caucasian Chalk Circle*, giving Brecht access to received images of martyrdom, which he can then deploy in unexpected and partly ironic ways. In fact, Christian images abound in Brecht, not least in the holy-family echoes in the last play and in the baptismal scene of Grusche's washing and dressing the child; Brecht's fascination with maternal instinct is colored with a displaced religious reverence.

Not all these motifs can be said to have a precise denotation; some operate affectively and by intuition. There is, for example, the ominous motif of white faces, the origin of which (a suggestion by Karl Valentin) has been frequently repeated; it appears in Begbick's cosmetics in *Mahagonny*, in the faces of the soldiers in the prologue scenes of *Schweik in the Second World War*, in *Coriolanus*, and elsewhere, as well as in Brecht's early poetry, where it is always associated with decay and death.

Some of the symbols, or motifs, seem to change meaning from one play to another: milk and cheese are reminders of Galileo's unidealistic materiality, an aspect of his moral decline, yet the same products signify nurturing and protection in *Caucasian Chalk Circle*—a play that dwells much on recurring images of milk, blood, and water: a maternalized poetic vocabulary for a play about maternality. *Galileo*, too, claims its own symbolic tropes, appropriate to its subject: the sun and all other sources of light are used throughout as precise symbols of truth. Galileo's daughter—who at one point carries a shaded candle—faints at the sight of the sun when it is optically magnified and projected on a wall; and Galileo symbolically loses his capacity to see the light after his recantation.

One symbol that is put to exquisite use through intertextuality is that of snow. In *The Tutor*, it serves as an explicit sign of the desire to let problems be covered up, concealed, and left uncorrected—an image of vicious complacency. Always, snow has a threatening quality. It is a symbolic (as well as a physical) opponent to the hero in *Schweik*, too, as is the wintry chill of *Mother Courage*. Only once does snow become an affirmative presence— at the moment in *Caucasian Chalk Circle* when Grusche, having rescued the child and fully realized its importance to her, describes the world with the eyes of one who has become newly maternal, and entirely generous:

> GRUSCHE. (*looking around at Michael.*) Never be afraid of the wind, it's only a poor devil like us. His job is pushing the clouds and he gets colder than anybody.

(*Snow begins to fall.*)
The snow isn't so bad either, Michael. Its job is covering the little
fir trees so the winter won't kill them. And now I'll sing a song for
you. Listen! (*Sings.*)

Your father is a bandit
And your mother is a whore
Every nobleman and honest
Will bow as you pass

The tiger's son will
Feed the little foals his brothers
The child of the serpent
Bring milk to the mothers.

With this peculiar, unaccompanied song, Brecht shows a miracle beginning: imaginatively, Grusche's love transforms the world's evil into a momentary, idyllic vision, in a brilliantly composed and affecting image—made more
powerful by its compression and by its subtle reference to related figures in the
other Brecht plays.

In fact, a fuller understanding of Brecht's stage will demand that we see
it as a fully symbolized sphere, in which any routine element may unexpectedly
take on special meaning, such as Mother Courage's non-progress on the moving
turntable floor, or Galileo's Pope exiting into darkness. Like Ibsen, Brecht
moved from a boldly poeticized language in early plays to an apparent realism
that nevertheless functions as a transmogrified poetry, a seemingly conventional
dramaturgy internally polarized by ideational schemes and complex revelations
of an "inner" meaning. For Ibsen, a spiritual meaning is evoked, whereas for
Brecht it is more a vision of concrete social facts, but each is reached through
a subtle and complex theatrical poetry that has been too long ignored.

4.   Prescriptions and Questions: Can a Post-Brechtian Theater Reinvent
      Brecht?

It would be wrong to claim that ignorance or violation of these principles
is the sole cause of our difficulties in staging Brecht. But insofar as these
principles permit a clearer and more precise vision of the correspondences
between Brecht's writing and directing, they may provide a basic understanding
through which Brecht's directorial example can be put to better use.

I would tell directors who want to undertake Brecht's plays to use these
principles, to look for the significant patternings Brecht has put into the action:
patterns of spatial juxtaposition and reversal of symbolic images across time,
patterns of symbolic reference, patterns of shifting and complementary tones
as the work moves from the explicit to the suggestive realms of Brecht's

complex discourse. Always, I would advise a director to approach the work with playfulness and sensuality, while honoring a Brechtian tightness of focus.

But perhaps most important, I would encourage a director of Brecht to learn to say no—to make distinctions among the various elements of Brecht's *Modellbuch* legacies, to discover the difference between the decorative and the fundamental, the temporally bound and the still powerful solutions to the challenges of the dramatic texts. I would encourage clearing out everything that has grown customary in Brecht stagings and reaching for a new vision, but a vision strengthened by a firm understanding of the dramaturgic structures and strategies that must shape any vivid retelling of these plays.

4.1 Separating Out the Inessential

Saying no is an aspect of any criticism, and it has operated somewhat tacitly in my own analysis. While sorting out these few essential principles of staging, I have deliberately ignored those principles or elements that I find inessential. Since this list of calculated omissions includes some of Brecht's most famous and most imitated habits, some of which are still seen as quintessentially Brechtian, I may be on controversial ground here.

But every great director, Brecht included, has quirks that somehow prove lively in his hands but only secondhand in others'. Brecht was perhaps unusually liable to develop such idiosyncratic personal codes in his stagings: he had a decidedly eccentric visual taste (which colors every page of his diaries and nearly every other page of *Theaterarbeit*), and he loved to play with certain historically rooted theatrical devices and with the *frisson* of then-recent developments, like revolving stages and projections, or, arguably, the scene titles that he seemingly borrowed from silent movies.

Some of the qualities that I relegate to the status of "quirks" (or what a semiotician might call "idiolect") include: the exposed lighting instruments and scaffolding, the ungelled and unmodulated white light, the half-curtain, the revolving stage, the monochromatic color schemes, the generally utilitarian look, and the affectionately (one could almost say sentimentally) detailed attention to whatever routine labor the characters perform during their onstage action. Undoubtedly, each of these elements can be justified in terms of Brecht's themes and his desire for an earthy (proletarian) tone; certainly they have proven effective in Brecht's own hands (and in his theatre, his culture, his historical moment).

But by now, all these devices have become the common clichés of mounting a Brecht classic, the calling cards of obedient acolytes, and a sure signal of a kind of sentimental unoriginality; they are almost unvaryingly used *instead* of deeper and more original insights. If Brecht is a living poet, something not unlike a living prophet, then these superficial stage dressings have become his whited—or dutifully grayed—sepulcher. What is needed is a new practice of staging Brecht that either replaces them or finds a way to render them fresh.

For now, I would argue polemically to begin all new Brecht productions by violating one of these less essential stylistic rules. Why not Brecht with colored light, so long as it is used to illumine the play? Why not a masked Grusche and an unmasked, naturalistic Natella Abashwili, in a production that tacitly assumes the normalcy of Natella and the strangeness of Grusche's selflessness? Why not a circus-clown Setzuan, a *Mother Courage* performed outdoors, or a brassy, brightly colored *Puntila*?

4.2 Restating the Essentials in New Theatrical Contexts and Vocabularies

If Brecht is to be re-connected to contemporary theatrical practices and experiment, one element in his staging practice must necessarily be challenged, although that challenge could disorient many of our most fundamental assumptions about Brechtian drama. That is the element of the lifelike itself: mimesis in acting, properties, and set—the limited, abstract mimesis around which Brecht organized his productions.

4.2.1   Brecht's Privileging of the Lifelike

There is a risk involved here: Brecht's naturalism is more than a superficial affectation; it is written into his language and is planned as a grounding element in the visual style. Brecht not only chose to include a dash of naturalism; he gave it a privileged position within his array of styles.

Consider the issue of characterization. Brecht's characters are depicted in a range of abstraction from essentialized political types to detailed individuals whose conflicting social roles produce profound inner disorientation. In staging, Brecht actualized this range of abstraction by using a range of theatrical devices, including facial masks, extreme postures, and caricatured vocal patterns on the one hand for the more "essentialized" characters, and unadorned, precisely imitated naturalistic behavior on the other, for his protagonists. Thus, he *grounded* his productions in a kind of histrionic naturalism, defining the central characters in lifelike performances so that the peripheral or emblematic (and usually antagonistic) characters displayed their difference through their stylistic distance from verisimilitude. Despite Brecht's demonstrative discrediting of naturalism as a delimited theatrical idiom, it is still the natural, the lifelike, that grounds his performance style.

4.2.2   The Lifelike Here and Now

But surely such a dependence on verisimilitude is partly determined by theatrical history. Eric Bentley reminds us that Brecht's lifelikeness was a breakthrough in its time, a startling move into a recognizable reality in the face of the hysterical rantings of the Nazi theater.[12] Later, the lifelike quality became the saving grace of Brecht's work under the dicta of socialist realism. But now, in America, the same resemblance to quotidian reality is the common assumption of our least challenging entertainments; Brecht's subtle experimentation is absorbed into our customary ways of seeing. That is why, on American stages, Brecht tends to read as a somewhat mannered realist, and not much more.

Brecht was not naive. To an extent, he anticipated this problem. When, in the preface to *Roundheads and Peakheads*, Brecht made some very early stabs at defining his own staging style, his suspicion and encouragement of non-realistic impulses are revealed at the same time: he was interested in placing a phonograph onstage to accompany the songs in the play, but retreated from the idea for fear that it would "shock the audience unduly or give too much cause for amusement."[13] A concern for his audience's level of theatrical experience and flexibility imposed limits on his stylistic excursion.

Perhaps the time has come to try the phonograph onstage without fear of disorienting the audience. In the age of rock concerts and performance artists, the audience is less likely to laugh at a little visible musical equipment; in the age of Serban, Sellars, Ciulei, and Foreman, little that Brecht ever dreamed of would seem too unorthodox to try.

4.2.3   Intimations of a Future Practice: Abandoning the Lifelike?

What would happen, then, if we were to jettison the lifelike, that one seemingly central element of Brechtian staging?   After discarding the monochromatic color and lighting schemes, the revolving stage and the peculiarities of Eisler's or Dessau's music, what might be the result if the naturalistic borrowings were discarded, too?   None of the principles I have listed depend upon verisimilitude; in fact, they tend to defy it. What then, if the defiance were taken further—if Grusche's internal conflicts were enacted by more than one actress at a time, or if Mother Courage's moments of "bargaining too long" were somehow reduced to a single, repeated gestural motif in a production that eschewed lifelike movement for choreographic extremity? What if Brecht's plays were theatrically reconceived as boldly as Shakespeare's, Chekhov's, Ibsen's, Calderón's, or Wagner's have been of late?

There is no guarantee of any sort of success; I raise these questions fully aware of that.   After all, Brecht wrote the naturalistic element into the plays painstakingly, and the loving care with which he did so is one of the signal traits of his achievement.

But where there might be losses, there also might be significant gains: Brecht himself recognized and feared the danger of even seeming to belong to or resemble the realistic commercial theater. (That is why, in his final period, he put such stress on the "poetic" qualities of his work, as he did in the notes to *The Tutor*: he feared that these qualities would be ignored, that his work would not stand out against the compelling customs of conventional theater.) To divest these plays of their likelike pretensions might forcibly awaken us to Brecht as a theatrical poet with a passionate and visionary consciousness, and unseat the somewhat mannered socialist Zola that he has tended to become on American stages.

In the United States, there have already been some hints of this kind of liberating experiment. Having seen none of them, I can only surmise about how well they illuminated the plays (or, for that matter, whether they embodied any of the "first principles" I noted above). But they have been described vividly enough for one to sense in them the validity of passionate experiment. Productions like the Living Theater's *Antigone*, the San Francisco Mime Troupe's *Turandot*, and Travis Preston's *Good Person of Setzuan* seem to have been thoughtful, poetic re-creations of Brecht's works. The presence of such stagings grants these plays their thinkability, their richness, their open appeal to the imagination; these stagings seek, in their irreverent way, to restore to Brecht his status as a poet of the theater, again a living and surprising—rather than tiresomely familiar and predictable—presence on our stage.

NOTES

All translations from the plays are taken from *Brecht: Collected Plays*, ed. Ralph Manheim and John Willett (New York: Vintage Books).

[1]Eric Bentley, "The Brecht Memoir," *Theater*, 14 (Spring 1983), p. 8. I have retranslated the phrase that Bentley quotes.

[2]Daphna Ben Chaim, *Distance in the Theatre: The Aesthetics of Audience Response*, Theater and Dramatic Studies, No. 17 (Ann Arbor, Michigan: UMI Research Press, 1984).

[3]Bertolt Brecht, "A Short Organum for the Theatre," in *Brecht on Theatre: The Development of an Aesthetic*, trans. John Willett (New York: Hill and Wang, 1964), pp. 191-192.

[4]I have avoided using Brecht's celebrated adjective "epic," since I find it rather eccentric and misleading. Augusto Boal's etymology of the term is perhaps the best: while tracing Brecht's usgage to Hegel rather than to Aristotle, Boal finds that the word was probably not the best choice for Brecht's purposes (*Theater of the Oppressed*, trans. Charles A. McBride and Maria-Olida Leal McBride [New York: Urizen Books, 1979], pp. 83-94). Brecht himself seemed to acknowledge this when, late in life, he toyed with the idea of replacing "epic" with "dialectical"—but here, too, Brecht's intention is unclear and the new term, like the old, can be interpreted in a number of ways.

[5]*Theaterarbeit: 6 Aufführungen des Berliner Ensembles*, comp. Berliner Ensemble (Dresden: Dresdner Verlag, 1950), p. 45.

[6]*Theaterarbeit*, pp. 348-386.

[7]Bertolt Brecht, *The Messingkauf Dialogues*, trans. John Willett (London: Methuen, 1965), pp. 78-79.

[8]This instance was first brought to my attention by Augusto Boal, *Theater of the Oppressed*, pp. 96-97.

[9]Alfred D. White, *Bertolt Brecht's Great Plays* (Hong Kong: Macmillan, 1978), pp. 75-84. White's book has suggested a number of examples in this essay.

[10]Bertolt Brecht, "Notes to *The Tutor*," trans. Ralph Manheim and Wolfgang Sauerlander, in *Brecht: Collected Plays*, Vol. 9 (1973), p. 334.

[11]John Fuegi, *The Essential Brecht*, University of Southern California Studies in Comparative Literature, Vol. 4 (Los Angeles: Hennessey and Ingalls, 1972), pp. 88-90.

[12]Eric Bentley, "The Stagecraft of Bertolt Brecht," in his *The Brecht Commentaries: 1943-1980* (New York: Grove Press, 1981), pp. 56-71.

[13]Bertolt Brecht, "Notes to *Die Rundköpfe und Die Spitzköpfe*," in *Brecht on Theatre*, p. 103.

III. FILM/DIRECTORS

My Keaton

Janice Paran
Drew University

"Love laughs at locksmiths." —Houdini

Excuse the proprietary title, but grant, if you will, the indulgence. Every writer, every critic, I suppose, maintains a private collection of artists whose works have given unending, nearly unconditional enjoyment; after a while these works become like the oldest of friends, thoroughly familiar (though not without surprise), always endearing, specially cherished. You begin to think you understand them better than most do, that, in a sense, they exist solely for you. Buster Keaton (I can't type his name without smiling) occupies such a place in my consciousness. I have known many pleasures, small and large, in his gentle, puzzling, wise and wily company, and have come to rely on him as secret soothing ballast in my own life. It is no exaggeration to state that he sustains a part of my being. I think of him as "my" Keaton, presuming that if fate ever allowed our paths to cross in some imagined place, he should recognize me.

There's a shot of Keaton in *Balloonatic*, the first time we see him, tumbling out of a funhouse chute, landing on his backside, feet straight out (Buster's body always moves in lines and angles, never curves). The entrance to the attraction frames the picture, and it's as if Keaton has literally fallen into the film, much as he later jumps into *Sherlock, Jr.*—a notion that more or less describes his actual introduction to silent film comedy.

Keaton's entry into the film world was accidental, though he was no stranger to accident, in film or in life. His childhood was characterized by freakish happenstance, if one is to believe Buster's father and chief promoter, Joe Keaton. Buster, born Joseph Frank Keaton in 1895, earned his nickname at the age of six months when he survived a fall down a flight of steps, prompting Harry Houdini, a family friend, to exclaim, "That's quite a buster your baby took!" On another occasion, young Buster was swept up and out of a second-story window by a cyclone, only to be deposited unharmed in the street a few blocks away. Whether true or not, stories such as these grew up around Buster from an early age, creating a personal mythology that he sometimes drew upon in his films (*Steamboat Bill, Jr.* is full of preternatural echoes of his past). Notoriety also accompanied Buster almost from birth: when still a toddler he

149

joined his parents' vaudeville act and quickly became the star attraction, learning to take a fall and to rise unruffled whenever and wherever his father threw him. The family act broke up when Buster was 21; bookings were becoming scarcer, Buster was getting too old for the act, and Joe was drinking heavily. In 1917 Buster was booked for a solo engagement at the Winter Garden in New York. He broke the contract before rehearsals even began, however, because of a chance encounter with Fatty Arbuckle on the street. Arbuckle, the story goes, invited Keaton to take part in the filming of the two-reel comedy *The Butcher Boy*. Buster went along, loved it, and started his film career. He didn't deliberate over the decision, as might be expected from a performer whose career up till that time had been entirely confined to the vaudeville stage; he simply walked into film and made it his natural habitat.

Chaplin made the transition from stage to screen a few years prior to Keaton, but for Chaplin the challenge was in adapting his mimetic skills to a new medium; he had to learn what he could do on the screen and shaped a character suited to his talents and temperament. For Keaton, though, the reevaluation of his performing abilities was less pressing than his curiosity about the properties and possibilities of film itself. He began his apprenticeship by dismantling a camera and figuring out how the darn thing worked.

Without question, Keaton took to film intuitively and adroitly, though his pictures still bear the stamp of his theatrical background. Both Chaplin and Keaton use interiors very much like stage sets, but while Chaplin is at home in them, cozying up to their familiar boundaries, Keaton can't seem to wait to break out of them into larger spaces. Why settle for a parlor, in *The High Sign*, when you can show the whole house in cutaway?

To be sure, theatres and theatrical imagery figure in a number of Keaton's films, and he explores the differences between stage and screen realities while acknowledging their respective illusions. The famous opening sequence of *The Playhouse* is one of Keaton's most inventive bits of film wayfaring. It's set in a vaudeville house, and, thanks to an exacting and imaginative bit of camera work, Keaton plays all the roles. He's the ticket taker and all of the audience members, he's the curtain puller, the orchestra musicians, and every member of every act, including all nine performers in a minstrel show. What's even more interesting, though, is the way the sequence ends. Keaton is discovered sleeping in bed, an older man shakes him awake, and yes, Virginia, it was all a dream. But it doesn't end there. Suddenly, the walls of his room pull apart and are carried off by stagehands, and we see that Buster was acutally backstage in a theatre, napping in a make-believe bedroom. Not what you thought, twice.

Environments in Keaton's films are apt to dissolve, transform; they're not to be taken at face value. The most paradigmatic expression of this is in the charming, curious *Sherlock, Jr.* Buster plays a film projectionist who falls asleep at the job. In his dream he leaves the booth, walks through the aisles of the theatre, and scrambles up into the film being shown. He is not immediately successful in entering the film, though; at first, he's at the mercy of wildly changing backdrops depositing him, perplexed, in ever shifting locales. Stranded on a rock in the middle of the surf, he dives in, but before he hits the water, it turns into a snowbank, leaving him stuck upended. And so on. The cuts bear no relation to the film (lushly titled *Hearts and Pearls*) that contains them; they exist only as an aside, worth lingering over for a moment. Much has been written hailing the sequence as a brilliant illustration of the theory of editing, a literal voyage into film's discontinuous nature. Well, all right. Keaton never much cared for discussion of this kind, insisting he was just trying to be funny. Still, this minute or so of film fancy is particularly memorable because it isolates Keaton as the constant in an unpredictable universe—something that happens in all his films.

It has been noted that Keaton, by virtue of his pragmatism, his ingenuity in the face of impossible circumstances, is more down-to-earth than Chaplin, whose presence manages to suggest exile from some divine and slightly mischievous place. There is a sigh in Chaplin, a hint of ancient loss; Keaton has no history, he is only here and now. He is superficially similar to Harold Lloyd's character in his dogged and resourceful efforts to succeed. Lloyd is the boy-next-door, though, in a way that Keaton could never be. Lloyd's goals are concrete and middle-class—status, popularity, material gain—and when he achieves them, he responds with button-popping self-satisfaction. He has his charm, but he must bulldoze his way into your affections. Keaton's aspirations are more modest. He doesn't want to show off, he just wants to fit in. His inability to slip unnoticed into normality is the beginning of his screen character and allows his extraordinary attributes their expression. Keaton seems to operate in a kind of parallel universe to our own, one recognizable, often tangential, but subject to different rules, Keaton's rules. At the center of that universe is Keaton himself, not just the famous deadpan or the ever present porkpie, not even the infinitely adaptive body or the gymnastic finesse, but something more fundamental: the fact of Keaton, durable, reassuring, peerless. And funny.

"Think slow, act fast," Keaton said, and the combination is deadly droll. He is a walking time/motion study, always observing, assessing, figuring out, moving through space like a guided missile, though pausing for frequent brief scans atop trains, astride sculptures, underwater, you name it. Chin lifted, eyes on the horizon, he is all tensile concentration, and he is soberly, hilariously empirical. In *Cops* he takes refuge from the armies of pursuing policemen in a trunk that has fallen into the street. A patrolman spies him, straps the trunk shut, and lifts it. It has no bottom, however, and Buster springs out. The cop stops, momentarily baffled, and examines the faulty trunk. Buster, before resuming his flight, looks too, as if to ascertain the agent of his escape. Chaplin would never stop for that, Lloyd wouldn't do it, but Buster must take the time to satisfy his curiosity. In *Steamboat Bill, Jr.* Buster visits his father (endearingly played by Ernest Torrence) in jail and, with skipping nonchalance, tries to sneak him a loaf of bread filled with tools. The father doesn't pick up on Buster's hints, thinking only that his panty-waisted son has, of all the useless things, baked him a loaf of bread. While Buster is holding the bread, the bottom falls out, spilling the loaf's incriminating contents all over the jail floor. Buster sees them and surreptitiously steals a glance inside the bread before trying to make excuses. No sense jumping to the conclusion that the tools at his ankles are from his loaf of bread until the evidence supports that interpretation!

It's not a bad idea to double-check, if you've got the time. The world can catch you off balance, can thwart your efforts and give the lie to expectation. This is the premise of comedy and tragedy alike; the difference is a matter of degree. Chaplin and Keaton both understood how fine a line distinguishes the two; both crossed that line from time to time. Chaplin refuses to meet the world on its own harsh terms. He sweetly and courageously creates a repertory of poses in counterpoint, ruse for ruse. Keaton, on the other hand, bows to the universe's baffling properties and discovers he can make them work for him. Even pratfalls he takes in stride, because it makes more sense to ride them out than fight them. His strategy is tht of the jumproper: wait till your body matches the rhythm of the rope, then make your move. In *The High Sign* Keaton pauses at a carrousel, puts out his hand, and a passing newspaper is delivered into it. In a scene from *The General* he is clearing the tracks of debris thrown down by Union soldiers in the train ahead. While trying to lift a railroad tie, he topples onto the cowcatcher of his own train, balancing the length of lumber as if it were an oversized trapeze pole. Another beam lies on the tracks just ahead. Without so much as a flicker of uneasiness, Keaton waits for his moment, then spears the wooden tie on the tracks with the one in his arms, sending both pieces over the edge and out of harm's way. Like tiddlywinks, only bigger. (Archimedes must have been Keaton's patron saint.) The physical world, as if in return for Keaton's trust, has a few small concessions of its own. It allows him, for instance, to hang his hat wherever he likes: on blank walls, on horses' flanks—wherever Keaton puts his hat, it stays.

All the same, he is never presumptuous about his bargain with the powers that be. He trusts, but warily, in case things turn out badly. He is ready to change course midstream if need be; habit and reflex and an enviable aplomb have cultivated the ability. He certainly doesn't waste time getting agitated about the change in plan. When the automobile he's driving overshoots its chassis and catapults into a river, without missing a beat he maneuvers the collapsible hood upright into full-sail position and takes his place at the helm, the consummate yachtsman. Nothing fazes this man (except for recalcitrant heroines), and there seems to be nothing he cannot do. That's not to say he'll do it conventionally—he's more apt to jerryrig solutions to his problems—but the task gets accomplished.

Keaton's relative neutrality in response to the unexpected and his willingness to serve as catalyst in no way imply weakness or lack of resolve; his containment has muscle. Still, there are those who disagree, who find his gravity coldblooded, even inexpressive. Two minutes at any Keaton film should be enough to convince anyone that his face, as serious as a child's, is anything but inexpressive. It is, as many have noted, sublimely iconographic. That chiseled face, all planes and hollows, governed by his dark, slightly exotic eyes, seems made for the camera. It is almost perfect in its beauty, though not blandly so. It is an intelligent, keenly perceptive countenance and its merest shift signals volumes. A sidelong glance, held for a fraction of a second, is enough to indicate with what abomination Keaton holds its recipient; a calculated dropping of the lids is a confession of Keaton's momentary world-weariness. Anything more would seem crass and histrionic (think of Harold Lloyd's facial gyrations: they would be sacrilege on Keaton).

Keaton's face is not his trademark, as Chaplin's is, because it is in long shot that he is most memorable. Keaton liked long shots because of the authenticity they guaranteed; stunts couldn't be faked if you showed the whole picture. The entire façade of a house really does come crashing down around him. The long shot also suited Keaton's character, juxtaposing his dynamic/calm compactness against the vastness of the physical world. A quintessential Keaton shot occurs in *The General*—it is one of many such shots in this film. After rescuing his train from Northern spies, Keaton makes it back to his own lines in time to warn the men of an impending attack. The camp explodes in response, as troops suit up and arm themselves, mount, and pour into the road. They stream by Keaton, hundreds of them, sending him scampering to and fro to avoid being overrun. Almost as quickly as it went into action, the camp is empty. It's a ghost town now, its only inhabitant this sad and solitary figure in an oversized uniform, stranded in the middle of the street. Keaton doesn't milk the pathos of the shot; in the next instant he draws his sword and charges after the army. And trips.

Silent film comedians employed their bodies as comic instruments, useful for running, colliding, cavorting, and a host of other functions, including dancing. Keaton, like Chaplin, dances, but he is a dancer of a different order. Chaplin's dance is gratuitous and makes you smile: a flourish of the wrist here, a nimble foot there. Keaton's, always, is functional, goal-oriented, and makes you marvel at how effortlessly and gracefully he moves. When working opposite and with machines, Keaton is at his ablest. On trains and ships he's in his element, sleek and sure and reliable. In repose his body brims with momentum, poised for instantaneous release; in motion it suggests quiescence.

At times his physical control is simply awesome, as in the magical, mystifying *Steamboat Bill, Jr.* The cyclone sequence in this film ranks with Keaton's most spectacular work. A Keaton fantasia, it's full of bizarre and lucid images. A bed hurtles through the streets with Buster patiently aboard. An airborne house lands gingerly atop Keaton, then collapses into a pile of matchsticks the instant he shuts its "cockeyed" door behind him. A stage set offers no sanctuary: its doors lead back into itself; its painted backdrop, for once, is impervious to Keaton's well-practiced dives. Keaton finally is reduced to opposing the blasting eddies of air with only his body as armor. He faces the winds head on, his body willed forward at an impossible angle of resistance. Unable to gain an inch of ground, he tries, ridiculously but gamely, to hop ahead. That fails, too, and he is swept offscreen. A moment later, he is blown back into view, and the sight makes me shake my head in disbelief every time I see it, though I know it's coming. He skids into the lower left-hand corner of the screen; then, balanced upside down on his neck, he flips himself into an upright split and, without using his hands for propulsion, lifts himself straight up and out of his spread eagle. Who else will ever do that? One of the compensations in an otherwise overextended dressing-room scene in *The Cameraman*, showing Keaton and another actor battling for space in a cubicle as they try to change into swimsuits, is the chance to see Keaton's body. You want to know what this man looks like under his clothes—a matter of purely architectural interest, of course.

One final aspect of Keaton's screen persona remains to be discussed, and that is his essentially tragic rhythm. Its presence is muted, even subterranean, but felt. A Keaton film depends not on irrepressible comic misrule but on the inexorable, wry completion of a movement earlier begun. James Agee speaks of the "freezing whisper of melancholia" in Keaton's work. There is a minute and disturbing sense of dislocation in the films, usually kept at comic bay but occasionally creeping into consciousness. It is related to Keaton's strange passivity, his disinclination to resist. His character rarely puts up a fight when he's been misunderstood or wrongly accused; instead he lets his actions themselves or outside circumstances effect an eventual vindication. (In *Sherlock, Jr.* he succeeds only in his dream; at the end of *Cops*, rather than confront his disdainful girlfriend with evidence of his tribulations, he gives himself up to the avalanche of policemen he's been fleeing.) Deep within the body of his films is a wish to disappear into anonymity, into oblivion. *Cops* ends with a shot of his porkpie hat perched on a tombstone. Keaton, who is defined not by what he thinks or feels but by what he does, wants to be relieved of the necessity to act, wants to escape into the cool consolation of the void.

Or so it seems. Onscreen, Keaton is the most private of the silent comedians. He keeps himself at arm's length from his audience, forcing us to come to him, which may explain why his appeal has always been rather limited. Chaplin is instantly and universally adored; he gives himself to his audience as a gift. Keaton requires his audience to become his collaborators and keeps a part of himself in reserve. This quality of his, simultaneously inviting and off-putting (which, by the way, makes me think of Brecht), gives his work a tension that defies understanding and insures his continuing, enigmatic appeal.

Beckett saw it and used in it *Film*. Keaton was 70 years old in 1965. This was to be one of his last screen appearances, a fact that gives his performance chilling poignancy. It is a perfect performance. The film, though Beckett's, is an extension and distillation of what was always implicit in Keaton's being. His inner remove, which can be sensed in all his films, is made the subject here. We know, of course, that it is Keaton whose back is to us, whose aged but unmistakable face is being kept from us. *Film* is about the burden of consciousness and the longed-for release from it. "O" (the character Keaton plays) systematically shuts off every avenue of approach, everything that confirms his being: mirror, window, eyes, photographs. Not being is not enough: he wants never to have been. There is perfect fatal symmetry in Keaton's presence; he withholds himself for the last time. His utterance, unspoken, has always been "No." Thanks to the legacy of his films, that's not his final word. Houdini christened him, after all. New generations of filmgoers have appropriated him and made him theirs. He may have the last laugh yet.

The "Boom" of David Lean's *A Passage to India*

Rustom Bharucha

State University of New York at Stony Brook

In E.M. Forster's *A Passage to India*, there is a seemingly inconsequential dialogue on the subject of mangoes. Godbole is wondering what can be offered to Mrs. Moore and Adela so that they can be tempted to stay on in India. Aziz suggests, "Mangoes, mangoes." Everyone laughs, then Fielding says, "Even mangoes can be got in England today . . . You can make India in England apparently, just as you can make England in India."

David Lean's epic film ostensibly on India was made almost entirely in India. Nearly 80 per cent of the film was shot on the grounds of the Mysore Maharaja's Palace in Bangalore—a colonial edifice modeled after Balmoral Castle—and this included everything from scenes at bazaars and on streets to those in court and even on ship. One has reason to doubt that shooting the film in India provided the predominantly British cast with an atmosphere of the "real" India. Nothing is particularly real in David Lean's film: his "India" has been constructed out of plywood and glass by the renowned production designer John Box. Perhaps a more pragmatic motive for doing the film in India was to save money, not to create "genuine" atmosphere for the actors. India—the real India—is a poor country where labor is proverbially cheap. No wonder foreign investors in the movie industry have been drawn to India in recent years. The goddess Laxshmi has been hospitable to them.

The producers of *A Passage to India*, Richard Goodwin and Lord John Brabourne, have cause to be pleased with their investment. Despite its reduced costs, *A Passage to India* looks as expensive and slick and lush as any big-budget Hollywood film made entirely at Universal Studios. The film reeks of money and of the professionalism associated with money. One can believe the stories one hears about how David Lean had to have just that particular shadow of light on a rock, and if he missed it by a second or one of the actors wasn't around, well, too bad for the producers: he'd just wait for that shadow of light to be exactly as he wanted it before shooting again. It seems that the producers could afford Lean's particularities. The film as a product exemplifies how the machinery and *mentality* of Hollywood can be transplanted to India. What we find in the film is a construction of "India" that has nothing to do with the actual place.

Beyond the synthetic spectacle of Lean's "India," there is another vision of India that has been trivialized beyond recognition. I mean E.M. Forster's celebrated vision of the country—compassionate, sharp, and contradictory— that is conspicuous by its very absence from the film. Now it may be argued that a film based on a novel should not be viewed as a representation of a representation, but as a representation in itself. A film has its own language, its own sense of time, rhythm, and tone. More important, it has visionary possibilities through editing and the mobility of the camera that are denied to the novelist. But if great films like Satyajit Ray's *Pather Panchali* and Eric Rohmer's *The Marquise of O. . .* are any criteria, then it must be acknowledged that films can be astonishingly true to the visions of great novels while being entirely true to themselves. Lean's *A Passage to India* is untrue in essence to Forster. It substitutes a touristic and sensational "treatment" of the Orient for Forster's deep and elusive vision of India. Whereas the novel is oblique, "dull," and unresolved, the film is obvious, climactic, and fully resolved. It is almost as if David Lean has empathized with Adela when she envisions her life in India:

> Colour and movement would remain, brown bodies, white turbans, crowds in the bazaar, but the force that lies behind the colour and movement would escape her . . . She would see India always as a frieze, never as a spirit.

David Lean sees India as a Hollywood extravaganza. Not inappropriately, his film has a reconciled, if not happy ending. One of the last shots focuses on Adela when she is back in England. With the rain dripping in the background— a comforting contrast to heat and dust—she reads a letter from Aziz that asks her to forgive him. Moments after this, we see Aziz and Fielding shaking hands with a great deal of British restraint. No, they are not on horses and there is no suggestion of an unfriendly universe separating them. "I've got rid of that 'Not yet, not yet' bit," Lean told Derek Malcolm of *The Guardian*. "You know, when the Quit India stuff comes up, and we have the passage about driving us into the sea?" Well, needless to say, none of this is there in the film.

The earth in David Lean's film, if nothing else, seems to accept this decision with benign grace. We are in Kashmir, as we can see from the glow on Stella's face and the obvious panorama of the Himalayas—far, far away from the dusty, messy, smelly Hindu state of Mau where Forster situates the last section of the book for important, rather than picturesque reasons. Here in Mau, Aziz does not fit in. As a Muslim, he is a stranger to Hindu customs and ceremonies. The last place in India where Forster would have placed him would have been Kashmir. This poetic landscape with its rich associations of Mughal culture lies outside Aziz' destiny as a character. "No holidays in Kashmir for you yet," his friend Hamidullah reminds him. Aziz himself writes to Fielding that "all hopes of Kashmir have vanished forever." All he can afford is a "poor little holiday" in Musoorie.

Not only does Kashmir serve as a romantic backdrop for Lean's recon- ciliatory attitude toward Forster's characters—commercial Hindi films themselves are ridiculed for using Kashmir in such a way!—it negates the complex vision of cosmic unity and historical difference embodied in the final section of the book. The "Temple" has simply been cut. In the film's "edition," one realizes Lean's total lack of awareness of the religious dimensions in the novel. For that matter, the Hindus and Muslims in his film are undifferentiated even on a social level. Aziz looks *mussalman*, but as the actor Victor Banerjee himself has observed, "Aziz was a very staunch Muslim in the book, but Aziz is nobody here." This is precisely what is so disturbing about the film: the Indians are homogenized, or, at best, conveniently categorized in generic rather than racial or social terms. Hamidullah is a "nice" Indian, Das is a "dutiful" one, and Mahmoud Ali is a "militant" Indian. But as Forster's Aziz (and Forster himself) knew so well: "There is no such person in existence as the general Indian."

Consequently, when in the film Aziz says, "I am an Indian at last," dressed in resplendent *mussalman* garb, the moment is dignified but also fake—as fake as the *kajal* around his eyes. It is not balanced or counterpointed with any suggestion that Aziz has, in Forster's words, "no real affection for his motherland." If Lean's depiction of the Muslim identity of Aziz is at most theatrical, his understanding of Hindus as revealed by Alec Guinness is positively weird. In a sense, the interpretation of Godbole serves as the high point of the film in its sheer absurdity and self-referentiality. Alec Guinness represents no conceivable Hindu one is likely to meet in India. He is simply Alec Guinness playing Alec Guinness Godbole. In his performance, one realizes how little "representation" and "reality" can have in common. If the rest of the film were as outrageous, yet oddly honest as this performance, I would be more prepared to accept Lean's film on the level of oriental kitsch, perhaps as the quintessence of such kitsch.

Unfortunately, the film attempts to be "serious" à la Hollywood when it is not indulging itself with colonial vignettes and picturesque scenery. Lean builds the script with systematic briskness to the "event" in the Marabar Caves (undoubtedly the Big Moment in the film) and the subsequent trial of Aziz. The sequence in the caves, which has been much acclaimed by the critics, is romantically nuanced in a way that seems totally false to Forster and entirely true to Hollywood. First, there is an inclusion of pregnant pauses and suggestive lines. Remembering his wife, Aziz tells Adela, "We were a man and a woman. And we were young"—words of eloquence that stand in counterpoint with Maurice Jarre's saccharine score. Then, there is that sexy shot of Aziz clasping Adela's hand, brown and white fingers interlocked. The camera lingers over this intimate detail, and the shot reappears during the trial scene, ostensibly from the depths of Adela's repressed libido. Finally, there is an undeniably virtuoso evocation of "what actually happens to Adela" inside the cave. The tension is priceless. She lights a match, the sound echoes; Aziz calls to her, his footsteps sound nearer, the voice echoes, the footsteps echo; then we actually see the beast silhouetted in the entrance of the cave. I mention all these details, so seductively embroidered by Lean, in order to point up the sexual tension generated by this scene in the Marabar Caves.

By contrast, there is no such heterosexual heat in Forster's novel, not only because "Forster wasn't very good with women" (as Lean observed in an interview), but for a more technical reason: Adela is never shown inside the cave in his novel. The "rape" takes place, figuratively speaking, in a blank— between Chapters 15 and 16. At the end of Chapter 15, Adela (who "does not admire Aziz with any personal warmth") nonchalantly enters a cave, thinking with half her mind about marriage and with the other half about sightseeing. And then, at the opening of Chapter 16, Aziz hears the car in which the presumably battered Adela has sought refuge. One can understand why Forster was so non-committal about "what happened in the Marabar Caves." As an artist, not a sensationalist, he left the possibilities of its interpretation open, preferring blanks to explanations.

David Lean fills in the blank. One would have to be exceptionally thick-skinned not to realize that his Adela has hallucinated the whole thing. As played by Judy Davis, she is represented in so repressed a manner that she is constantly quivering, twitching, and tightening her throat muscles. At the risk of offending feminists, one is tempted to accept Aziz' recommendation that she needs a husband, or at least a stint in a sanitarium equipped with a good sauna. Actually, feminists have reason to be outraged by Lean's representation of Adela because she follows in the long and vicious tradition of the victimized woman, essentially weak and susceptible to her own sexual desires.

This view of Adela becomes explicitly clear in the only sequence of the film that Lean has written into the script. We are shown Adela on a deserted stretch of land where she explores the remnants of a temple. She is alone. Gradually, her attention is attracted to erotic sculptures—bejewelled dancing girls, a woman with voluptuous breasts, lovers in intimate embrace—all the familiar figures of Hindu temple architecture, divested by Lean of their spiritual contexts and presented as objects of titillation. Naturally, his strategy succeeds in exciting Adela—she begins to sweat and linger over the images. As if this aura of the "sensual" Orient were not enough, Lean then introduces another stereotype that any child associates with India—monkeys. Not one or two— Hollywood isn't cheap—but a band of monkeys, chattering, screeching, and threatening. They leap over the sculptures and advance on Adela with an almost lascivious menace. In sheer panic, she cycles away, chased by the beasts.

Not being enamored of monkeys myself, I cannot really object to Lean's demeaning portrait of them, but I am offended when later in the film I see Indian youths dressed as monkeys, screaming and leaping around, thereby confirming yet another European stereotype of Indians as savages. One of these menacing figures makes a threatening move towards Adela when she is in the car on the way to court. A policeman smashes the skull of this "monkey" and blood spatters. By using monkeys to intensify the erotic scene with Adela and later to underscore the violent crowd scenes, where the "monkeys" are rebel Indians, Lean creates unavoidable associations between bestiality, sexuality, and common Indian behavior.

It is not coincidental that the monkeys (both real and human) threaten Adela, because it is through her point of view that we see much of the film.

She opens and closes it, and she is probably the only character whose part has grown rather than diminished in relation to the novel. In contrast, Aziz is almost a sidekick on her Indian adventure. His complexities and nuances of emotion, his outbursts and moments of vulnerability, his sense of betrayal and his feeling of community—all these are barely touched on in Victor Banerjee's monochromatic, carefully edited performance of the role. Fundamentally, Aziz is a passive character, so we get only a few glimpses of his state of mind. "Things just happen to him. He can't help it," Lean explained to Derek Malcolm. His Aziz is a "goose." And like geese in general, he can't be taken too seriously.

Clearly, the focus of the film is on the British in India. Lean's sympathies for his own countrymen are scarcely concealed in the following comment:

> I think [Forster] was rather unfair to the English . . . except for Fielding they come out a pretty good lot of idiots, and I don't think they were. In those days, colonialism was fashionable, now it isn't. Everybody's trying to make jokes about those people, and I don't know that they were particularly funny. Of course there was a funny side, but in fact I think they did some very good things.

> (Interview with Amita Malik in
> *The Statesman*, 20 November 1983)

Truly, as Salman Rushdie has remarked, Lean's interviews merit reviews—perhaps more than his films themselves. The comment is fascinating to me—colonialism was *fashionable* once upon a time? Wouldn't it be more appropriate to call it the reality, the base historical reality, of an arbitrary distribution of political power that gave one country the right to rule over another? To whom was it "fashionable"? The Turtons and Burtons, perhaps, but not the vast majority of Indians.

As long as we are speaking of colonialism as being fashionable, I must point out that this "fashion" is what we are experiencing today through Oriental extravaganzas like *The Far Pavilions* and the British Raj soap opera, *The Jewel in the Crown*. David Lean's *A Passage to India* is simply part of this phenomenon in making the bad old days of the British Raj seem not so bad after all. There was glory in it, a great deal of color—maybe an ass or two around, a little repression here, some intolerance there, but fundamentally, so the film seems to say, the British were a pretty decent lot of people. In this fraternal view of colonizers, imperialism is almost entirely divested of its political context and becomes something of a virtue, a lost state of innocence, a time conjuring up military brass bands, afternoon tea, and evenings at the club. Needless to say, it is precisely this apolitical aura of the Raj revival that makes it so conservatively and insidiously political.

Much has been written about the revival in relation to the aura of nostalgia sweeping over America and England at the moment. Both countries are poorer than they once were, or, more precisely, there are many poorer people within these countries—the poor are, perhaps, less visible in America than in England.

And both countries are led by militantly conservative governments. At such times—the cliché is almost cruel—people need to be entertained (or is it the entertainment industry that decides this for them?). Waiting for another war to break out, another repressive regime to be supported on humanitarian grounds, another famine not caused by drought, another Bhopal in West Virginia perhaps, people want nothing more than to be able to forget these realities through the consumption of a new myth, right? "The Raj": distant enough, not threatening anymore, with stories galore, exciting locations, different people—brown not black—alluring women, monkeys, elephants, savages, and other sights . . . the fiction overpowers the history underlying it. Besides, does history really matter, especially if it is not your own? The Indian colonial experience is a new *story* for scriptwriters, and its emergence could not be better timed. Now that the world wars and Vietnam have lost their commercial appeal and even Auschwitz is old hat, the Raj is on.

How do people in India feel about this? After all, it is their country being represented. Clearly, they are not entirely nostalgic about the Raj. Even the brown sahibs and retired colonels and Anglicized communities must have some unpleasant memories of the Raj to temper its romantic revival. At least, I hope so, though this may be an optimistic assumption on my part. What is clearer, however, is that Indians, particularly in the business and political spheres, seem to be proud that their country is attracting the world's attention. It doesn't really seem to matter whether Indian history is being misrepresented or confronted at all. Richard Attenborough's factual errors in the script of *Gandhi*, for instance, were pointed out in a few articles, but these were incidental to the wave of appreciation that swept the country (with the possible exception of West Bengal, where Gandhi has never been idolized) when the film won eight Academy Awards. Indira Gandhi's only regret was that it didn't win more. The more awards, the greater the image of India as a "developing" country. Perhaps the most disturbing aspect of the appreciative acceptance of India's misrepresentation by most Indians themselves is its undercurrent of deference. "Thank you for putting us on the map" is essentially what characterizes this acceptance.

What map is this? The map of the world as patiently charted by cartographers over the centuries? No, this one is much less noble in dimension—it is a blueprint of the world as defined by businesses and corporations, financial speculators and movie moguls, cable networks and Hollywood. This is the map that some "progressive" Indians want their country to be a part of: a map of recognition by the controllers of the First World. In this context, it is significant to know what Victor Banerjee has to say about maps:

> It's not easy being put on the international map as an Indian because you're not just a minority community, you belong to a community that has not really appeared on the international commercial scene as an actor.

> (*The Telegraph*, 10 February 1985)

The "commercial scene" is what the map is all about. It is dominated by figures like David Lean. In fact, Banerjee goes so far as to say, "When Sir David Lean introduces you to the world, the introduction is so much more important than when you're Sir Richard Attenborough." Banerjee's adulation of Lean expressed in *The Telegraph*, almost colonial in its deference and excess, is what encourages him to "sell" the film on the most objectionable grounds. Of course, it is only natural that he should praise the film, but to say that Indians will "love" it and then promptly add, "There's no poverty, no squalor, none of the suffering of the Indian masses, nothing of that" in the film—this reads like the worst kind of publicity.

One is reminded of the time when Satyajit Ray was taken to task by the late Hindi film actress Nargis Dutt, who was then a member of the Rajya Sabha (one of the Houses of Parliament in India). Dutt voiced a predominantly elitist concern that Ray's concentration on poverty and destitution had presented a false image of India to the world. Though this charge was totally inaccurate because Ray's artistic milieu is middle-class, if not aristocratic, rather than working class—he may be criticized for *not* sufficiently focusing on problems like poverty—the charge itself indicates how certain influential forces within India can support commercial tinsel over exposures of reality for the sake of an image. Only the image of India in the eyes of the world, the image of India in relation to "the international map," matters to these forces.

It appears that *A Passage to India* will figure prominently in the forthcoming Festival of India in America and that David Lean will receive a special award from the organizers of the Festival. This official endorsement of what I must bluntly call Lean's commercialization of India is what Edward Said would refer to as the perpetuation of Orientalism within the Orient itself. As an Indian, I have come to accept certain misrepresentations of my culture (and I know that I am not exempt from them myself), but what is intolerable is to see these blatant misrepresentations being honored, quoted, and, in some cases, used as reference points for their affirmation of Indian culture. It is bad enough to know that your culture needs some kind of foreign stamp of approval, but it is worse when this approval comes through a distorted interpretation of the culture. Though fortunately there are Indians who are critical of the "Orientalization" of Indian culture—and it is encouraging that our Indian ambassador to the United States has publicly declared that Lean's film and *The Jewel in the Crown* "do not have much to do with India"—I fear that the film will be almost as great a hit in India as in America, and, ironically, for the very same reasons.

The film is big, colorful, scenic, and entertaining in the best (worst?) tradition of Hollywood. When I saw it in New York, the audience was so "psyched" by the publicity for it that they applauded even before the movie began. Large quantitites of popcorn were consumed during the two hours and 45 minutes of the film. Tickets were sold out. Business was booming. And that's just the sound I associate with the film—"boom." Not "bou-oum" or "ouboum" as in Forster's novel, but plain, old BOOM. Perhaps, when the revival of the Raj has died a natural death and Hollywood discovers a new fashion, we can hope that the "boom" of Lean's film, like the echoes in the Marabar Caves, will amount to nothing.

For Valor: The Career of Ingmar Bergman

Steve Lawson

Williamstown Theatre Festival

"Heroic" is a word of innumerable definitions, but three in the *Random House Dictionary of the English Language* strike me as relevant to Ingmar Bergman: "extraordinarily bold, altruistic, determined"; "being larger than life-size"; "valiant, gallant, brave." Diehard critics of Bergman's long, long career—and there are a lot of them—would seize on the second of these; Bergman partisans would prefer the first and last. All seem true to me.

In a time when cults and trends rise and fall with the nightly news, Bergman's career is, proportionately, immense. He made his first film in 1944 (the year of D-Day, when—to use filmic touchstones—Frank Capra was deep in his "Why We Fight" series and Marcel Carné was shooting *Children of Paradise* in the back streets of occupied Paris). By my count, Bergman has made 40 features since, at least nine of which I'd call fine and half a dozen great (*The Naked Night, Smiles of a Summer Night, Winter Light, Persona, Shame, The Passion of Anna*). Perhaps only now when—if his public statements are true—Bergman's film career is over, is it possible to look back and really gauge its scope.

Like many of my generation, I first became familiar with Bergman through college film societies. (In my case, at Williams College, where a superb scholar and film lover, the late Charles Thomas Samuels, held sway in the late sixties and early seventies.) I knew dimly that Bergman had burst into international vogue a decade before with a string of highly picturesque, much-debated pictures—*Smiles of a Summer Night, The Seventh Seal, Wild Strawberries, The Magician, The Virgin Spring*—and that he had since consciously reverted to "chamber" films with very small casts, somewhat irritating the critics who had showered him with praise for his showier works.

But that was all I knew. At age 18, I was seeing foreign films for the first time in bulk; I was lolling in Antonioni and Bresson and Truffaut and Olmi. It seems gently ironic that my first Bergman film was a lesser one—*The Seventh Seal*. At the time, it was Parnassus. Bergman was a demigod, a secular saint, we were really getting the Middle Ages on screen for the first time. If all this weren't enough, the picture had been shot in 35 days—take that, Hollywood! Incense hung heavy in the air; the word "masterpiece" was tossed around like a Frisbee. By coincidence I saw *The Seventh Seal* again a few weeks ago, and when one minor character on screen, waiting nervously for Death to scoop him up, peered at the full moon and observed, "*The moon!*"—well, I'm afraid I laughed aloud.

I don't mean to kick this particular film around. My intention is to point out how the perception of individual moments in a titanic career can alter with time. When I first saw *The Virgin Spring* and *Hour of the Wolf*, I was (to put it judiciously) knocked out by them. Today, granting some soaring sequences— the rape or the little boy vomiting in the former, the Mozart pieces or the opening and closing monologues in the latter—both seem arid at their cores, more *willed* than felt out of full Bergman conviction. Conversely, "slight" films such as *Monika* come across as delightful now.

Swings and arcs, valleys and hills. The young Ingmar Bergman was indebted to the French *film noir* of the thirties and the war years. This was his first period, the apprentice one of *Prison* and *A Ship Bound for India* and *Port of Call* when Bergman was finding his cinematic legs.

In 1950 came a change. At age 32, Bergman made his tenth film, *Summer Interlude*. The raw materials—a ballerina thinking back to her boyfriend's death, torn between remorse and her career—are, to put it gently, attenuated. But the shooting is adroit, the performances persuasive, and some of the imagery startling. I don't think I'll ever forget the vacationing ballerina suddenly seeing an ancient woman cross her path, umbrella unfurled, as if Death itself had popped up. (A shot that would recur to some extent in *The Magician, Hour of the Wolf*, and *Face to Face*.) Thematically, there was a new sense of resolution, too, of coming to grips—however tentatively—with the world. Marie, the ballerina, accepts a new boyfriend; she isn't egregiously "doomed" like most of the earlier Bergman prototypes.

With occasional dips into slice-of-life realism (*Secrets of Women, A Lesson in Love*, and *Monika*—Harriet Andersson's memorable debut with Bergman), this second period, stretching roughly until 1955, shows the director's preoccupation with *performance*, with people who impersonate others—sometimes to applause, often to catcalls. By his mid-thirties, of course, Bergman was known throughout Sweden as a theatrical *enfant terrible*. So it's unsurprising that "theater" should enter the film side of his life, notably through an ensemble of gifted actors from the Malmö, Gothenburg, and Royal Dramatic companies. What *is* amazing is that Bergman often manages to move beyond performing-as-subject into something far more insidious and suggestive.

In *The Naked Night* (1953), the traveling circus owner—sick of his work, suspicious of his mistress, jealous of the "higher" art of drama, and writhing under the taunts of the actor who has cuckolded him—makes an abortive effort at reconciliation with his ex-wife. She remembers the circus world with loathing; she feeds him but refuses to take him back. The actor adds injury to insult by kneeing him in the ring before hundreds of spectators. There is nothing left for Albert but suicide with a clown's gun. But he spurns this way out, this exit (a *theatrical* gesture!), and orders the caravan readied. In the last moments of the film, his contrite mistress joins him in the road, and they move off together. All the masks are stripped off; all roles played out; all finery lost. And the performers travel again at dawn, continuing their lives.

Something similar could be said of the actress in *Smiles of a Summer Night*, the acting troupe in *The Seventh Seal*, the mesmerist's band in *The Magician*, the musician couple in *Shame*, or the concert pianist mother in *Autumn Sonata*. (Or—supreme example—the mute Elizabeth of *Persona*. "Life trickles in," cautions the therapist in that film. "Your hiding place isn't watertight . . . You should keep on playing this role, just like all your other roles.") Identity—the great, tantalizing question—cannot be fixed, can only be guessed at, played at, tried out.

Bergman's next period—that of his first vogue—covers the late fifties, up to *The Devil's Eye* (1960). What's most intriguing about this time is that it no longer seems like an apogee, a mountaintop against which all subsequent Bergman must be measured. *Wild Strawberries* is still beautiful and Victor Sjöström's performance as the doctor who relives his life is magnificent, yet much of the plotting plods and the dream symbolism drags. But at this juncture, having just turned 40, Bergman altered his course yet again.

The most obvious change came in setting and style. Between 1953 and 1959, Bergman directed nine films—six of them wholly or partly in period. After *The Virgin Spring*, he was not to make another period picture for 13 years (until *Cries and Whispers*, in 1972). Some critics had found the Bergman of the late fifties either grandiose, intellectually suspect, melodramatic, or all three; as if in direct response, he turned his back on the stylistic flourishes that had brought him his reputation. And, perhaps most important, Bergman switched cinematographers.

"For me a film's suggestiveness lies in a combination of rhythm and faces, tensions and relaxations of tension. For me, the lighting of the image decides everything." Thus Bergman, in a 1968 interview, recalled his break with longtime cameraman Gunnar Fischer and his joining forces with Sven Nykvist. Anyone who has seen *Persona*—the indescribable mingling of faces and bodies, the pre-credit sequence that virtually summarizes 20 years of Bergman images— and compared its abstract miracles with the eerie "naturalism" of *Shame* or with the juxtaposition of light and shadow in even a failed work such as *The Serpent's Egg*, will have some idea of Nykvist's extraordinary contribution to the later Bergman's oeuvre—a contribution as vital and inseparable as that of Nino Rota to Fellini or Raoul Coutard to Godard.

And, initially at least, Nykvist's camera was in the service of a new, spare, contemporary-minded filmmaker. Except for a silly, damn-the-critics effort, *All These Women*, the Bergman of the early sixties rejected big gestures of any kind. *Through a Glass Darkly*, *Winter Light*, and *The Silence* were distinct works, but all shared a bleak, post-modernist vision of the world. As if inspired by Nykvist's presence on his creative team, Bergman banished gorgeousness in favor of immense close-ups and an increasing use of monologues. To see Ingrid Thulin retell the schoolmistress' anguish in *Winter Light* (to cite one powerful sequence) in intense, head-on proximity to the lens is to recognize a new, subtle interweaving of theater (rhetoric) and film (the closeup).

This juggling of art forms increases in Bergman's next and arguably greatest period—that of *Persona* (1966), *Shame* (1968), and *The Passion of Anna* (1969). It is almost incredible, considering the classic status *Persona* has acquired in the 20 years since it was released, to recall that the film came about as the result of an ear infection: that Bergman, dizzy and ill in his hospital bed, suddenly conceived the image of two women comparing hands. Further accident: Bergman had met Norwegian actress Liv Ullmann the previous year and instinctively likened her to his longtime friend and colleague Bibi Andersson. Out of sickness and coincidence came a film that I think will last as long as people care about the medium.

For all its unsparing nature—and much of *Persona* is terrifying, as two human beings unravel, then coalesce in front of us—this picture reveals Bergman in a teasing frame of mind, playing with the boundaries and possibilities of the medium as never before. From the rapid-fire pre-credit montage, we cut to a hospital office. A nurse meets a mute patient, a famous actress who has elected to stop speaking. (Mystery: *why?*) The two women adjourn to the seashore; the nurse tells the actress all about herself. (Realism: walks, sun hats, mushroom-picking, coffee cups, smoking.) It's late: the actress tells the dozing nurse to go to bed. (She *what?*) That night, the nurse sees/dreams the actress coming to her room and embracing her.

Morning. (Reassurance: for us and the nurse.) But, driving to the post office, she sees an unsealed envelope and reads the actress' letter to the therapist. It lightly mocks the nurse; muses that "it's fun studying her." The nurse sits immobile in shock as the rain slides down the windshield. Suddenly we see her on the edge of a pond, staring into the water at her blurred reflection.

Brilliant sunlight. (A condition Bergman hates.) Sunbathing, the nurse breaks a glass, then deliberately leaves a shard of glass—contradicting her entire persona, her presumption of nursing, of coaxing back to health. The actress steps on it. She and the nurse stare at each other. The film breaks.

From this midpoint on, there is a feeling that anything can happen, that all our notions about these women have been destroyed. The actress' husband appears; he and the nurse make love. The latter babbles nonsense words, then bares a vein for the actress to suck. The nurse tries to analyze her patient— a scene shot twice, from both women's points of view. We hear the actress whisper "Nothing." The actress is seen packing. The nurse closes up the cottage and catches a bus back to town. Bergman and Nykvist appear on a crane, filming the actress as Electra, her last role. The celluloid unwinds; the experience—the "case"—is closed.

"On many points I am uncertain," Bergman wrote in his preface to the published script of *Persona*, "and at one point at least I know nothing." This utter denial of what we like to think of as a film—a "movie," an object to be consumed with a beginning, middle, and end—is not Bergman being coy. What he does in *Persona* is smash coherence, in order to explore the flashpoints beyond which artistic representation cannot hope to go.

Having probed the psyche with such ferocity, Bergman slummed a bit in *Hour of the Wolf*, throwing in allusions to American horror movies and Gothic literature in order to whip up a (spurious) case for artistic crackup. With *Shame* and *The Passion of Anna*, he reverted to peak form, examining human frailty under the stresses of war and loneliness. In the first film, Bergman is objective, observing the disintegration of Jan and Eva Rosenberg with scrupulous realism— abstraction is employed only at the very end to fortify Eva's sensation of being caught up in a malevolent dream. In the second—the first major Bergman film in color—the director takes up, in a sense, where *Shame* leaves off. (We even see a black-and-white dream of Liv Ullmann coming ashore from the boat in the earlier film.) Only this time, there is no war needed to break these people down, merely human nature: the jealousies and longings of Bergman's all-too-contemporary characters.

In his next period, Bergman alternated between badly flawed projects (*The Touch*, *Face to Face*) and three huge successes—*Cries and Whispers*, where a blatant color scheme undercut an attempt to weld Chekhov and Strindberg, *Scenes from a Marriage*, and *The Magic Flute*. The last two were both adapted from television, reflecting Bergman's growing interest in that form. Even in the feebler works of this period, there were memorable scenes: Ullman's collapse in *Face to Face*, Harriet Andersson's final paroxysms in *Cries and Whispers*. And if none of these films achieved the spendid level of *Persona*, the best of *Scenes from a Marriage* or *The Magic Flute* clearly demonstrated that Bergman was still taking chances, trying something new every time.

Then, disaster. An overzealous Swedish bureaucracy arrested Bergman in mid-rehearsal for supposed tax evasion (a charge eventually dropped). In reaction, Bergman suffered a nervous breakdown and fled Sweden. Happily, his compulsion to work remained alive, which under the circumstances seems to me a concise summary of that third definition of heroism. It's almost irrelevant that the first film he made during his self-imposed exile was *The Serpent's Egg*, one of his weakest; the important thing was that Bergman's determination was undiminished. (And, as if to prove himself to those who felt separation from Sweden would be aesthetically fatal, he then proceeded to make *Autumn Sonata*, in which he raised internecine family anguish to its highest pitch since late O'Neill.)

Two aspects of Bergman's art haven't been mentioned yet, but any discussion of the man would be hopelessly hobbled without them: his gifts as a writer and as a director of actors.

First, his dialogue. He can be epigrammatic, as in old Mme. Armfeldt's advice to her daughter in *Smiles of a Summer Night*: "You can never protect a single human being from suffering. That's what makes us despair." Or satiric, as with the vain Count Malcolm in that film: "I can tolerate someone dallying with my wife, but if anyone touches my mistress, I become a tiger!" The joke is doubled when Malcolm reverses wife and mistress later in the film.

But Bergman's skill isn't limited to period dialogue. After an explosion of hatred in the schoolroom of *Winter Light*, the minister mumbles, "I'd better be going before I say anything worse." Slumped at a child's desk, the teacher responds softly, "*Is* there anything worse?" Near the end of *Shame*, Jan, brutalized by the war, has this exchange with Eva:

JAN. Let's pack. We have to make the boat by dawn.

EVA. I'm not going.

JAN. Easier if you stay.

EVA. We'd better eat something before leaving.

And there are phrases that glint: the architect in *The Passion of Anna*, "building a mausoleum over the meaninglessness of Milan"; the nurse in *Persona* being "professional" with the actress: "I think art's so important in life—especially for people with problems." Even stage directions shine: try to read Bergman's guidelines and quick sketches in the screenplay of *Wild Strawberries*, say, without being moved by their evocative power.

Then, Bergman's actors. What good fortune—for him, to be blessed with talented men and women; for them, to be working over and over with an artist so willing to investigate their range. Gunnar Björnstrand—the hapless lawyer in *Smiles of a Summer Night*, the cynical Squire in *The Seventh Seal*, the cold-fish doctor in *The Magician*, the minister, the agent, the husband, the mayor. Max von Sydow, playing leading roles in *The Virgin Spring*, *The Magician*, *Shame*, and *The Touch*, and walk-ons in *Wild Strawberries* and *Brink of Life*. Liv Ullman, moving from a silent debut in *Persona* through *Hour of the Wolf* and *Scenes from a Marriage* to *Autumn Sonata*. Bibi Andersson, so charming as the ingenue in her first films for Bergman, returning to his troupe after a five-year absence with a galvanizing performance in *Persona*. Or Harriet Andersson, who started as the erotic Monika and played various tomboys and seductresses in her youth, then came back with three utterly different portrayals over the last two decades—the schizophrenic heroine of *Through a Glass Darkly*, the dying sister in *Cries in Whispers*, and the sinister housemaid in *Fanny and Alexander*. Eva Dahlbeck, Ingrid Thulin, Naima Wifstrand, Anders Ek, Gunnel Lindblom, Erland Josephson . . . tracing these wonderful actors in and out of Bergman's career is one way of telling time in the last half of the twentieth century. It's like subscribing to a matchless repertory company, season after season, and watching the roles multiply and shift while the faces and voices remain the same.

We all know careers can materialize and wither overnight. Others start and just keep on going without notable change for years on end out of sheer inertia. Ingmar Bergman's career is neither of these. Forty years of swings and arcs, of taking stock and leaping ahead, of telling tales and abandoning stories. More than a few times, his visions have let him down. More than a few times, they've been luminous. But—in a time and a world inimical to personal expression—they have indisputably been *his*.

The Real Fascination of *Citizen Kane*

Bert Cardullo

Louisiana State University

One aspect of *Citizen Kane* has always puzzled me: why, aside from the opportunity it afforded them to display virtuoso technique, did Orson Welles and Herman J. Mankiewicz make a film about the dead Kane instead of about Kane while he lived? To my knowledge, no one has ever attempted to answer this question; yet probably more has been written about *Citizen Kane* than any other American film. If, as most critics believe, the "message" of *Citizen Kane* is the mystery of the titular character,[1] then couldn't that mystery have been presented in traditional narrative form, a condensed "life of Charles Foster Kane"? Couldn't that mystery have been presented *more subtly* in this way? It is pretty clear once Thatcher's "story" about the young Kane is over and Bernstein's begins, with an immediate contradiction of Thatcher ("It wasn't money [Mr. Kane] wanted. Thatcher never did figure him out"), that what we are going to get in the film is several more or less conflicting viewpoints on the man, none with any real depth, as much because given hastily or sketchily to a newspaper reporter who did not know Kane, as because given by a biased individual. The "storytellers" simplify Kane, to make their own points about him. No matter how many times I see *Citizen Kane*, I always get impatient the moment the reporter, Jerry Thompson, begins his interview of Bernstein, Kane's former business manager and now chairman of the board. I know somewhere inside myself that this method will not deliver—at least not traditional results: an ambiguous but fully developed, complex, *sympathetic* character.

Kane is not sympathetic in the traditional sense because we get to know him only through others' eyes. Bernstein, Leland, and Alexander are sympathetic, because we get to know them through the eyes of the filmmakers, in the "narrative present." But the film is clearly not about these three, or about Raymond the butler, the last of the "storytellers" (Thatcher is dead; Thompson reads Thatcher's "story" of Kane from his memoirs). It is about Charles Foster Kane, and to believe the critics as well as Orson Welles himself, whose obfuscatory words these are, "the point of the picture is not so much the solution of the problem [the mystery of Kane] as its presentation."[2]

But my point is, the presentation is apparently loaded: anyone could tell you that if you ask five different people about a man, you'll get five different stories or interpretations. Those stories will tell less about the man than about the bias of the particular storyteller. They will add up to nothing in particular because a man's motives can never be satisfactorily fathomed by those closest to him. They can, however, be fathomed somewhat by the "objective author," or by this author posing as someone who knew the man. That is, presumably, what muct art is all about: the providing of "answers" or motives for particular characters so that larger questions of life and character can be explored. So I pose my question again: presuming that they were aware of what I have just said, why did Orson Welles and Herman J. Mankiewicz choose to make a film about the dead Kane, through the eyes of others, instead of about the living Kane, through their own eyes? Is *Citizen Kane* one large piece of chicanery, a contribution less to film art, according to Charles Thomas Samuels, than to the art of making films?[3] Or is the film, on the other hand, as David Bordwell claims, a great achievement because it fuses "an objective realism of texture with a subjective realism of structure"?[4] Bordwell believes that the method of *Citizen Kane is* its meaning. He writes that

> *Kane* explores the nature of consciousness chiefly by presenting various points of view on a shifting, multiplaned world. We enter Kane's consciousness as he dies, before we have even met him; he is less a character than a stylized image. Immediately, we view him as a public figure—fascinating but remote. Next we scrutinize him as a man, seen through the eyes of his wife and his associates, as a reporter traces his life story. Finally, these various perspectives are capped by a detached, omniscient one. In all, Kane emerges as a man—pathetic, grand, contradictory, ultimately enigmatic. The film expresses an ambiguous reality through formal devices that stress both the objectivity of fact and the subjectivity of point of view. It is because the best contemporary cinema has turned to the exploration of such a reality that *Kane* is, in a sense, the first modern American film. (p. 105)

Now Bordwell is on to something when he says that Charles Foster Kane is "less a character than a stylized image," and that as a character, Kane is pathetic. But he fails to tell us how exactly we "enter Kane's consciousness as he dies" and who owns the "detached, omniscient" perspective at the end of the film that caps the other perspectives on Kane.

Bordwell's oversights or omissions are characteristic of his argument in general: unlike the majority of critics on *Citizen Kane*, he believes that the "message" of the film, beyond being the mystery of Kane the character, is the mystery of reality or of life itself. Once one ascertains that the object of a work of art is to present the mystery of reality, it is very easy to become mysterious oneself in writing about that work of art: after all, what else is there to say once one says that the work depicts the mystery of reality? I don't believe that *Citizen Kane* presents the mystery of reality any more than *His Girl Friday* presents an argument for the equality of women. I think that the film is first and last about Charles Foster Kane, as its title indicates, but I do think it is up to something in its eschewing portrayal of the living Kane that no one has yet detected, although David Bordwell begins to touch on it.

Two events occur in the film that, I believe, are clues to the filmmakers' real intentions and the work's true status. No one has ever incisively questioned the actions of Kane's mother toward her son, which actions form a part of Thatcher's story.[5] Mrs. Kane runs a boarding house in Colorado with her apparently alcoholic and abusive husband. It is discovered that some property of hers contains large deposits of silver, and she instantly becomes rich. Although she appears to have a very loving relationship with her son, she now decides to entrust Charles to the banker Thatcher, who will manage the boy's large inheritance and see to his education. The film does not provide her with sufficient motivation to commit this act: ostensibly she is worried about her husband's influence on the child. But father and son seem to get on well enough, and Mrs. Kane seems more than in control of her husband's actions (apart from the fact that the "Colorado Lode" is in her name). Let us keep in mind in addition that on the evidence of the film, once she gives her son over to Thatcher, *she never sees him again* (Thatcher takes him back East to live).

Why is Mrs. Kane so eager to do this? She herself is quite rich, so why doesn't she retain custody of her child while having Thatcher look after her business affairs and advise her on her son's education and opportunities? Why can't she simply leave her husband (again, *she* owns the mine), with whom she appears to have anything but a loving relationship, instead of give up her son? I am not saying that Mrs. Kane's action cannot be made believable, although this would require great delicacy, but that Welles and Mankiewicz do not make it so. And I am not interested in whether this happened in real life to William Randolph Hearst, on whom the character of Charles Foster Kane is in part based (I do not know if it did). Truth is often stranger than fiction, it is said; that does not relieve fiction of the burden of believability, however. That does not relieve Mr. Thatcher of the burden of believability, either. He may narrate this part of Kane's life, but Welles and Mankiewicz "narrate" him. In short, neither anything we are told about Mrs. Kane nor all that we know about mothers and their offspring can make Mrs. Kane's act comprehensible. (My argument is strengthened by the fact that Charles is the only child and surely at the same time the last one of the middle-aged Kanes.) It seems an outrage. What, then, is it doing in the film? Of course it is there to motivate Charles's search for love and for control over his environment throughout his life. But, to repeat, why is it not made more believable?

I want to submit that this was not a simple oversight on the part of Welles and Mankiewicz, not another instance of hasty or one-dimensional Hollywood filmmaking. I believe that this is the first substantial clue we get in *Citizen Kane*, aside from the film's treatment of the dead Kane and not the living one, that what we are witnessing is not intended primarily as a character *study*—the approach most critics take to the film—but as the *experience* of character, the experience of a character's foremost desires and frustrations, not through identification with the figure himself, but through identification with the narrative method of the film that is about him. (This is quite different from David Bordwell's assertion that the film's narrative method per se is its meaning.) Welles and Mankiewicz "clue" us in that their film is not intended as a character study of Charles Foster Kane because he appears, on screen in Thatcher's memory, fabricated from the very start, the unnatural product of his mother's unnatural act.

Looked at in this light, the film's showy camera work, editing, and use of sound make more sense: they are the constant reminder, in their artificiality, of the unreal world the protagonist inhabits, in others' memory. These devices and the world they embellish account for the unsettling effect the film has even on a viewer who has seen it many times. We have been conditioned by most narrative film and literature to want to identify with the main character; in the case of film, we are encouraged to do so by a camera that often comes close up on the main character or otherwise isolates him, and that adopts his point of view at crucial moments. We get none of this in *Citizen Kane* (we get everything but this), yet the film purports to be about Charles Foster Kane. We are confused. Even Welles's celebrated deep-focus photography works to unnatural effect, when one would think, with Bazin, that it would work to the opposite end. What deep focus in *Citizen Kane* gives us initially is a sense of life, of dramatic space, continuous with our own. But ironically, at the same time it seems to be opening Kane up to us more, the "flashbacks," buttressed by salient technique, are frustrating our desire to decipher Kane and thus to identify with him. We are enabled to inhabit this character's space, but not him. We are confused. But we are held. That is the advantage of depth of focus over Eisensteinian montage for this particular film, where the use of the multiplaned image is called attention to as never before: the image continually teases us, by seeming to include us within its confines, that we will be able to know Charles Foster Kane completely, even as we know his "space," his entire domain, completely. For this reason, *we* never leave "Charlie," unlike virtually everyone else who knew him.

We never "leave" Kane, yet we cannot be said to identify or empathize with him. On balance, we do not find his personality so appealing; we do not warm to him. As I have already indicated, we are, however, identified with the narrative method of the film that is about him. That method, for which the reporter Thompson supplies the cue, is the search for knowledge of Charles Foster Kane, and thus in a sense power over him, and it is by extension therefore the search for love of him, through the finding of what in him is most like ourselves. It is precisely the method of the film *Citizen Kane*, I am maintaining, that corresponds to (and itself signifies) the major experience of Charles Foster Kane's life: the search for power or control over his environment, for total "knowledge" of it, and the quest to love and be loved by all who surrounded him. One of the reasons, I suspect, that Orson Welles not only played Kane, but also directed the film, was so that identification with the film's narrative method, that is, with the one imposed on it by the director Welles, would substitute even more easily for identification with the character played by the actor Welles. The main character and the director would become almost indistinguishable, and thus the experience of the film's narrative method, charted by Welles, would become all the more the experience of Kane's foremost desires.

Ira Jaffe, in an article entitled "Film as the Narration of Space," gives another reason why we are identified with the narrative method of *Citizen Kane*. Not only does deep focus seem to include us within the confines of the film, to make Kane's space and thus him accessible to us, but Welles's moving camera also does this. The moving camera duplicates for us the central experience or conflict of Kane's life: his search for open space, for the freedom, security, and motherly love of his childhood, and his entrapment in closed space, in the responsibilities that his money brings, in the snares that it plants, and in the materialism and coldness it engenders. Jaffe writes, for example, that

> from the beginning we are caught up in a spatial action as the camera travels up in the night from the forbidding NO TRESPASSING sign on the outer fence of Xanadu, and numerous dissolves through the dark, often hilly terrain bring us closer to the lit window of the mansion ahead. Almost instantly we experience ourselves as overcoming obstacles in space including the layers of fences, gates, and hills, as bypassing odd sentinels such as the caged monkeys and the gondolas, and as dissolving space itself. Starting from a position of relative containment outside the fence, we rapidly obtain a certain release by transcending barriers in space, and by penetrating space itself.[6]

Once "we have penetrated the window and gained the access we found ourselves seeking," however, "we also are confined in a new way. For instead of occupying the presumably open, limitless space of the outdoors, we are, though in view of the window and within reach of nature, enclosed in the space of a room in the mansion" (Jaffe, pp. 100-101). In a spatial analogy to Kane's inner experience, we desire knowledge of the character and the freedom to pursue it, only to be hoist by our own petard. The same spatial analogy to Kane's inner experience applies to the reverse camera movement. In the scene at the Colorado boarding house where Mrs. Kane gives responsibility for Charles to Thatcher, the camera begins to pull back from the child, who is outside playing in the snow and seems to revel in the open, unencumbered space. The movement of the camera, says Jaffe,

> does not reveal, as it would in Kubrick's *Barry Lyndon*, yet more majestic space around the young hero. Instead, the camera retreats through a window into Mrs. Kane's boarding house . . . The camera continues all the way back to a table toward which Mrs. Kane and Thatcher walk from the window in order to sign the legal agreement which will turn Charles over to the bank and result in his removal from Colorado and his parents. In the move back through the window into the house, the camera diminishes rather than expands the child's space. . . . The camera movement changes the appearance of the space the hero occupies from open to closed. . . . Now he appears tiny within the firm frame of the distant window which remains visible from the table at which sit his mother and Thatcher. (pp. 103-104)

As a result of the camera's retreat, we see, not more of little Charles, but less; we are locked away from him by the window that his father closes on his playful shouts, just as Mrs. Kane is by the agreement that she signs giving custody of her son to Thatcher. No matter how cautious we are in seeking knowledge and freedom, no matter how certain we are that our next move will increase both of them, we become victims of our own curiosity. We are trapped by the narrative method of the film, even as Charles Foster Kane is by his own experience.

The second clue to the filmmakers' intentions and the one that identifies the audience absolutely with the narrative method of their film is the word Kane speaks before he dies: the name of his childhood sled, Rosebud. Now no one is within earshot of Kane on his deathbed when he says this word. The nurse comes in after she hears the glass ball smash onto the floor from the dead Kane's hand. Raymond is nowhere to be seen. How is it, then, that Jerry Thompson and all his news associates know that "Rosebud" was Charles Foster Kane's dying word? No one has ever asked this question; yet it is clear that no one could possibly have heard Kane's last word—except us, the audience. No one except us finds out that "Rosebud" is the name of Kane's childhood sled, either. That Thompson and his associates, as well as Raymond, know what Kane said before he died is the film's contrivance; it is what makes the film possible, what makes the dead Kane accessible to us. "Rosebud" is the identification of the audience with the search for knowledge of Charles Foster Kane and love of him. We are identified with this search from the start, because we receive information about Kane that no one else does. *We* search for the meaning of "Rosebud," thinking that it will give us total access to Kane, even as he said the word in a last attempt to gain total access to his past, so as to be able to reorder it. We get the meaning and, like Kane's "knowledge," his power, it proves incomplete and unsatisfying. Kane wanted to be President, to be known and loved by all and to govern them. He wound up a recluse. We want to know Kane and to love him, and thus in a sense to be known and loved by him, and what knowledge we get serves only to isolate us from him, in his death, just as he was isolated from himself in life: Kane neither knew nor loved himself, and that is why he needed so much recognition and love from others, yet could not respond to them in kind however much he may have wanted to. We are isolated from Kane, and like him, we are even isolated from all who loved or knew or even just heard about him: we know the meaning of "Rosebud," whereas they do not. That meaning returns us to Kane's childhood and abandonment by his mother. It returns us, in other words, to what I have called the first clue to the strategy of the film about him.

Other interpreters of *Citizen Kane* feel that "Rosebud" returns us to Kane's childhood and abandonment by his mother, but they view the sled as a conventional symbol, whereas I see it, or rather I see the revelation that the sled bears the name Kane called out on his deathbed, much more as a final confirmation of the film's unique artistic strategy. Alan Stanbrook, for example, believes that " 'Rosebud' becomes the symbol of [Kane's] youthful innocence, lost when he was adopted into a family of bankers. Money and the pursuit of wealth have robbed him of his humanity and left him isolated and lonely, vainly seeking happiness in an endless acquisition of gimcracks."[7] Peter Cowie takes Stanbrook's interpretation of "Rosebud" one step further when he states that "['Rosebud'] stands as a token of Kane's unhappy relations with people in general. He has no friends, only acquaintances, because he insists on setting himself on a pedestal above those who seek to know him."[8] Stanbrook and Cowie, then, represent the minority view of the film: they believe that the "message" of *Citizen Kane* is not the mystery of Kane the character, but his *depiction*, and they find the appearance of the burning sled at the end to provide the information for a definitive interpretation of Charles Foster Kane.

Robert L. Carringer rightly attacks such critics as Stanbrook and Cowie, saying, "If this interpretation were valid, *Citizen Kane* might indeed be vulnerable to charges of intellectual shallowness and of attempting to pass off a creaky melodramatic gimmick in place of real analysis of its subject" (p. 185). But then Carringer goes on, curiously, to interpret in the same way as Stanbrook and Cowie, not the sled, but the little glass globe that Kane drops from his hand as he dies. The glass globe, he writes, is

> self-enclosed; self-sustaining; an intact world in miniature, a microcosm. . . . Sealed off to intrusion from outside. Free also of human presence—and therefore of suggestions of responsibilities to others. But by the same token, free of human warmth—a cold, frozen world of eternal winter. Suggestive of Charles Foster Kane . . . The little glass globe, not Rosebud, incorporates the film's essential insight into Kane. It is a crystallization of everything we learn about him— that he was a man continually driven to idealize his experiences as a means of insulating himself from human life. (pp. 191-192)

Carringer wishes to have his cake and eat it, too, however, for no sooner has he found the presence of the glass globe in the film to provide information for a definitive interpretation of Charles Foster Kane, than he is claiming, at the other end of the spectrum from Stanbrook and Cowie, that the "message" of *Citizen Kane* is the mystery of the titular character and that "Rosebud" confirms that mystery, for it "does not add significantly to our understanding of Charles Foster Kane . . . Rosebud finally yields up a figure at once clear and indistinct who is always less or more than the sum total of what is said about him. While appearing to give its assent that sentimental or facile notions like Rosebud can sum up a man's life, the film actually works to rescue Kane from them" (p. 192).

Most critics take this view of Carringer's, that the identification of "Rosebud" only serves to confirm the mystery of Charles Foster Kane. Significant among these critics are David Bordwell and Joseph McBride. Bordwell sums up the received wisdom on the film and "Rosebud":

> Although it stands for the affection Kane lost when he was wrenched into Thatcher's world, the sled is clearly not to be taken as the "solution" of the film. It is only one piece of the jigsaw puzzle,

"something he couldn't get or something he lost." The Rosebud sled solves the problem that Thompson was set—"A dying man's last words should explain his life"—but by the end Thompson realizes that the problem was a false one: "I don't think that any word can explain a man's life." The appearance of the sled presents another perspective on Kane, but it doesn't "explain" him. His inner self remains inviolate (NO TRESPASSING) and enigmatic. The last shots of the sign and of Xanadu restore a grandeur to Kane's life, a dignity born of the essential impenetrability of human character. (p. 111)

McBride sees the revelation of "Rosebud" as a very necessary part of *Citizen Kane*, not simply one more piece of a large jigsaw puzzle. "The revelation of Rosebud," writes McBride, "far from explaining the mystery of Kane's futile existence, adds another dimension to it. If Welles had not shown us Rosebud, we would have continued to think that there could be a solution, and that Thompson is merely unable to find it. We would be left to conjure up our own solutions" (p. 42). Also, McBride sees the revelation of "Rosebud" as a character device, not to shed light on Kane, but to "fill in" Thompson: "Thompson is dignified by our realization that we had to see Rosebud to reach his understanding" (p. 42).

Welles himself said of "Rosebud" in a 1963 interview that "it's a gimmick, really, and rather dollar-book Freud."[9] Certainly "Rosebud" *becomes* dollar-book Freud if one interprets it in the manner that Alan Stanbrook and Peter Cowie do. I'll leave the last word on "Rosebud" to Welles's self-styled spokesman, Pauline Kael, who takes the master at his word and elaborates on it in the way only she can: "The mystery in *Kane* is largely fake, and the Gothic-thriller atmosphere and the Rosebud gimmickry (though fun) are such obvious penny-dreadful popular theatrics that they're not so very different from the fake mysteries that Hearst's *American Weekly* used to whip up—the haunted castles and the curses fulfilled."[10]

I have attempted to explain how I think *Citizen Kane* works, but a question still remains, the one I posed at the start: why specifically did Welles and Mankiewicz make a film about the dead Kane instead of about Kane while he lived? Although traditional narrative film form—a film about the living Kane—could not give us the *experience* of the character's foremost desires and frustrations in the same way that *Citizen Kane* does, it could do well enough by a complex *study* of him. The method is different, but the outcome would be about the same: greater understanding of the character and of ourselves. But *would* the outcome be the same in the case of Charles Foster Kane? I don't think so, because I believe that Welles and Mankiewicz conceived of Kane as a fundamentally pathetic character—that is, one not truly aware of what was happening to him—and that they felt the best way to treat him was after his death, through the reports of others. In other words, I am saying that they deliberately chose to make a film about a pathetic character, but to do so in a way that would make the film itself rise above pathos. To have told the story of Kane while he lived would have been to achieve pathos and nothing more.

Kane is not tragic because he is not self-aware, or is unable to be; he suffers, but learns nothing from his suffering. (It would have been easy to feel sorry for Kane in a film of his *life*, because he was helpless. It is much harder to feel nothing more than sorry for a tragic figure, who is not helpless and in whom one therefore imagines that one truly sees oneself.) But to tell the story of the dead Kane, through others, and have us approximate his experience aesthetically, is to resurrect him through us and to show us the Kane in ourselves far better than any identification with the living Kane on screen could have. We want to possess Kane, but cannot. In the same way that Kane sought to dominate the "storytellers" in his life, we seek to "dominate" them in their stories: we almost forget that they are doing the telling as we search restlessly for knowledge and understanding of Charles Foster Kane. By the end of the film our knowledge has got us nowhere, and we are untouched. Like Kane on his deathbed. The filmmakers have ensured that. But unlike Kane we know this, or can admit it to ourselves on reflection.

Kane's "flaw," as I have suggested, was that he did not, or could not, reflect on or criticize himself. The "flaw" of his "storytellers" is that not one of them can see himself in Kane. Each thinks that he has the answer to the riddle of Charles Foster Kane, but not one has the answer to his own problems; not one appears self-critical. (Even Bernstein, who appears the most successful and happy of the "storytellers," has reason to be self-critical: he seems to have devoted his life to Mr. Kane—his former boss's portrait dwarfs him in his own office—and now that life is made up of distant memories of girls in white dresses, of a life of his own with a woman that was never to be.) On reflection, we do see ourselves in Kane, and we separate ourselves from him. We are left to know and love ourselves before we can know and love another person or conquer the worlds of business, politics, or the arts. That is the triumph of *Citizen Kane* as art: we are enabled by the film's imitation of a subjective experience, as opposed to an objective action, to reflect on ourselves in a way that no character in the film reflects on himself. The characters in the film *assert*; we *reflect*. This kind of art falls, finally, somewhere between pathos and tragedy. It does not make a pathetic figure tragic, but, ironically, through his absence from the film, it helps him to give us what tragedy at its best gives us: knowledge of ourselves. He gets to do more than simply play out his days pathetically, and we get to do more than feel sorry for him.

Citizen Kane's technical daring, I think, pales beside its thematic daring in treating a pathetic figure so.[11] It is time that critics stopped overpraising the film for its brilliant technique, on the one hand, and criticizing it for its supposedly shallow theme and main character in the service of all that technique, on the other. *Citizen Kane* represents a different kind of film art, and one for which it could scarcely be said a sufficient critical language exists at this point.

NOTES

[1]See especially Joseph McBride, *Orson Welles* (New York: Viking, 1972), p. 42; Andrew Sarris, *The Primal Screen* (New York: Simon and Schuster, 1973), pp. 120-121; Robert L. Carringer, "Rosebud, Dead or Alive: Narrative and Symbolic Structure in *Citizen Kane*," *PMLA*, 91 (1976), p. 192; and James Naremore, *The Magic World of Orson Welles* (New York: Oxford University Press, 1978), pp. 66-68. McBride and Carringer hereafter cited by page number in the text.

[2]Orson Welles, *"Citizen Kane* Is Not about Louella Parsons' Boss," *Friday*, 14 Feb. 1941, p. 9; reprinted in Ronald Gottesman, ed., *Focus on "Citizen Kane"* (Englewood Cliffs, New Jersey: Prentice-Hall, 1971), pp. 67-68.

[3]Charles Thomas Samuels, *Mastering the Film and Other Essays* (Knoxville: The University of Tennessee Press, 1977), p. 171. For a doubly negative view, that *Citizen Kane* is both essentially one large piece of chicanery and a *retrogression* in screen technique, see *The Film Criticism of Otis Ferguson*, ed. Robert Wilson (Philadelphia: Temple University Press, 1971), pp. 369-371.

[4]David Bordwell, *"Citizen Kane,"* in *Focus on Orson Welles*, ed. Ronald Gottesman (Englewood Cliffs, New Jersey: Prentice-Hall, 1976), p.   105. Hereafter cited by page number in the text.

[5]Joseph McBride begins to question the actions of Mrs. Kane in sending young Charles away, but he then ends his speculation by passing everything off unaccountably to fate:

> The family tensions are sketched in quickly and cryptically: the mother is domineering but anguished as she commits her son to Thatcher; the father is pathetic and clumsy in his objections. Why is she sending Charles away? To get him away from his father, who apparently abuses the boy when drunk? Perhaps. But more likely, given the aura of helplessness with which Welles surrounds the entire family, it is simply that the accident which made the Kanes suddenly rich has created its own fateful logic—Charles must 'get ahead.' What gives the brief leave-taking scene its mystery and poignancy is precisely this feeling of predetermination. (*Orson Welles*, p. 43.)

[6]Ira S. Jaffe, "Film as the Narration of Space: *Citizen Kane,"* *Literature/Film Quarterly*, 7 (1979), p. 100. Hereafter cited by page number in the text.

[7]Alan Stanbrook, "The Heroes of Welles," *Film* (Great Britain), March/April 1961, p. 14.

[8]Peter Cowie, "The Study of a Colossus: *Citizen Kane,"* in *The Emergence of Film Art*, ed. Lewis Jacobs, 2nd ed. (New York: Norton, 1979), p. 265.

[9]Orson Welles quoted by Cowie, "The Study of a Colossus," p. 264, from a 1963 interview with Welles conducted by Dilys Powell of the *Sunday Times* (London).

[10]Pauline Kael, "Raising Kane," in *The "Citizen Kane" Book* (Boston: Little, Brown, 1971), p. 5.

[11]Peter Cowie states the case for the film's technical daring:

> *Citizen Kane* is of primary importance in the history of the cinema because of the audacity and virtuosity of Welles' technique, and because of the influence that the style was to exert on films in all parts of the world for the next two decades. . . . [Welles's] brilliance stems from his ability to synthesize and harmonize all possible stylistic methods into a coherent instrument for telling his story. ("The Study of a Colossus," p. 267.)

Jorge Luis Borges, writing in 1945, seems to endorse Cowie's view, albeit negatively: "I dare predict . . . that *Citizen Kane* will endure in the same way certain films of Griffith or of Pudovkin 'endure': no one denies their historic value but no one sees them again. It suffers from grossness, pedantry, dullness." (Borges' essay was published originally in *Sur* [Buenos Aires], no. 83 [1945]; reprinted in French translation in *Positif* 58 [Feb. 1964], pp. 17-18; and reprinted in Mark Bernheim and Ronald Gottesman's English translation of the *French* translation, in Gottesman, ed., *Focus on "Citizen Kane"*, pp. 127-128 [this quotation is from p. 128].)

Citizen Kane has endured, of course, in a different way: people see it all the time. In my view, that is because it "fascinates" in the manner I describe in this essay. If technical daring were all that *Citizen Kane* had going for it, it would indeed have suffered the fate of, say, *Birth of a Nation* by now: to be studied in film class for its advances in technique, and to be snickered at in a public screening for its naiveté of theme and primitiveness of characterization.

Bibliography of the Writings of

STANLEY KAUFFMANN

NON-FICTION BOOKS

A World on Film: Criticism and Comment (Harper & Row)	1966
Figures of Light: Film Criticism and Comment (Harper & Row)	1971
Editor, with Bruce Henstell, *American Film Criticism: From the Beginnings to "Citizen Kane"; Reviews of Significant Films at the Time They First Appeared* (Liveright)	1972
Living Images: Film Comment and Criticism (Harper & Row)	1975
Persons of the Drama: Theater Criticism and Comment (Harper & Row)	1976
Before My Eyes: Film Criticism and Comment (Harper & Row)	1980
Albums of Early Life (Ticknor & Fields)	1980
Theater Criticisms (Performing Arts Journal Publications)	1983
Field of View: Film Criticism and Comment (Performing Arts Journal Publications)	1986

NOVELS

The King of Proxy Street, a Story (John Day)	1941
The Bad Samaritan (Cassell)	1943
This Time Forever, a Romance (Doubleday, Doran)	1945
The Hidden Hero (Rinehart)	1949
The Tightrope (Simon and Schuster; *The Philanderer* in England)	1952
A Change of Climate (Rinehart)	1954
Man of the World (Rinehart; *The Very Man* in England)	1956
If It Be Love (M. Joseph)	1960

PLAYS

The Red-Handkerchief Man (three acts, Samuel French)	1933
The Mayor's Hose (one-act comedy, in *The Second Yearbook of Short Plays*, Row Peterson)	1934
How She Managed Her Marriage (one act, Samuel French)	1935
The Singer in Search of a King (one act, Samuel French)	1935
The True Adventure (three-act comedy, Samuel French)	1935
Altogether Reformed (three-act comedy, Samuel French)	1936
Father Spills the Beans (three-act comedy, Walter H. Baker Co.)	1936
A Million Stars (one-act farce, in *Ladies night!*, Eldridge Entertainment House)	1937
Cyrano of the Long Nose (one act, Eldridge Entertainment House)	1937
The Marooning of Marilla (one-act comedy, in *Tournament Plays*, Samuel French)	1937
A Word from the Wise, for Three Women (Eldridge Entertainment House)	1937
Come Again: A South Seas Vignette in One Act (Dramatists' Play Service)	1937
Coming of Age (one-act comedy, Samuel French)	1937
Eleanor on the Hill: A One-Act Fantasia on Comic Themes (Samuel French)	1937
His First Wife (one-act farce, in *Ladies night!*, Eldridge Entertainment House)	1937
The Cow Was in the Parlor (one-act comedy, Denison)	1938
Mr. Flemington Sits Down (one-act comedy, Samuel French)	1938
Right under Her Nose (one-act comedy, Penn Publishing Co.)	1938
The More the Merrier (in *One-Act Play Magazine*)	1939
Overhead (one-act farce, in *Sixth Yearbook of Short Plays*, Row Peterson)	1940
Play Ball! (under pseudonym Barry Spranger; Samuel French)	1940
Close Courting (under pseudonym Barry Spranger; one-act comedy, Willis N. Bugbee Co.)	1940
The Prince Who Shouldn't Have Shaved: A Frolic in One Act (Ingram)	1940
The Salvation of Mr. Song (one-act comedy, Ingram)	1940
Bobino, His Adventures (two-act children's play, Row Peterson)	1941
Pig of My Dreams (under pseudonym Barry Spranger; one-act comedy, Dramatic Publishing Co.)	1942
Food for Freedom: A United Nations Play for Elementary School Children in One Act (Food for Freedom, Inc.)	1944

ESSAYS AND ARTICLES

"Whole Actors, Please." *Theatre Arts*, XLV, No. 10 (October 1961), pp. 21, 74-76.

"The Trail of the Spendid Gypsy [on Edmund Kean]." *Horizon*, 4, No. 4 (March 1962), pp. 13, 114-119.

"End of an Inferiority Complex." *Theatre Arts*, XLVI, No. 9 (September 1962), pp. 67-70.

"Literature of the Early Sixties." *Wilson Library Bulletin*, 39 (May 1965), pp. 748-756 +. Reprinted from *Great Ideas Today*, 1964, annual to *Great Books of the Western World*.

"Focus on Film Criticism." *Harper's Magazine*, 230 (June 1965), pp. 113-116.

"Can Culture Explode? Notes on Subsidizing the Arts." *Commentary*, 40 (August 1965), pp. 19-28.

"Greatness as a Literary Standard." *Harper's Magazine*, 231 (November 1965), pp. 151-156.

"Germany 1967." *The Atlantic*, 219, No. 5 (May 1967), pp. 55-56.

"Drama on the [New York] *Times*." *New American Review*, No. 1 (September 1967), pp. 30-49.

"Films." In *Quality: Its Image in the Arts*. Ed. Louis Kronenberger. New York: Atheneum, 1969.

"A Year with *Blow-Up*." In *American Literary Anthology 3: The Third Annual Collection of the Best from the Literary Magazines*. Ed. George Plimpton and Peter Ardery. New York: Viking, 1970. Reprinted from *Salmagundi*, Spring 1968.

Intro. *The Art of the Moving Picture*. By Vachel Lindsay. New York: Liveright, 1970. Reprint of the 1922 edition with a new introduction by Stanley Kauffmann.

"The Public Arts: Film." In *The Cosmos Reader*. Ed. Edgar Z. Friedenberg et al. New York: Harcourt, Brace, Jovanovich, 1971.

"Middling Ages: Notes on Some American Film Directors." *Yale Review*, 60 (June 1971), pp. 626-640.

"*Lady Chatterly's Lover*." In *The Critic as Artist: Essays on Books, 1920-1970*. Ed. Gilbert Harrison. New York: Liveright, 1972.

"Film Negatives." *Saturday Review of the Arts*, 1, No. 3 (March 1973), pp. 37-40.

"Notes on Theatre-and-Film." In *Focus on Film and Theatre*. Ed. James Hurt. Englewood Cliffs, New Jersey: Prentice-Hall, 1974. Reprinted from *Performance*, September/October 1972.

"Saul Bellow: A Closing Note." *Salmagundi*, 30 (Summer 1975), pp. 90-91.

"Life in the Theatre." *Horizon*, 17 (Autumn 1975), pp. 80-85.

"Literary Criticism." In *The Creative Expression*. Ed. Stanley Rosner and

Lawrence E. Abt. Croton-on-Hudson, New York: North River Press, 1976.

"Theatre As You Like It: A Round of Applause for Repertory." *Horizon*, 18, No. 4 (Autumn 1976), pp. 98-103.

"*La Notte*." In *Awake in the Dark*. Ed. David Denby. New York: Vintage, 1977. Reprinted from *A World on Film*.

"Dialogue: Theatre in America." *Performing Arts Journal*, 3, No. 1 (1978), pp. 19-34.

"Point of View: The Ghost of Films Past." *American Film*, 4 (November 1978), pp. 10-11.

"Director as Star." [London] *Times Literary Supplement*, No. 3997 (10 November 1978), pp. 1305-1306.

"Take Two: *General della Rovere*." *American Film*, 4 (April 1979), pp. 54-56.

"Melodrama and Farce: A Note on a Fusion in Film." In *Melodrama*. Ed. Daniel Gerould. New York: New York Literary Forum, 1980.

"A Theoretical Auteur." *American Film*, 5 (January/February 1980), pp. 65-67.

"George Konrad." *Salmagundi*, 57 (1982), pp. 87-91.

"Album of Mr. Cohen." *The American Scholar*, 52 (Winter 1982-1983), pp. 49-64.

"The Landscape of Alberto Moravia." *Harper's Magazine*, 266 (April 1983), pp. 63-66.

"Album of Job Interviews." *Michigan Quarterly Review*, 23 (Winter 1984), pp. 21-29.

"Album of a European Year." *Kenyon Review*, new series, 6 (Winter 1984), pp. 87-110.

"Album of Lili." *Michigan Quarterly Review*, 23, No. 4 (Fall 1984), pp. 563-575.

"Why We Need Broadway: Some Notes." *Performing Arts Journal*, 9, Nos. 2 & 3 (1985), pp. 193-198.

BOOK REVIEWS

Selected Writings of Truman Capote. *The New Republic*, 23 February 1963, pp. 21-22+.

Letters from the Earth, by Mark Twain. *The New Republic*, 6 April 1963, pp. 20-22.

Beatrice Webb's American Diary, 1898, ed. David A. Shannon. *The New Republic*, 22 June 1963, pp. 28-30.

My Life and Loves, by Frank Harris. *The New Republic*, 28 December 1963, pp. 23-27.

The World in Vogue. The New Republic, 11 January 1964, p. 17 + .

The Moveable Feast, by Ernest Hemingway. *The New Republic*, 9 May 1964, pp. 17-18 + .

My Autobiography, by Charles Chaplin. *The New Republic*, 3 October 1964, pp. 19-21.

Max, by David Cecil, and *Max Beerbohm's Letters to Reggie Turner*, ed. Rupert Hart-Davis. *The New Republic*, 10 April 1965, pp. 19-22.

Starting Out in the Thirties, by Alfred Kazin, and *Part of the Truth*, by Granville Hicks. *The New Republic*, 18 September 1965, pp. 17-20.

The Music School, by John Updike. *The New Republic*, 24 September 1966, pp. 15-17.

The Great Leap, by John Brooks. *The New Republic*, 1 October 1966, p. 18 + .

Black Angels and Other Stories, by Bruce Jay Friedman. *The New Republic*, 8 October 1966, p. 20 + .

The Birds Fall Down, by Rebecca West. *The New Republic*, 15 October 1966, p. 14 + .

La Chamade, by Françoise Sagan. *The New Republic*, 29 October 1966, p. 21 + .

Book Publishing in America, by Charles A. Madison. *The New Republic*, 5 November 1966, p. 24 + .

Harold Nicholson: Diaries and Letters 1930-1939, ed. Nigel Nicolson. *The New Republic*, 12 November 1966, p. 22 + .

The World of Modern Fiction, ed. Steven Marcus. *The New Republic*, 19 November 1966, p. 17 + .

The American 1890s, by Larzer Ziff, and *The Awakening*, by Kate Chopin. *The New Republic*, 3 December 1966, p. 22 + .

The Most of Malcolm Muggeridge. The New Republic, 17 December 1966, p. 23 + .

The Smart Set, A History and Anthology, by Carl R. Dolmetsch. *The New Republic*, 24 December 1966, p. 24 + .

Letters of James Joyce, Volumes II and III, ed. Richard Ellmann. *The New Republic*, 7 January 1967, p. 33 + .

The Ravishing of Lol Stein, by Marguerite Duras, trans. Richard Seaver, and *La Maison de Rendez-Vous*, by Alain Robbe-Grillet, trans. Richard Howard. *The New Republic*, 14 January 1967, p. 26 + .

Aden, Arabie, by Paul Nizan, trans. Joan Pinkham, intro. Jean-Paul Sartre. *The New Republic*, 11 May 1968, p. 28 + .